OREGON FIRSTS

Firsts For Oregon
Past and Present

The only book that details and describes over
1,500 chronological and other ranking "firsts"
for Oregon

by
James Andrew Long

Oregon Firsts Media
Books and Database

Pumpkin Ridge Productions
P.O. Box 33
North Plains, Oregon 97133-0033

International Standard Book Number   1-882635-00-0

Library of Congress Number   TX 407 974

First Printing   1994

10   9   8   7   6   5   4   3   2   1

Cover photo descriptions

The 23-foot **Pioneer** gilded in gold atop the Oregon Capitol faces north, looks west, reflects a blue sky, and is unique. Most states have capitols with domes, and only a few other state capitols have a statue on top. Oregon is the only state with a pioneer on its capitol. The gold-covered Pioneer, which represents the women, children, and men who came to Oregon, holds a tent over his shoulder and a sledge-ax for construction. Thousands of Oregon schoolchildren donated nickels and dimes (about $40,000) to pay for regilding of the 8.5 ton statue and base in 1984. The statue moved one-eighth inch to the east during the earthquake on March 25, 1993.   (See #464)

Thirty members of the **Harney County "Sagebrush Symphony" (in Burns) on the largest wooden violin** before a musical trip to the Willamette Valley in 1915. **Harney County is so big** (10,288 square miles), that the states of Rhode Island, Delaware, and Connecticut combined could fit inside it.   (See #488)

Portland was chosen to host the Olympic basketball Tournament of the Americas. Cover photo shows the **Venezuela team and the first USA "Dream Team," felt to be the best basketball team ever assembled,** and thousands of local fans before the tournament championship game on July 5, 1992, in the Memorial Coliseum, Portland.   (See #1121, #1139)

Joseph Lafayette Meek was a mountain man and public official with many Oregon Country and Territorial "firsts." (See #112, #118, #130, #166, #1075)

Refundable can with non-detachable tab. (See #574)

Equitable Building, innovative 1948 skyscraper.
        (See #466 to #473)

This book is dedicated to my mother
Josephine Marie Rogers Long
(1915-1951)

Table of Contents

In-State Firsts

Introduction

People have been native to the land now called Oregon for thousands of years. From every state and many countries, immigrants and pioneers came out the Oregon Trail in search of a better life. The labors, sweat, tears, creativity, and lives of many generations of people have contributed to both our internal thoughts and the external life we enjoy every day.

Oregon is deep, diverse, and inspiring. All countries and states have their own "firsts": pioneers, unique geography, government, inventors, and business innovations. This is both an historical and contemporary study of one state's activities, contributions, and achievements.

Oregon trails other states in various ways; for example, less than half of one percent of all patents issued by the U.S. Patent Office in the past twenty years were issued to Oregonians. Still, Oregon is outstanding and at times astounding, ranking first in many other significant things.

The impetus for this book and some of the most significant "firsts" are Oregon's five dozen legislative innovations. These unique laws are significant because they were enacted by the citizens or their elected representatives. These laws affect all Oregonians, and many Oregon laws have been used by other states and countries. Legislative innovations take political will, tactics, and maneuvering to survive unbelievably powerful lobbying, usually by industry, to gain approval.

The most essential ingredients to both prevent and solve problems are communication, courage to take action, and tenacity to follow through and evaluate results. Creative and successful problem-solving ideas are exportable and importable person to person, community to community, state to state, and country to country.

Imagine the dedication, effort, courage, and focus it took to achieve the "firsts" described in this book.

The purpose of this book is to provide both chronological and top rankings for a wide variety of "firsts" that contribute(d) to life in Oregon and beyond. The social significance of a chronological "first" is the number of people who have followed a similar path or that it affects.

Chronological "first," in this book's contents, generally refers to the initial occurrence on record. Of course, items described may have been recorded inaccurately, credit misplaced, or not noted at all in previous societies.

Academicians are often leery of chronologically describing anything as "the first." In that sense this book may be controversial. Studying history is a learning experience. Remembering past contributions keeps their lessons alive. The world is full of extraordinary assertions, marketing, and public relations. Oftentimes the men and women credited with accomplishments have drawn upon the ideas of earlier workers in that or a related field of endeavor. Some people "re-invent the wheel" and other people "put wheels on ideas" (e.g., elected officials often utilize and are credited with ideas suggested by citizens). Some people establish claims that are not challenged, and other firsts are hard to pin down.

Each of us creates personal firsts (e.g., your first steps as a baby, first words, first class, first job, first day, first impression, first-person singular, first blink upon awakening, first grade, etc.) and daily firsts. Other firsts fill our lives (first time, first place, safety first, first aid, first drafts, "first come first served," First Avenue, First Amendment, first degree, first-hand knowledge, etc.).

Our future depends upon innovation, changes, new solutions to pressing problems, and hence more firsts. Solutions to problems need local actions, at times bold experimentation, and objective evaluations. Opportunities for non-partisan cooperation can fulfill positive visions of the future. Firsts mean change, transition, and, usually, progress.

This book is dedicated to the challenges of the future. It attempts to give credit where it is due for accomplishments from one state. This book is informative, debatable, arguable, contentious, and fun. It contains something for everyone, and, like us, it's imperfect. In addition, this book became more incomplete upon its "first" printing. Please accept our apologies for any errors or omissions. Let us hear from you. Future editions will contain corrections and additions. Written or printed corrections and additions are helpful for future editions and will be acknowledged if used.

How This Book Is Organized

There are over 1,500 "firsts" described in this book. The firsts are numbered or bulleted (•) for indexing and impression, and generally are chronologically described within the chapters. A bibliography and two indices (numerical and alphabetical) help the book serve as an easy reference.

Interrelated chapters group the "firsts" entries. Geographical landmarks and prehistoric evidence of habitation come first, followed by explorers, settlers, laws, regulations, businesses, and people. "Firsts" entries are numbered 1-1541. Years identified are from 1542 to 2011 or prehistorically by numerical estimates of years before present.

The primary part of this book is the 1,195 "firsts" which are defined as **inside and beyond Oregon's current borders**, including the Oregon Country (1542-1843), the Oregon Provisional Government Era (1843-1848), and the Oregon Territory (1848-1859). The final 300-plus firsts are **"In-State Firsts,"** occurring within Oregon's state borders.

The ranking **"firsts"** include top rankings by various measurements, e.g., uniqueness (only/sole), oldest, most, longest, shortest, deepest, largest, smallest, highest, fastest, finest, last, et cetera, and by place.

This is the first edition of **"Oregon Firsts"** and it covers only a small portion of all the firsts in our database. It is the first in a series of books about Oregon and other states and localities. Future, revised editions will include new firsts and more details about past, present, and future accomplishments. Research to compile this guide consisted of many questions, interviews, and comparisons of secondary sources. In addition to original research, this book summarizes information gleaned from a variety of publications and individuals. Historical and contemporary supplementary information and corrections (evidence, citations, documentation, etc.) will always be welcome and acknowledged if used. Please address comments, claims, citations, inquiries, and book orders to:

Oregon Firsts Media
Books and Database

Pumpkin Ridge Productions
P. O. Box 33
North Plains, Oregon   97133-0033
U.S.A.

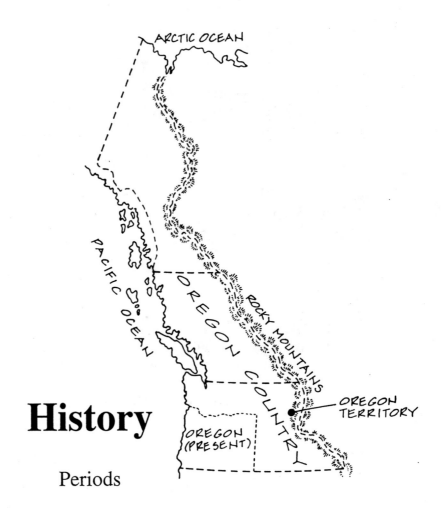

History

Periods

Prehistory	Pre-1542
Oregon Country	1542-1843
Oregon Provisional Government	1843-1848
Oregon Territory	1848-1859
State of Oregon	1859-present

Oregon Firsts and Beyond

Geography and Geology

About fifty million years ago the ocean waters covered the western coast of North America to the Wallowa Mountains. Erosion, volcanoes, earthquakes, and lava flows shaped the current and course of the rivers. Hundreds of thousands of years ago the Ice Age rivers of the Northwest held many times more water volume than today's flows, and most of western Oregon was under the Pacific Ocean.

1 The **John Day Fossil Beds display 45 to 50 million years of earth's history.** Oregon is one of the most geologically diverse areas on the continent, with fossilized records dating more than 60 million years ago, including evidence of dinosaurs, saber-toothed tigers, crocodiles, bear dogs, camels, three-toed horses, and rhinos. This was a subtropical climatic setting 30 to 40 million years ago. The John Day Fossil Beds are some of the richest fossil beds in the world, thoroughly showing complete sequences of tertiary plant and animal populations. The beds were created when volcanic ash entombed plants and animals. The John Day Fossil Beds were made a National Monument in 1974 at three different places: Clarno (oldest), Painted Hills, and Sheep Rock. The beds of fossils were discovered by Reverend Thomas Condon.

First photo of Crater Lake was by Peter Britt in 1863, engraved by staff at West Shore (courtesy of OHS Negative OrHi 89395)

2 **Crater Lake is the Deepest Lake in North America** (at 1,996 feet deep). **Crater Lake** was formed by the volcanic eruption of Mt. Mazama, which was estimated to be 14,000 feet high, about 7,000 years ago. Crater Lake has neither an inlet nor an outlet. The water is very clear and blue at **Crater Lake** (elevation 6,179 feet). Wizard Island (6,940 feet) is inside **Crater Lake,** and Applegate Peak at about 8,135 feet is nearby. On June 12, 1853, prospectors hunting for gold and led by John Wesley Hillman found Crater Lake. Crater Lake was declared a national park on May 22, 1902, by President Teddy Roosevelt.

Rivers

3 **Hell's Canyon is the Deepest River Canyon in North America.** It's a natural state border dividing Idaho (Seven Devils Mountains) and northeast Oregon (Wallowa Mountains). **The forty-mile Hell's Canyon** averages 6,600 feet deep, with some peaks towering nearly 7,900 feet above the **Snake River** at its deepest. Hell's Canyon is 1,000 feet deeper than the Grand Canyon of the Colorado River, and narrower. Over 67 miles of the Snake River are federally designated as wild and scenic.

4 **The Columbia River is the Mightiest River of the West,** and the third largest in the nation. It flows 1,242 miles, with a 2,654-foot fall to the ocean from the Canadian Rockies through eastern Washington and along over 200 miles of the Oregon border to the Pacific Ocean. **North America's largest single source of hydroelectric power is the Columbia River. It serves one of the nation's largest irrigation systems. The Columbia River creates one of the most dangerous bars for ship navigation, and it had the largest wild salmon runs in the U.S.**

5 **The Willamette River**, which is totally within Oregon, is one of the few large American rivers **flowing from south to north.**

6 **Oregon has at least one big fault. Abert Rim is the largest and highest exposed fault in North America** and the second largest in the entire world. It's a 30-mile-long exposed fault that rises 2,000 feet above Crooked Creek Valley and Lake Abert. John C. Fremont discovered the Abert Rim on December 20, 1843.

The first mass immigration to Oregon occurred about 100 million years ago when the Klamath Mountains broke with the Sierra Nevada Mountain Range and moved sixty miles north and west to sit within the state's border.

7 One of **the largest concentrations of high waterfalls in the nation sprays a** ten-mile stretch of the Columbia River Gorge National Scenic Area. There are six dozen waterfalls in the Columbia River Gorge, 11 of which are taller than 100 feet.

8 Multnomah Falls (620 feet) is the second tallest year-round waterfall and seventh tallest of all waterfalls in the U.S. **Multnomah Falls is the tallest waterfall in the Northwest.** Multnomah Falls was dedicated as a public park in 1915, and it is Oregon's most visited place.

9 **Jordan's Crater Lava Flow in Malheur County is the largest in the U.S.** Geologists claim the relatively young volcano was active as recently as 500 years ago. The flow is about 28 square miles.

10 **Mt. Hood,** 60 miles east of Portland, is a strato-volcano that was once 500 to 1,000 feet higher than it is now. Around the year 1800, ash was spewn near the north face of Mt. Hood.

One fairly recent seismic shock on Mt. Hood was recorded at a magnitude of 4.1 on the Richter scale in 1974. Increased steam was seen coming from the mountain on June 20, 1992.

Mount Hood's Cascade-sister Mount St. Helens erupted violently in Southwest Washington on May 18, 1980.

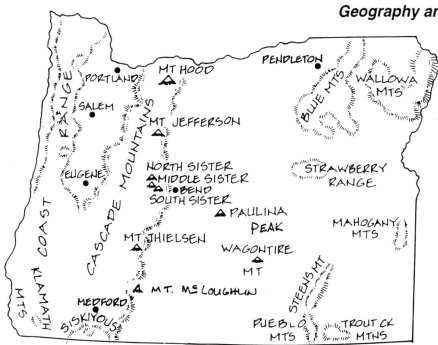

There are 40 mountain peaks with

Eleven Mountain Ranges.

1. **The Cascade Range stretches from Lassen Peak in California north to British Columbia. The Columbia River Gorge is the only water-level gap in the 5,000+ foot Cascade Range.** The Cascade Range was almost named the President's Range (each peak would have been named after a president). The summit of the Cascade Range is the boundary for many counties, e.g., Clackamas and Hood River counties border at the summit of Mount Hood. From a distance, and up close . . . see these Cascade peaks and other mountain ranges (with elevations above sea level of tallest peaks listed):

   Mount Hood (11,240 feet/3428 m.)
   South Sister (10,358 feet/3157 m.)
   North Sister (10,085 feet/3074 m.)
   Middle Sister (10,047 feet/3062 m.)
   Mount Jefferson
      (10,497 feet or 3199 meters)
   Mount McLoughlin (9,495 feet)
   Mount Thielsen (9,182 feet)
   Three Fingered Jack (7,841 feet)
   Mount Washington (7,794 feet)

2. **Wallowa Mountains** (Wallowa Co.)
      (Matterhorn Peak, 9,845 feet)
      (Mt. Sacajawea, 9,838 feet)
3. **Steens Mountain** (9,350 feet),
      west of the Alvord Desert in south east Oregon's Harney County, is the **largest fault-block mountain in North America**.
4. **Blue Mountains** (Umatilla County)
      (Rock Creek Butte, 9,103 feet)
5. **Strawberry Mountains**
      (9,038 feet)   (Grant County)
6. **Siskiyou-Klamath Mountains**
   (Jackson Co.) (Mt. Ashland, 7,533 feet)
7. **Trout Creek Mountains** (Harney
      County) (Blue Mountain, 7,420 ft.)
8. **Pueblo Mountains**
      (8,725 feet) (Harney County)
9. **Wagontire Mountain**
      (6,504 feet) (Harney County)
10. **Mahogany Mountains** (Malheur)
      (Cedar Mountain, 5,740 feet)
11. **Coast Range**
   (North Range: Mary's Peak, 4,097 ft.)
   (South Range: Chetco Peak, 4,660 ft.)

12 **Oregon Dunes** (now a National Recreation Area) stretches 47 miles from Florence to North Bend, and is one and a half miles at its widest, with some dunes 500 feet tall. This rainy place has over 400 different species of wildlife. **It's the tallest and one of the largest coastal dunes areas on earth.**

13 The **volcanic crater at Mt. Tabor Park** (in southeast Portland) **is the only volcanic crater within the city limits of a major city in the continental U.S.** Geologists estimate formation of the volcanic crater at Mt. Tabor from basalts about 35 million years ago. There are fifty extinct volcanoes within twenty miles of Portland, with the epicenter near Boring, Oregon.

14 Oregon has two of the nation's tallest ocean monoliths, and **both are named Haystack Rock.** Haystack Rock in Clatsop County towers 235 feet above Cannon Beach. The taller Haystack Rock off Tillamook County's coastline is about one mile southwest of Cape Kiwanda, and rises 327 feet above the sea.

15 **Cape Blanco,** an Oregon state park with a 225-foot ridge, is the westernmost point in Oregon.

16 **Oregon's Sea Lion Caves are some of the largest in the United States.** The caves are 38 miles south of Newport and 11 miles north of Florence. There's an elevator 208 feet down to the caves. More sea lions inhabit these caves during fall and winter than at other times.

17 The Oregon Caves in Josephine County were **discovered** in 1874 by Elijah Davidson while following his dog, who was pursuing a bear. Davidson made a torch, entered the hole, killed the bear, and discovered the caves. A National Monument since 1909, there are year-round tours of the caves with hanging stalactites and standing stalagmites inside the marble cavern. The temperature ranges from 38°-45° F.

18 Sauvie Island in Multnomah County, twelve miles northwest of downtown Portland, is the **largest inland (freshwater) island in the U.S.** It was the site of a sunken Indian village.

19 At Oneonta Gorge many unique species of wildflowers, flowering trees, and shrubs grow and thrive in this cool, protected, and moist environment. Six species are found nowhere else on earth.

20 Newberry Crater Lava Beds has **one of the largest obsidian (volcanic glass) flows in the world.** It's between Paulina Lake and East Lake a few miles off Highway 97 south of Bend in central Oregon. Astronauts trained there for lunar exploration.

21 A clearly unique place in North America is the continent's most varied collection of basalt vent structures at the Diamond Craters field in Harney Basin. The basalt lava flows from fissures to form spatter cones and cinder cones.

Lava flows in Oregon have created many other unique forms, e.g., the Lava Cast Forest of pine trees and the Lavacicle Cave with drip formations in Deschutes County.

22 Only 20 feet across at the bay entrance, Depoe Bay has the distinction of being the **smallest navigable harbor in the U.S.**

23 The swift-flowing **Metolius River,** an excellent fly-fishing stream in central Oregon, is one of the few and largest spring-fed rivers in the United States.

24 The Smith River is the **last remaining undammed wild and scenic river in California.** The upper reaches or headwaters of the north fork of the Smith River are in the Illinois Ranger District of the U.S. Forest Service in southwest Oregon. There is a Smith River in Umpqua County, Oregon, also named after explorer Jedediah Smith; its main tributary is the north fork Smith River.

25 The **Umpqua River** is the largest river flowing into the Pacific Ocean between the Columbia River and San Francisco Bay.

26 The **"D" River** in Lincoln City is 440 feet long at low tide and 120 feet at high tide, making it the shortest river in the world and the river with the shortest name. This Guinness Book of World Records status was contested by a fifth-grade class in Great Falls, Montana, for a tideless 201-foot stream known as the Roe River.

27 The high Cascade Mountains receive ocean-moderated precipitation and winds, causing **at times some of the deepest snowfall in the U. S.** Seven peaks have permanent glacial snow fields. (*See also* Weather #1513 to #1519)

Government stockpile at the nickel mine at Riddle, 1960s (OHS Neg. C006313)

28 The **nation's only producing nickel mine and smelter** is operated at a serpentine deposit in Nickel Mountain, west of Riddle in Douglas County. In 1991 Glenbrook Nickel Company produced 19.3 million pounds from Nickel Mountain ore and 6.4 million pounds from New Caledonia ore.

28• When Alaska and Hawaii attained statehood, Oregon became the precise center of the U.S., from Point Barrow, Alaska (north), Cape Prince of Wales, Alaska (west), Quoddy Head, Maine (east), and the southern beaches of Hawaii (south).

Oregon is halfway between the equator and the North Pole. The 45th parallel passes a few miles north of Salem, the state capital. With a latitude of 45 degrees 32 minutes north, **Portland, Oregon is north of Portland, Maine,** which has a latitude of 43 degrees 41 minutes north. Oregon's southern border with California is 42 degrees north latitude.

Oregon's borders were formed with these countries and territories: Spain (1819), Idaho (1863), Nevada (1864), and Washington (1853).

Oregon Firsts

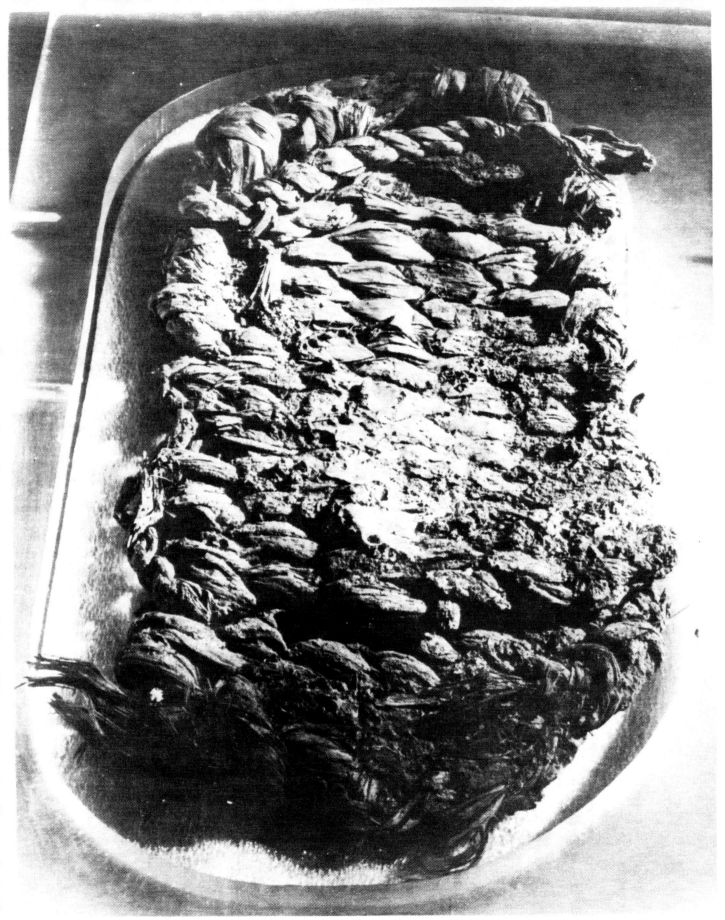

This is one of the sagebrush sandals discovered at Fort Rock in the 1930s. This sandal is about 10,000 years old and is one of the oldest artifacts found in Oregon and the North American continent. *(OHS Negative OrHi 88346)*

Prehistory
(pre-1542)

There are over 16,900 prehistoric archaeological sites in Oregon recorded at the State Historic Preservation Office in Salem as of April, 1993. Many sites are not recorded and only a small portion of the recorded sites have been surveyed.

The First Oregonians

29   The first people have been chronologically placed earlier and earlier as new evidence of past life is uncovered. For decades, experts believed North America began to be settled about 2,000 years ago. From 1932 to 1935, Dr. Luther S. Cressman studied the area near Lake Abert in Central Oregon, finding petroglyphs, camp sites, burials, and remains of mortars that suggest continuous human use for the past 6,000 years.

Western North America's earliest known people took shelter near a large lake in a cave at Fort Rock. The Fort Rock people lived in a cave facing the lake in part of an old volcano that towers 325 feet over the terrain. Well-preserved sandals woven of sagebrush bark excavated at Fort Rock in Lake County by archaeologist Dr. Luther Cressman in 1938 were later (1949) carbon-dated as being **about ten thousand years old**. These sandals are on display at the Oregon Museum of Natural History in Eugene. The Fort Rock Cave became a National Historic Landmark in 1962, and a plaque was placed at this archaeological site in recognition of its scientific significance. Charcoals from a hearth carbon-date to 13,200 years ago.

30   Several historians have calculated that there were about 100,000 Indians living in the Oregon Country before the coming of non-native explorers and settlers about 185 years ago.

Projectile points found at the Bureau of Land Management's Dietz site in eastern Fort Rock Basin date to about 11,500 years Before Present (BP). The Dietz site is probably the most important Clovis site in the Northwest because the stone tools provide detailed descriptions.

The Dalles five-mile rapids site is the oldest known occupied location on the Columbia River, with salmon bones which date to over 10,000 years BP.

The Dirty Shame Rockshelter, currently BLM lands in the far southeast corner of Oregon, yields evidence of occupation from 950 BP to 5,800 BP and from 2,750 BP to 365 BP (1628 AD).

The Marial site is on the interior Rogue River, about fifty miles inland from the Pacific coast. The Mack Canyon area is an interpretive BLM site on the Deschutes River. In Mack Canyon, 29 housepits were identified and diagrammed. The two housepits that have been excavated were 15 and 20 feet in diameter. Domestic tools such as hopper mortars, pestles, milling stones, pounding stones, flaked stone cutting and scraping tools, and projectile points were used.

The oldest archaeological site on Oregon's Pacific coast is south of Florence at Tahkenitch (Lake) Yaquina Head, and it yields radiocarbon dates that suggest a timespan from roughly 8,000 to 6,880 years Before Present for occupation and use.

Archaeologists have found evidence of **Spanish, Chinese, and Japanese** vessels that may have drifted and wrecked along the Oregon coast. Chinese and Japanese cargos of beeswax and ceramics, including wares, arrowheads, and scrapers, date from the 1590s to 1610s.

The Indians probably came from Asia 15,000 years ago or earlier during the most recent Ice Age, when the Bering land bridge connected the Asian and North American continents between Siberia and Alaska. A recent Siberian excavation dated evidence of human activity to 120,000 years BP.

There is a vague reference in Chinese written history that the earliest purported landing in the 5th Century AD was by a Chinese vessel in areas near the mouth of the Columbia River and the state of Alaska. In theory, the Kingdom of Fu Sang, founded by Hwui Shan, a Buddhist monk sailing from China, and his disciples, flourished somewhere on the Oregon coast about 500 AD.

31   The **single largest Federal archaeological collection in North America came from the Columbia River Gorge**.

The Center for the Study of the First Americans has been located at the Anthropology Department at Oregon State University in Corvallis since 1991.

32   The Museum at Warm Springs, opened in 1993, has the most Native American artifacts (2,600) of any collection still in Indian hands in the country. *(See map page 158)*

Exploration

33   Oregon's coast was **one of the last unexplored parts of the earth**. The Pacific Northwest was one of the nation's last isolated areas.

34   **The first European men to see the southern coast of Oregon were Spanish seamen from Mexico in 1543.** Some of the earliest voyages to the western coast of the continent were under the **Spanish** flag. A pilot for Juan Rodriguez Cabrillo, named Bartolome Ferrelo, sailed north near the vicinity of the Rogue River on the southwest coast of Oregon.

35   In 1578, **Sir Francis Drake of England** explored the north Pacific coast in the *Golden Hind*. There are many suppositions as to where he first landed, including Tillamook Bay, Little Whale Cove, south of Cape Arago, Chetco Cove, and the southwest coast of Vancouver Island. (Wherever Sir Francis Drake landed, it predates the landing of the Mayflower at Plymouth Rock in November, 1620, on the continent's east coast.) Sir Francis Drake first mentioned sighting a river in 1578, the first recorded sighting of Oregon's coast by Europeans. He was 33 years old at that time.

36   Sebastian Vizcaino of Spain exploring north from Mexico on January 20, 1603, saw a cape and named it **Cape Sebastian**.

37   Also in 1603, Martin d'Aguilar sailed along the Oregon coast and saw a "rapid and abundant river." For the next 150 years, maps showed the **"Rio d'Aguilar."** The Columbia River was later discovered and entered in that vicinity.

38   The first recorded **shipwreck** was in 1707, when the *San Augustin* wrecked on Oregon's coast at the base of Neahkahnie Mountain (Tillamook County) with beeswax in its cargo.

    Russian explorers had journeyed east since 1720 across the northern Pacific peninsula and down the northwest coast to Northern California by boat. **Russian ships** with hopes of starting colonies sank north of the mouth of the Columbia River.

39   **"Oregon" is probably a word of Indian origin; otherwise it may have a French origin meaning "windy."** The word is perhaps from the Sautee or Chippewa branch of the Sioux. The **first known written** use of the word was in a proposal by Major Robert Rogers in 1765 for an exploration of the "Ouragon" country. It was **first used in print** by Jonathan Carver as **"Oregon"** in his 1779 book about his travels, as "...River Oregon, or River of the West." Other name theories explain cartographer errors from the river "Ouaricon."

40   Spaniard Juan Perez in 1774 became the **first person to sail along the entire Oregon coast.** On board the *Santiago* with the Perez expedition were the first Catholic priests in the Pacific Northwest, Franciscans Juan Crespi and Thomas de la Pena.

41   On August 17, 1775, Don Bruno de Heceta, another Spanish explorer, sailed across the mouth of the Columbia River but Heceta's ship did not enter it. When his ship landed in the Oregon Country on what is now the Washington shore, **he and his crew became the first Europeans known to stand on Northwest soil.**

42   The Columbia River mouth was first mapped during the 1775 visit by Bruno Heceta.

43   On March 7, 1778, Captain James Cook, sailing on the *HMS Resolution,* sighted the Oregon coast at Yaquina Bay. **Capes Foulweather, Perpetua, and Flattery** were named by Cook; he missed the Columbia River due to inclement weather. Before sailing to the Northwest, Cook took possession of Australia's east coast for Britain, circumnavigated Antarctica, discovered the Sandwich Islands (Hawaii), and charted the dangerous west coast of North America for 3,000 miles, from what is now Oregon to beyond the Bering Strait. Captain Cook's crew started trade of sea otter furs with journeys to China.

44   Connecticut native John Ledyard served on Cook's third voyage. He recognized the potential of trade among China, the Northwest, and Europe. In the 1780s in France, Ledyard met the U.S. Minister to France, Thomas Jefferson, and sparked Jefferson's interest in western exploration.

44•   The first French government exploring expedition sailing in waters off Northwest America was in 1786, with the frigates, *Astrolabe* and *Boussole.*

45 English Captain John Meares, commanding the ship *Nootka,* arrived in the Northwest at Prince William Sound in 1786. After sailing to China, he established a company, sending numerous trading vessels to the Oregon Country. In 1788 he moved back to the Northwest. Meares is responsible for several regional firsts: the **first ship launched,**
46 the **first lumber shipped**, and
47 the **first time Chinese workers were employed**.

48 In 1787, Francis Trevor, the wife of English Captain William Barkley, was apparently the first European woman to see the Northwest Coast.

49 Captain Robert Gray's crew became the **first Americans to land on the west coast of North America** in 1788, near the bay now called Tillamook. The first time on record that Europeans or Americans set foot on what is today the State of Oregon was on May 14, 1788, from the *Lady Washington.* Captain Gray traded with natives for sea otter pelts, which he later traded in the Orient, before returning to Boston as captain of the **first American sailing vessel to circle the earth**. Tillamook Indians helped him understand the location of the great river.

49• In 1788, Markus Lopius, became **the first Black man to set foot on Oregon soil,** served aboard Captain Gray's sloop *Lady Washington.* Markus Lopius, who was from the Cape Verde Islands, was killed by native's arrows.

50 Over 200 years ago, the Columbia River, the "**River of the West**," was entered by American explorer Captain Robert Gray on May 11, 1792. He named the river after his ship, the ***The Columbia Rediviva,*** a 220-ton, 83-foot long vessel built in Plymouth, Mass., in 1787. The ***Columbia Rediviva*** was the first ship to enter the Columbia River. Captain Gray found an ancient forest. He traded for sea otter skins and salmon with the Indians. He and the crew spent ten days on the lower parts of the river charting anchorages and soundings as far as 35 miles upriver. **His entering of the Columbia River gave the U.S. its first claim to the Oregon Country and established U.S. presence for the first time in western America as well as on the Pacific.** The Indians informed him that there were 50 Indian villages on the banks of the lower river. Later, at Nootka Sound on Vancouver Island, Captain Gray proudly presented his charts to Spanish Commander Bodega y Quadra and British Captain Vancouver.

51 Two weeks before Gray's entered the Columbia River, British Captain George Vancouver sailed near the same area and examined Cape Disappointment without discovering the river. He sailed north with Lt. Peter Puget, Mr. Whidbey, and other crew members, making numerous discoveries.
Later, in October, 1792, Captain George Vancouver traveled south and laid the basis for joint occupancy of Oregon with fur traders. British Lt. William Broughton anchored the Armed Tender *Chatham* inside the mouth, then rowed 100 miles ascending the Columbia River and **took possession of the territory in the name of the British Crown.** He named bays, capes, sounds and mountains, e.g., Mount Hood was named for Samuel Hood, a British vice-admiral with French Revolutionary War fame.

52   Twelve years before the Lewis and Clark Expedition, Sir Alexander McKenzie of the North West Company led **the first group of white men to cross the Rocky Mountain range to the Arctic Ocean** in 1789 **and to the Pacific Ocean** in 1793 **overland from Canada** north of the Oregon Country. He and his traveling companions reached the continental divide on June 12, 1793, and they traveled in canoes down the Bella Coola River, reaching the Pacific Ocean on July 22, 1793, at 52 degrees 30 minutes north latitude.

53   The Louisiana Purchase was a very significant real estate transaction made between the U.S. (President Thomas Jefferson) and France (Napoleon Bonaparte) in April, 1803. The Louisiana Purchase doubled the size of the U.S., adding 827,192 square miles of land, now fifteen U.S. states. Napoleon sold unknown lands, the entire Louisiana Territory (bounded roughly by the Mississippi River, the 49th parallel, the Rocky Mountains summit, and the Gulf of Mexico) for $15 million. Although a tremendous westward expansion of the nation, the Louisiana Purchase made the U.S. a border neighbor to the Oregon Country, which was claimed by four countries. The Oregon Country, which was in dispute via claims by England, Spain, Russia, and France, was not purchased.

In 1804, the young nation of the United States consisted of seventeen states and the newly acquired Louisiana Purchase, a vast unknown territory. An overland route to the Pacific Ocean was only an idea.

The southern border of the Oregon Country (and thus the Oregon Territory and later the State of Oregon) was fixed at 42° north latitude by the U.S. treaty with Spain in 1819.

Lewis and Clark Trail from the U.S. through the Louisiana Purchase to the Oregon Country.

54   **The overland Lewis and Clark Expedition** across the continent to the northwest coast, **a 3,555-mile round trip, was President Thomas Jefferson's idea.** President Jefferson persuaded Congress to fund an expedition. The **"Corps of Discovery"** had three purposes:

1) to determine a route between the Missouri and the Columbia rivers;
2) to report on flora, fauna, and geography; and
3) to establish friendly relations with the Indians.

Thomas Jefferson chose his secretary, 26-year-old Meriwether Lewis, to lead the expedition. Lewis chose William Clark to assist him. Captain Lewis obtained and read a copy of Sir Alexander McKenzie's book, which was first published in London in 1801. Lewis left Washington, D.C., on July 5, 1803.

The expedition left St. Louis on May 14, 1804, traveling up the Missouri River in a 55-foot square-rigged boat. In October, 1804, 1,600 miles later, they spent a comfortable winter at the Indian village of Mandans (near the present site of Bismarck, North Dakota). Thirty-two men started on the Lewis and Clark Expedition.

55 On April 7, 1805, the expedition started westward again. Captain Lewis saw for the **first** time the crests of the "Rock Mountains" on May 26. The expedition **crossed the continental divide** on August 12, 1805. The expedition followed these rivers west: Lemni, Salmon, Clearwater, Snake, and Columbia. The expedition made friends with various tribes of Indians and they left their horses with the Nez Perce tribe and traveled by canoe most of the rest of the way west. On October 19, 1805, they sighted Mt. Adams and Mt. Hood. On October 22 they saw the great Celilo Falls. When Lewis and Clark arrived at The Dalles, they found at an Indian village that Euro-American goods had already been introduced into the region via the native trade routes. The expedition members sighted and named Beacon Rock.

56 On November 7, 1805, nineteen months and 2,200 miles from their beginnings, Captain Clark was traveling in a canoe. **When the fog cleared he first saw the Pacific Ocean** at the mouth of the Columbia River. He entered in his journal, **"Ocian In VIEW! O! the joy."**

57 The expedition originally landed on the north bank of the Columbia River. Captain Clark visited Cape Disappointment and the ocean beach as far north as Long Beach. On November 26 the weather conditions permitted them to cross to the south side.

58 The Lewis and Clark Expedition first camped on the Pacific coast on land that projected into the river over a mile (now called Tongue Point). Two weeks later they entered what is now called Young's Bay.

59 The only black man on this expedition was Captain Clark's servant York, who was born at Clark's home in Virginia and was his lifelong companion.

60 Sacajawea was a Shoshone Indian who later was the wife of the French Canadian trapper Toussaint Charbonneau, who was hired for the Lewis and Clark Expedition. They both served as guides and interpreters from what is now North Dakota to the Pacific. **Sacajawea was the only woman on the expedition** and she carried her baby (Jean Baptiste Charbonneau). She lived a long life and is the subject of many statues.

Members of the Lewis and Clark Expedition existed in Oregon on a diet of elk, salmon, and wapato. Wapato resembles potatoes with a slightly sweeter taste.

61 The **first American salt works on the Pacific coast** was built January 2, 1806, by three Lewis and Clark Expedition members (Joseph Fields, William Bratton, and George Gibson) at an area now within the City of Seaside. Four days later, a large 105-foot whale skeleton was found on a beach to the south.

62 After the winter, the expedition **started the return journey east** on March 23, 1806, going upriver the same route by which they came. The journey up the Columbia River against the current was slower and more difficult.

63 Captain Clark located an island village of the "Multnomah Nations" on Wapato, the modern Sauvie Island. **He saw and named Mt. Jefferson** on March 30, 1806. He also saw three other snow-covered mountains: Mt. Hood, Mt. Adams, and Mt. St. Helens. On April 2, 1806, Captain Clark explored the Multnomah/Willamette River about ten miles from its mouth.

64 On September 23, 1806, the expedition landed back at St. Louis, two years, four months, and nine days after it started. Lewis and Clark and five other members of the expedition kept journals or notebooks of their findings. The **first official published edition of the journal** was printed in 1814.

65 The Lewis and Clark Expedition was the **first U.S. expedition** and exploration of the North American continent, and the first government-sponsored exploration of the Oregon Country.

66 The **first group of U.S. citizens to cross North America** was the 31 surviving members of the Lewis and Clark Expedition. The end of the Lewis and Clark trail is along the northern stretches of the Oregon coast, south of Seaside.

67 The following 31 Lewis and Clark Expedition members completed the lengthy 2,200-mile exploration and were the first individuals to traverse the continent within the present U.S.
Captain Meriwether Lewis, Captain William Clark.
Sergeants: Patrick Gass, John Ordway, Nathaniel Pryor.
Privates: William Bratton, John Colter, John Collin, Peter Cruzatte, George Droulliard, Reuben Fields, Joseph Fields, Peter Frazier, George Gibson, Silas Goodrich, Hugh Hall, Thomas Proctor Howard,
Francois La Biche, Jean Baptiste LaPage, Hugh McNeal, John Potts, George Shannon, John Shields, John B. Thompson, Richard Windsor, William Werner, Peter Weiser, Joseph Whitehouse, Alexander Willard, York, Toussaint Charbonneau, Sacajawea, Baptiste (Pomp) Charbonneau.
Others: John Newman (discharged); Moses Reed (deserted).

68 Death struck just one man, Sergeant Charles Floyd, on the entire Lewis and Clark Expedition. He was the first U.S. soldier to die west of the Missouri River. He died of an unknown illness (perhaps appendicitis) on August 20, 1804.

69 The Lewis and Clark explorers were the first white men to explore the upper Missouri River Basin and large parts of the **Columbia River basin.**

70 The documented observations contributed by Lewis and Clark and their partners in discovery provided extensive new knowledge to the scientific world, specifically in the disciplines of botany, zoology, geography, and ethnology. In the field of botany, **a total of 178 plant species new to science** (e.g., red-flowering currants and Oregon grape) were found throughout their transcontinental journey and were reported by the explorers. The new animal species they found included the rufous hummingbird, mountain quail, and Townsend's chipmunk.
Politically, the brilliant success of the Lewis and Clark exploring enterprise created a vital strengthening of U.S. claims to the Oregon Country and had long-range effects upon international relations. The expedition's achievements set the stage for America's westward expansion and fulfillment of America's dream of "Manifest Destiny."

72 **Abiel, Jonathan, and Nathan Winship,** who had traded profitably with China and the Sandwich Islands for years, arrived by ship *(The Albatross)* with 30 men from Boston, entered the Columbia River on May 26, 1810 and settled about 45 miles from its mouth (between the current cities of Clatskanie and Rainier). A shelter was begun and a garden planted. Chinook Indians threatened them. After high waters flooded their log structure, on June 12 they packed their remaining belongings on their vessel, boarded it, and never returned. **The Winship brothers' eight-day settlement, though temporary, existed a year before the Astor party arrived to establish a permanent settlement.**

73 David Thompson was a fur trader, explorer, geographer, and cartographer for the British North West Company. From 1807 to 1812, he became the **first white man to see the entire length of the Columbia River.** He established trading posts upriver.

74 Bold New York businessman John Jacob Astor financed the Pacific Fur Co. enterprise in 1810, sending a copper-clad ship, The *Tonquin,* **to found a trading post.**

75 The **first disaster** for Americans on record in the Oregon Country was aboard the ship *Tonquin,* when eight crewmen were lost near the mouth of the Columbia River.

75• The Burns Paiute Indians' first contact with non-Indians occurred when fur trappers came in search of beavers.

76 In April, 1811, the Pacific Fur Company, **which was first headed by Duncan McDougall,** located itself near the mouth of the Columbia River in the Oregon Country where **Astoria** now stands.

77 Marie Aioe Dorion, the Iowa Indian wife of Pierre Dorion, was the **first woman to cross the plains and settle in Oregon.** She gave birth to her third child near North Powder on December 30, 1811. Her child was the **first person born in the Oregon country with European ancestry.** (A week later, however, her baby died.)

78 **South Pass, a way through the Rocky Mountains,** was discovered on an eastward trip by Robert Stuart of the Pacific Fur Company in 1812. **South Pass** was well used later by pioneers, animals, and wagons over the Oregon Trail.

79 In December, 1813, the British warship *HMS Raccoon* seized Astoria. **Fort Astoria** was sold by the Pacific Fur Company to the Canadian North West Company. The seizure was later considered a result of the War of 1812. Fort Astoria was renamed Fort George until 1846. The first acting governor and partner of the North West Company was John George McTavish, who served from October 16, 1813 to December 1, 1813.

80 Itinerant French Canadian fur trappers established the **Willamette Post** on French Prairie in 1813.

81 John Jacob Astor's **Pacific Fur Company** laid the basis for U.S. claims in Oregon under the "status ante bellum" clause of the Treaty of Ghent in 1814.

82   The **first treaty with Indians**, permitting white men to peacefully enter the Willamette Valley, was made in 1815 by Alexander Ross and his group.

83   In 1814, Jane Barnes, the **first white woman to land on the Pacific Northwest coast,** arrived at Fort George on the ship *Isaac Todd* from England. Her blonde hair and blue eyes caused quite a stir amongst the natives.

84   There were six negotiations between the British and Americans from 1818 to 1846 to partition and share the Oregon Country. The **first joint-occupancy boundary treaty** between the U.S. and Great Britain regarding the Oregon Country lasted ten years. English occupancy of the Oregon Country was the general status, though the law was "joint occupancy." The second treaty in 1827 lasted to June 15, 1846, when **the United States was conceded sole rights to the country south of 49° latitude.** Spain had given all its claims north of the 42° parallel to the United States in 1819.

85   Dr. John Floyd of Virginia introduced in Congress the **first two bills to establish the Oregon Territory,** the first on December 19, 1820. The bills were not passed but were initial steps that used the word "Oregon" to describe a region.

86   The Hudson's Bay Company, Canada's oldest corporation, which was chartered in 1670 in England, merged with the North West Company in 1821. Afterwards, Thomas McKay guided Dr. John McLoughlin and Sir George Simpson and their companions into the Oregon Country to further establish Hudson's Bay Company in the region. John McDougald Cameron was the first authority of Hudson's Bay Company Headquarters, Columbia District, in the spring of 1821.

87   Donald McKenzie was the first European to conduct much of the exploration of the Snake River Country and the Willamette River Valley. A river was named for him.

88   The 1824 treaty between the U.S. and Russia limited the latter's southern boundary to 54 degrees 40 minutes north.

89   The (de facto) British government shifted from the North West Company at **Fort George** in Astoria to the Hudson's Bay Company, which moved its headquarters to **Fort Vancouver**, on the north bank of the Columbia River in 1824. Dr. John McLoughlin was the chief factor at this post for 22 years.

90   The **first white female to cross the continent** was Miss Eloisa McLoughlin, daughter of John McLoughlin. She was born on the shores of Lake Superior on February 13, 1817, and she came west with her father in 1824.

91   In the fall of 1825, Peter Skene Ogden's trapping party made the first recorded journey over the Siskiyou Mountains to south central Oregon. Ogden became the first European to discover Mt. Shasta in California (1826).

92   In 1826, Peter Skene Ogden and his group were probably the first Europeans to cross into the Willamette Valley over the Cascade Range via the Santiam Pass.

93 Explorer and fur trapper Jedediah Smith made the first recorded overland travel from California to Oregon (1828). **His party was the first group to traverse from southern California through to northern Oregon.**

94 The Hudson's Bay Company at Fort Vancouver was a commercial venture by a large multinational corporation with exports to Russia and Alaska. The Hudson's Bay Company employed a number of Sandwich Islanders (Hawaiians). **Fort Vancouver was the hub of the Northwest Territory and site of many firsts** in the Oregon Country (1825-1860), including the first farming, formal garden, orchard, sawmill, and church. *(See #352-#361 for more details)*

95 The **first grist mills** in the Oregon Country were built in 1828 by Hudson's Bay Company at Fort Vancouver and Fort Colville, and used ponies for power.

96 The **first bakery** in the Oregon Country was built at Fort Vancouver.

97 The Hudson's Bay Company, with Dr. John McLoughlin in charge, had strict laws. The first **jail stockade** in the Oregon Country was at Fort Vancouver.

98 Dr. John McLoughlin in 1829 established a **claim at Willamette Falls**, a former Indian fishing village. He moved there (the present Oregon City) in 1842.

99 In 1829, Dr. McLoughlin allowed French Canadian trappers who had completed contracts with the Hudson's Bay Company to settle at the first open prairie along the banks of the Willamette River, hence the name **French Prairie**. First of these French Canadian settlers was Etienne Lucier.

100 In the 1830s, the **first shipyard** to build more than one ship in the Oregon Country was at Fort Vancouver.

101 The Hudson's Bay Company (HBC) established the **first fort in southern Oregon** on the Umpqua River in 1832.

103 U.S. Captain Benjamin Eulalie de Bonneville led a party of 110 men west on exploration of the Oregon Country in 1832. He was in command at Fort Vancouver in 1853.

104 A junk wrecked at Cape Flattery in 1833 and three Japanese sailors were taken to the British Fort Vancouver, where they met residents. Dr. John McLoughlin sent them to England, and the sailors were taken as far as China. *(See #1076)*

105 On July 3, 1834, the **first petition** by French Canadians in the Willamette Valley was sent northeast to the Catholic Bishop at Red River to send missionaries to the Oregon Country.

106 HBC's *Beaver* was built in England. She sailed around South America's Cape Horn and became the **first steamboat on the northwest Pacific Ocean** coast. She steamed into Ft. Vancouver in 1836.

107 Traveling with their Protestant missionary husbands, on July 4, 1836, Narcissa Whitman and Eliza Spalding became the first two white women to have crossed the continental divide and come to the Oregon Country. This was also the **first group to bring a wheeled cart west of Fort Hall.**

108 **The oldest records at the old and new State Archives buildings are for the Oregon Country's first corporation.** The Willamette Cattle Company, organized by Ewing Young and Lt. William Slacum (January 13, 1837), imported cattle from California. Twelve Americans and three Indians went on the brig *Loriot* and bought 800 head of Spanish Longhorns. They returned the next fall to the Chehalem Valley with 15 horses and 630 head of cattle on the **first major cattle drive in the west. This was the start of the commercial cattle business in Oregon.**

109 The first white American child born and living in the Oregon Country was the Whitmans' daughter, Alice Clarissa, born March 14, 1837, near Walla Walla.

110 Missionaries planted statehood's **earliest seeds** in 1838 when Rev. Jason Lee rode horseback to the U.S. capital with a petition asking Congress to include U.S. jurisdiction to cover Oregon.

111 The **first printing press in the Northwest** was a gift from the Sandwich Islands mission. Rev. Henry Spalding printed religious literature (a primer), which was **the first book published in the Pacific Northwest** in 1839 at Lapwai. (*See #1100*)

112 The **first road for wagons from Fort Hall to Fort Walla Walla** was led by Robert "Doc" Newell in 1840. Joseph Meek, Caleb Wilkins and Frederick Ermatinger joined him.

113 The **first group of American settlers**, the "Peoria (Illinois) party" became interested in Oregon after hearing Rev. Jason Lee's lectures. Led by Thomas J.

Farnham, the "Peoria party" began its transcontinental journey west May 11, 1839, and arrived in the Willamette Valley in the spring of 1840. This represents the first endeavor of young persons interested in becoming settlers.

114 American settlers in the Willamette Valley **first met to create a civil government in 1841.** This attempt at government failed, in part because of pressure from British interests (Dr. John McLoughlin). Lieutenant Charles Wilkes of the U.S. Exploration Expedition said the attempt was premature.

115 The **first U.S. Naval Exploring Expedition** in history with Lt. Charles Wilkes, Commander, was in the Oregon Country near the mouth of the Columbia River on April 5, 1841. Its purpose was to visit lands along the Pacific Ocean, look after the whale fisheries, and survey the northwest coast and the Columbia River. Lt. Wilkes named "Saddle Mountain" since its summit resembles the contours of a saddle.

116 The **first recorded large meetings of British** (the French Canadians) **and American settlers in the Willamette Valley were the "wolf meetings"** which occurred near Champoeg in the French Prairie area in early February, 1843, to discuss and take actions for the reduction of roaming, hungry, and destructive animals. At the second wolf meeting in March, a committee was appointed "to take into consideration the civil and military protection of the colony."

117 John C. Fremont, along with two dozen soldiers, **mapped a route to California east of the Cascade Mountains** by going south from The Dalles in 1843.

Provisional Government and Early Oregon Trail Era 1843-48

118 On May 2, 1843, the settlers met again in an open field at Champoeg to hear the report of the wolf committee, which was organized for military and civil protection. Joe Meek called for a vote to form a government. **A close vote among the settlers of 52 to 50 favored "a divide." An American government was agreed upon and organized for the first time on the Pacific coast.** A committee was instructed to draft a constitution and present it at another meeting in two months.

119 The **first election was held to elect the officers of the Oregon Provisional Government** on May 14, 1843.

120 On May 22, 1843, **the first large wagon train of Americans left Independence, Missouri.** Earlier wagon trains had been fairly small but this one was gigantic—260 men, 120 women, and 602 children with 120 wagons. Horses, mules, oxen, and several thousand head of cattle accompanied them. **This first migration was so large, newcomers outnumbered both the American settlers and former Hudson's Bay contractors who were already in Oregon.** About 900 people from this migration settled in the Willamette Valley.

121 Jesse Applegate arrived in Oregon in 1843 as **one of the leaders of the first major covered wagon train** along the Oregon Trail. Jesse Applegate later completed the first survey of Oregon City.

122 **The settlers adopted the first constitution** on July 5, 1843, at Champoeg. The executive power was placed in a three-man committee, instead of in one governor. The government was to be financed by a volunteer membership fee, instead of taxes. Slavery was prohibited. The constitution incorporated the Northwest Ordinance, the Declaration of Independence, the Constitution of the United States, and since one settler happened to have a copy of the Iowa territorial laws, they were included too.

123 **The original three people** elected by settlers in 1843 to the Provisional Government's **first Executive Committee to officially govern the Oregon Country** were **Joseph Gale, David Hill, and Alanson Beers.**

The first Executive Committee's third member was Connecticut native **Alanson Beers**. Beers became George Abernethy's business partner, manufacturing lumber and grinding flour.

Joseph Gale, born in Washington, D.C., was a "mountain man" and a ship builder before serving on the first Executive Committee. Afterwards, about 1850, he moved to the Baker County area to farm and trap.

Connecticut native **David Hill** was a Champoeg settler in 1842. He moved north to Tuality County, the present site of Hillsboro, which he named Columbia in 1847. Hill served in both the provisional and territorial legislatures.

124 George W. Le Breton became the **first provisional secretary** at the Champoeg meeting.

125 William Holden Willson was elected **first treasurer of the provisional government** at the May 2, 1843, meeting at Champoeg. William H. Willson, a New Hampshire native, gave the land the State Capitol was built on.

126 The Oregon Country in 1843 consisted of all lands bounded by latitude 54° 40' on the north, by the crest of the Rocky Mountains on the east, by latitude 42° on the south, and on the west by the Pacific Ocean.

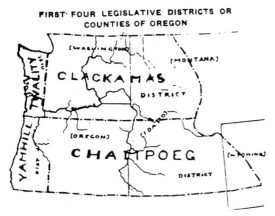

FIRST FOUR LEGISLATIVE DISTRICTS OR COUNTIES OF OREGON

The provisional government **created four large districts/counties:**
   Champoeg (later Marion County)
   Clackamas
   Tuality (Washington County) and
   Yamhill.

127 Massachusetts native Asa Lawrence Lovejoy was one of the founders of Portland and the **first lawyer to practice in the Oregon Country** in 1842. Lovejoy won elective office in Oregon City and Salem.

128 The provisional legislature created the office of county treasurer in 1843 to receive taxes collected by county sheriffs, distribute revenue, and receive fees.

129 Joseph Gervais *(pronounced jer-vay)* was one of the first Justices of the Peace appointed at Mission Meetings in 1841. Two years later, Justices of the Peace were incorporated into county governments when the provisional government formed.

130 The **first American taxes in the Oregon Country were collected** by Joseph L. Meek, Sheriff of the Provisional Government, in 1844. Family records show a sum of $455.93 collected. Initially, taxes were voluntary by subscription of members. Some people who could not pay money paid in wheat. Joe Meek needed a granary more than a pocketbook. This was **the beginning of American taxes on the Pacific Coast.**

$. ¢¢ *(See back cover photo of Joe Meek)*

131 **Oregon City was designated the first capital** of the Oregon Country by the provisional legislature in 1844.

132 The **first elected provisional legislature** met starting December 2, 1845, in Oregon City and passed the region's first laws.

133 The **Oregon Country's first jail in the** was commissioned by the provisional legislature (on December 20, 1844) and was completed in Oregon City (April, 1845).

135 A New York City native and Oregon merchant, George Abernethy was elected the **first and only provisional governor** of Oregon while in the Sandwich Islands on a business trip in 1845. Governor Abernethy quietly sent Jesse Quinn Thornton to Washington, D.C., to work towards achieving territorial status for Oregon. He narrowly won re-election as governor in 1847.

Oregon Trail History

136 **The Oregon Trail route was opened by fur traders** from 1810 to 1840 and by missionaries in 1836. The first white man on the Oregon Trail was Robert Stuart of the Astor Company, who, while traveling east, discovered the South Pass in 1812.

137 **The Oregon Trail carried the largest voluntary human migration in history.**

138 **The Oregon Trail is the longest emigrant trail in the country. The Oregon Trail was the longest continuous road** known in history for over 70 years. In 1840, Missouri was the gateway to the American frontier. The **Oregon Trail** was a rutted, rocky road that crossed over 2,000 miles of desolate country from Independence, Missouri to Fort Kearney, Nebraska; past Chimney Rock, a 500-foot sandstone column, up the Platte River north branch past Scott's Bluff to Fort Laramie, Wyoming; along the North Platte River to its Sweetwater branch; through the South Pass in the Rocky Mountains to the Green River Valley at Fort Bridger, Wyoming; then northwest to Fort Hall in the Snake River area, and on to Fort Boise, Idaho; across the Grande Ronde Valley and Blue Mountains to Marcus Whitman's mission at Walla Walla, Washington; and down the Columbia River to The Dalles, Fort Vancouver, and the Willamette Valley of Oregon. After 1845, when travelers reached The Dalles, they decided which treacherous way to go, down the Columbia River or around and over Mt. Hood.

139 In 1840, the **first non-mission family,** the Joel Walker family of eight, accompanied the last fur trade caravan and then missionaries to Fort Hall. At Fort Hall, Joel Walker and his family gave up their wagons and went by pack train.

140 Indians greeted and fed hungry pioneers salmon, roots and berries. The continuing influx of people dramatically limited the freedom of the Native Americans. The overland and over-sea newcomers (fur trappers, missionaries, and pioneers) introduced European concepts and customs of capitalism, "private property," and Christianity.

141 The **great migration of adventurers and covered wagons** westward across America to Oregon occurred primarily from 1841 to 1848. Lots of wagons were made and stocked in Independence, Missouri. Only 32 persons reached the Willamette Valley via the Oregon Trail in 1841. This was the Bidwell and Bartelson party of 70 persons, which intended to emigrate to California. The group split up at Soda Springs (southeast Idaho) where half continued on a southeast path to California, and half went to Fort Hall and then took a northwest route by pack train.

142 The first emigrant to die in a gun accident along the Oregon Trail was **William Shotwell,** who was a member of the Bidwell and Bartelson party in 1841. When he pulled a rifle from a wagon muzzle first, the gun discharged and shot him near his heart. He lived for about an hour afterward.

143 In 1842, the Dr. Elijah White wagon train of 16 to 18 wagons and about 107 pioneers rolled over the Oregon Trail to Fort Hall, left their wagons, and went to the Willamette Valley.

144 It was not until 1843 that the **wagons were first taken all the way through to The Dalles.** Initially, the journey from Independence, Missouri, to the Willamette Valley took five to six months. 1843 is called the year of the Great Migration, when about 1,000 people went by wagon all the way to the Columbia River and Fort Walla Walla. From here, many went downriver by boat and others went by wagon to The Dalles. The next large wagon train headed for Oregon left Independence in the spring of 1844. It included 225 heads of families, and over 800 people, many riding on the eighty wagons.

145 In May of 1844, Michael Simmons and George Washington Bush led **the Oregon Trail's first expedition of black men** on a seven-month journey from Independence, Missouri, 2,000 miles to The Dalles. When the 23-person Bush-Simmons group arrived they learned that the Oregon Territorial Government had passed laws prohibiting black people from living there. The group moved north to Fort Vancouver for the winter and eventually settled near the present city of Olympia. In 1854, a Special Act of Congress, a joint Resolution of the House and Senate, granted G.W. Bush his claim of 640 acres of land.

146 At Oregon City on June 27, 1844, the provisional government of the Oregon Country established the District of Vancouver, including all land north of the Columbia River, which then meant as far as the southern part of Alaska.

147 After the northern boundary of the U.S. was established at the 49th parallel in 1846, Fort Vancouver became an American military post. One of the most famous soldiers to serve at Fort Vancouver was Ulysses S. Grant, later the eighteenth U.S. president.

148 Over 3,000 emigrants and wagons headed west over the Oregon Trail from 1845-46. In 1847, **4,500 pioneers** arrived in the Willamette Valley.

149 During the Califonia Gold Rush (1848 to 1849) entire settlements in Oregon were deserted. In 1849, the provisional government did not have a quorum for transaction of business. The **pattern of the Oregon Trail was radically altered when gold was discovered in California** and many pioneers traveled southward before reaching Oregon.

150 About 315,000 pioneers traveled along the Oregon Trail by wagon from 1840 to 1860. **Many more emigrants** followed the Oregon Trail west over the next fifty years until the railroad and automobiles made the wagon obsolete.

151 Legend has it that when a wagon train that left the trail stopped to rest, the children found pebbles and rocks to play with. The **shiny yellowish rocks** which were their favorites turned out to be gold nuggets. The exact spot for the legendary find of yellow nuggets left in

a **"blue bucket"** by a wagon train that abandoned the rugged Oregon Trail in 1845 was never located, and remains legendary.

152 The **first road built over the Cascade Mountain Range** around Mt. Hood was the Barlow Trail. It was located by Joel Palmer, and built by Samuel K. Barlow, a pioneer from Kentucky. In 1846, Samuel Barlow obtained the first provisional legislative charter for construction of a road, a steep and treacherous trail for pioneers around the south side of Mt. Hood to Oregon City, cleared through the labor of 40 men. This toll road caused lots of IOUs until 1907.

153 There were many hardships along the Oregon Trail. It's perhaps the longest cemetery, with an average of five burials for every mile. Approximately one in ten pioneers died on the trail. A cholera epidemic claimed many lives in 1849 and 1850 and again in 1852, when 6,000 people died from it. Fighting between the emigrants and native Indians was only a small factor in the loss of emigrant's lives.

154 The migration of pioneers meant disruption, disease, and death for Northwest Indians and extinction of entire tribes. Diseases included chicken pox, measles, syphilis, tuberculosis, and tobacco-related illnesses.

155 Prior to 1845, all surveying in Oregon was completed either by the U.S. Surveyor General or the territorial surveyor. The office of county surveyor was created in 1854 and again in 1859.

156 At least 700 emigrants kept diaries of their crossing of the plains. It wasn't always peaceful on the Oregon Trail from 1840 to 1860; there were roughly 360 emigrants killed by Indians and 420 Indians killed by emigrants.

157 Of the approximately 296,000 pioneers who traveled the Oregon Trail from 1840 to 1860, **roughly 18% went to Oregon, 68% traveled to California, and 14% went south to Utah**. The gold and timber booms from the 1840s through the 1860s peopled southern Oregon.

158 Many people who did not travel the overland trails came to Oregon by boat either around the Cape Horn tip of South America or by crossing at the Isthmus of Panama. Other people came overland and by boat from Canada.

159 From 1843 to 1845, territorial peace officers provided law enforcement on the county level. In 1845, the legislature created the office of county sheriff for Oregon Country counties.

160 The office of County Clerk was first established in 1846 by the Oregon provisional government.

161 Justice Courts in the Oregon Country were established in 1846. Provisional and territorial prosecuting attorneys performed the duties of district attorneys from 1843 to 1853, after which the office of District Attorney was established for each judicial district.

162 The office of the County Coroner was created in 1847.

163 The "**Oregon Question**" about joint occupancy of the Oregon Country was finally settled by treaty with Britain in 1846. The treaty with Great Britain established the Oregon boundary at 49° latitude north.

164 The **first news sheet** on the west coast was established in Oregon City on February 5, 1845, and it was called the *Flumgudgeon Gazette and Bumble Bee Budget*. Each press run consisted of a dozen copies and the paper was printed twice weekly during the 1845 provisional legislative session at Oregon City. The news sheet was not only "**entirely original**," it was handwritten. California's first newspaper was published six months and ten days after the first issue of the *Flumgudgeon Gazette and Bumble Bee Budget*. Price: free.

OREGON SPECTATOR.

165 The *Oregon Spectator*, **the first printed newspaper in the Oregon Country,** made its debut in Oregon City on February 5, 1846. William Green T'Vault was its first editor; John Fleming was printer.

166 **Joseph Lafayette Meek** was an active founder of the first American provisional government in the Northwest. He also served as **the Oregon provisional government's first sheriff, first census taker, and first tax collector.**

In winter, mid-January, 1848, **Joe Meek started an overland trip east to Washington with a petition requesting that President James K. Polk declare Oregon a U.S. territory.** The petition

Meek carried **renewed** the plea for help, protection, laws, and arms. Meek and his party started on horseback, abandoned the horses at Fort Hall, then traveled by self-made snowshoes over the mountains and met an immigrant train headed west, before arriving in St. Joseph, Missouri, on May 4. This was called the "quickest trip east under any circumstances." They continued by horse, boat on the Ohio River, stage coach, and train. Joseph Meek, who was a cousin of President Polk's wife, was named the **first U.S. Marshall** in the Oregon territorial government.

(photo of Joseph L. Meek on back cover)

167 After it visited Honolulu and Nisqually, in August, 1848, the American ship *Honolulu* brought the **news to Oregon of the discovery of gold in California** seven months earlier. Ship Captain Newell bought up all the tools and provisions before he told the Oregonians. When gold was discovered in California, most men in Oregon went south to California seeking it.

167• One example of these gold seekers is Peter Burnett, who came out west to Oregon as part of the Great Migration of 1843. Burnett was an elected legislator in the Provisional Government and served as chief justice of its Supreme Court. In 1848, he was appointed **one of the first justices of the Supreme Court** of the Oregon Territory by President Polk, but he could not serve because he'd already gone south to the gold fields of California. In 1850, he became the **first governor of the State of California**.

Oregon Territory, USA (1848-1859)

168 The **Oregon Territory was established by Congress on August 18, 1848**. The Act of Congress which established the Oregon Territory in 1848 replaced the existing county circuit courts with U.S. District Courts. These courts were replaced in 1859 under the provisions of the state constitution with county circuit courts. *(See map at beginning of first chapter)*

169 After Abraham Lincoln declined the position, in 1848, President Polk appointed General Joseph Lane as the **first governor of the Oregon Territory**.

170 Governor Lane arrived on February 18, 1849, and gave his inaugural address from the balcony at William Holmes' house in Oregon City where **the first Territorial Legislature** met.

171 After the formation of the Oregon Territory, Samuel R. Thurston was elected the **northwest's first delegate to Congress** in 1849. He helped secure passage of the Donation Land Claim Act of 1850. The Act offered 640 acres of free land to each couple, encouraging people to settle in the less populated and relatively disease-free frontier. Over 7,400 settlers filed for 2.5 million acres between 1850 to 1855 when it expired. While returning from Washington, D.C., to see his constituents, Thurston died at sea.

172 King Hibbard, who settled on his land claim south of Silverton, on April 1, 1848, prior to when the legislation was in effect, became the **first man in Oregon issued a Donation Land Claim certificate** (Number 1).

173 After Samuel Thurston's death, Joseph Lane was elected the Oregon Territory's delegate to Congress (1851-1859).

174 In 1849-50, U.S. Naval Lt. William Pope McArthur directed the crew that made the Pacific Coast's **first hydrographic survey**.

175 Ohio native David P. Thompson discovered the source of the Columbia River and conducted numerous **early land surveys** in Oregon, Washington, Idaho, and Canada.

By the 1850s Russian ships were in the Columbia and Willamette rivers, trading for grain from the Tualatin and other valleys.

176 The first paid executioner in the Oregon Country was U.S. Marshall Joseph L. Meek, who hanged five Indians in Oregon City in 1850. They had been convicted of first-degree murder at the Whitman Mission Massacre near Walla Walla. His daughter, Helen Mar Meek, had died at the mission.

177 John R. Preston, the appointed first Surveyor General of Oregon, established the Willamette Meridian and Baseline intersection on June 4, 1851. **From this point all the lands of Oregon were sectioned**. These two lines appear on all official maps and deeds. The establishment of this stone started the sectioning of the public domain on the north Pacific Coast. A straight line north from the Willamette Meridian was projected to pass through the mouth of the Willamette River. The baseline was drawn south of the Columbia River to prevent surveying difficulties. The **Willamette Base Stone** is west of NW Skyline Boulevard and north of Burnside Road. It is the point of political subdivision from which Multnomah and Columbia counties were formed from Washington County.

Jesse Applegate favored **creation of an independent state comprising southern Oregon and northern California** in 1857. With Levi Scott, Applegate explored and laid out the Scott-Applegate Trail (or Southern Route), which ran past Klamath Lake and through northern California and Nevada to Fort Hall.

178 The Oregon Territory's **first penitentiary** was opened in 1856 (at what's now SW Hall and Front Street in Portland). Joseph Sloan was the superintendent.

179 **The Oregon Territory included the following counties, which became the Washington Territory in 1853:**
Clark County (created as Vancouver County on June 27, 1844, from portions of Clackamas and Tuality counties)
Lewis County
(established December 21, 1845)
Pacific County
(established February 4, 1851)
Jefferson County
(established December 22, 1852)
King County
(established December 22, 1852)
Thurston County
(established January 12, 1853)
Pierce County
(established December 22, 1853)
Island County (established 1853)
Because the Oregon Territory was so large and its low population so scattered, it was difficult to govern effectively from one capital south of the Columbia River. Congress established Washington as a separate territory on March 2, 1853, to alleviate the problem.

180 The peak year for emigrants on the Oregon Trail was 1852, when 70,000+ persons made the crossing to Oregon and California. There were over 400 wagons per day on the busiest days.

181 The first treaties approved by the U.S Congress **with Indians** in the Pacific Northwest were the September 10, 1853, treaty with the Rogue River Tribe and the September 19, 1853, treaty with the Takelmas-speaking Cow Creek Band of Umpqua Indians. These treaties, which ceded hundreds of square miles of land at 2.3¢ per acre, were ratified in 1854.

182 When the Oregon Territorial Government created Wasco County on January 11, 1854, it consisted of all of the Oregon Territory between the Rocky Mountains and the Cascade Mountains and from latitude 42° to latitude 46°. This was the largest county ever to be formed in the United States, originally consisting of 130,000 square miles. Gradually, 17 other counties in central and eastern Oregon were created from Wasco County.

183 In 1855, a wagon train with 250 people and 35 wagons, mostly family and followers of Dr. William Keil, was preparing in Independence, Missouri, for the 2,000-mile journey west. Dr. Keil had promised his son, Willie, that he would lead the caravan. An outbreak of malaria struck them; Willie Keil got sick, and he died five days before departure. Grief-stricken, Dr. Keil obtained a lead-lined coffin from St. Louis, which was filled with "Golden Rule" whiskey, and Willie's body was placed inside and strapped down on an open wagon. The wagon train left with a great herd of livestock, horses, mules, oxen, and milk cows on its journey to Willapa Bay. The many Indians who saw this wagon train

were amazed at Dr. Keil, a great medicine man who could preserve the dead. Willie was buried at Willapa Bay, the end of **the longest funeral procession in world history**. Later, Dr. Keil and most of his group, at Dr. John Mcloughlin's suggestion, settled south of Portland where the Pudding River and Deer Creek join. They named their new community Aurora, in honor of Dr. Keil's daughter.

184 Asahel Bush served as the first and only Oregon territorial printer in 1859.

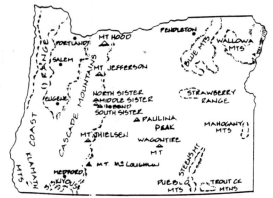

After Statehood (1859 +)

185 Oregon became the 33rd U.S. state and the first state in the current Northwest on Valentine's Day, 1859, when President James Buchanan signed the papers. It's interesting to note the news that statehood was granted took 29 days to get from Washington, D.C., to Oregon. It traveled to San Francisco by pony express, arriving on March 10, and arrived by ship (The *Brother Jonathan*) from San Fransisco in Portland on March 15. The next day, Stephen Senter rode horseback 30 hours from Oregon City to Salem around flooded rivers to deliver news of statehood. The large mural on the wall in the Oregon Senate chamber depicts news of statehood arriving in Salem on March 17, 1859.

By the time of statehood (February, 1859) the Oregon Territory was divided into 18 counties. Wasco County, the largest county at statehood, had an area nearly twice as large as that of the rest of the territory but its population numbered less than 1,500 people.

186 Joseph Lane was elected by the legislature to be **one of Oregon's first U.S. Senators**, serving from statehood, February 14, 1859, until March 3, 1861. Later, Joseph Lane ran for vice president on the pro-Southern Democratic ticket headed by John Breckinridge.

187 At a special legislative session in Salem, on December 5, 1865, 86% of the elected officials voted for ratification of the 13th amendment to the U. S. Constitution abolishing slavery.

188 Georgiana Pittock organized a rose show in 1888. The **first official Rose Show** was held May 21, 1889, in Portland, and founded at that time was the Portland Rose Society, the **first of its kind in the nation.**

189 In the 1890s, **Portland's Chinatown was the largest in the Northwest** and second largest in the United States.

190 In 1897, word of the gold discovery and rush in Alaska reached Oregon by ship. Many individuals and groups bound for the Klondike gold fields bought equipment and supplies in Portland. Many boats were used for transport to Alaska.

191 The Clatsop, Kathlamet, and Tillamook bands from Oregon were joined by the Chinookans from Washington in filing in 1899 the **first lawsuit won by Oregon Indians** in the U.S. Court of Claims. The first tribes to use the legal system received modest compensation for their lands when their suit was finally settled in 1912.

192 **The largest meteorite ever found in North America is the Willamette Meteorite, which was found in 1902 in Clackamas County** on the property of the Oregon Iron and Steel Company. The meteorite is the **sixth largest ever found on earth.** Originally discovered by the Clackamas Indians, the first white men to find the meteorite were Welsh woodsman Elias G. Hughes and prospector William Dale. The large meteorite was later moved down river to Portland and hauled by twelve horses to the Lewis & Clark Exposition where the public could view it. Mrs. William E. Dodge III bought it for $26,000. The huge 31,107-pound chunk from outer space was in the American Museum of Natural History in New York City until 1936, when it was moved to the nearby Hayden Planetarium. (It's too big to move out of the Planetarium.) Several small parts of the meteorite are in various museums. In 1991, Lake Oswego elementary school students tried to get the meteorite back to Oregon.

193 **The Lewis & Clark Exposition was the first international exposition of its broad scope and national character to be built and held west of the Rocky Mountains. The five-month Lewis & Clark Exposition** opened in the Northwest Portland industrial district on June 1, 1905, to celebrate the 100-year anniversary of the Lewis and Clark Expedition. The Lewis & Clark Exposition was initiated by the Oregon Historical Society. It was also known as the Lewis and Clark Centennial American Pacific Exposition and Oriental Fair. President Roosevelt officially opened the fair with an electric key. Every Oregon county, every state, and several nations had exhibits, contributing to the total expenditure of $25 million. The U.S. Government Building was the largest. **First-time displays included electricity, the Willamette meteorite, plywood, and automobiles.** *(See photo of world's largest log cabin, the Forestry Building, on page 105)*

194 The Portland Lewis & Clark Exposition fairgrounds served as the final destination of the **first transcontinental auto race** which took the winner forty-four days and five hours. Investors realized a 21% return, from one of the few profitable "world's fairs." Within five years, by 1911, Portland's population increased nearly 50% to 210,000 residents. **Portland was the smallest city ever to put on a world's fair.** Paid attendance was 1,588,000 with an additional almost one million free passes given to reporters, workers, and officials.

195 Beginning in 1906, Ezra Meeker (at age 76) marked the **Oregon Trail** when he retraced the route of the **Oregon Trail** from Oregon to Iowa. Over two dozen monuments were set up along the trail route, which has mostly disappeared. Ezra Meeker is the only person to travel over the trail by ox-cart (1852), horse (1906), automobile (1915), and plane (1924). The official U.S. monument for the Oregon Trail was established in 1923.

The "Salmon Seal" with three sheaves of wheat depicts two of early Oregon's principal products. The Oregon **Provisional Government Seal** was designed in 1846, and it was used until the territorial government seal replaced it in 1850.

The **Territorial Seal** shows a plow in the foreground and mountains in the distance, with a ship under full sail. The crest is a beaver. The shield is supported by an eagle with wings and an Indian holding a bow with arrow and a mantle of skins over his shoulder.

Oregon Territorial and State Motto

"Alis Volat Propriis"
or
"She Flies With Her Own Wings"

The Oregon State Seal

Oregon became the 33rd state on Februrary 14, 1859. The seal consists of a shield cradled by 33 stars with the inscription "The Union." Below these words appear a sheaf of wheat, a plow, and a pickax, which represent Oregon's mining and agricultural resources. The crest is the American eagle. Depicted in the middle are the mountains and forests of Oregon, an elk with branching antlers, a covered wagon and ox team, the Pacific Ocean with the setting sun, a departing British warship, and an arriving American merchant ship to signify the rise of American power.

Oregon Firsts

Legislative Innovations

Oregon's 70-plus legislative innovations were the impetus for this book because they are some of the most significant of Oregon's "firsts." Approved either by citizen participation or through their elected officials, good, sensible laws which affect all Oregonians have been enacted. Sometimes the effect of legislation surpasses even the vision of its authors.

Citizen lawmaking and initiative and referendum powers have been an important part of the Oregon process. Oregonians tend to seek and find solutions to problems through governmental processes.

The citizen lobby has been and can be effective. Paid industry lobbyists are an unbelievably powerful force in the legislative process. At times the tactics and maneuvers of successful legislators are the only ways that meaningful legislation is approved.

Oregon is one of seven states with legislatures meeting biennially, whereas forty-three state legislatures meet annually. The following legislation is unique if not totally original, and in many instances has been replicated and re-enacted elsewhere. Descriptions of legislative innovations are scattered in a dozen chapters in this book.

196 Labor Day was first celebrated in 1882 with a New York City parade. **Oregon was the first state to adopt a "Labor Day" law,** and New York, New Jersey, and Colorado soon followed. Shortly after Governor Sylvester Pennoyer's inauguration on February 21, 1887, Oregon officially designated a public holiday (the first Saturday of June each year) to honor workers. Seven years later, in 1894, Congress adopted Labor Day as a national legal holiday and changed it to the first Monday in September. The idea was suggested by carpenter Peter J. McGuire, founder of the United Brotherhood of Carpenters.

197 **Oregon was among the first in America to register voters on a statewide basis.** The 1899 Legislative Assembly approved a law directing each county clerk to register all electors. However, the law also enabled persons to vote even if they had not registered. Until this time, the county clerk or election boards had either to know the voter personally or to accept the voter's word. As a result, election irregularities had caused problems.

198 In 1903, during Governor T. T. Geer's term, the legislature made social history by passing **the first law limiting the employment of women in factories and laundries to 10 hours a day.** After a similar statute in New York had been ruled to be unconstitutional, the Oregon law was declared valid.

199 **The nation's first statewide distribution of initiative and referendum pamphlets was in Oregon in 1903.** This pamphlet contained the title and text for the ballot measures. County clerks were required to obtain postal addresses for each voter and to send the pamphlets on a specific day prior to the election to the Secretary of State, who would complete statewide mailing of pamphlets to voters ten days before the election.

200 **Oregon and Wisconsin were the earliest states with a direct presidential primary.** Oregon's closed primary law was the first to require citizens to state a party affiliation at the time they register. **Oregon's closed primary system was the result of an initiative approved by the voters in 1904.** The law allowed the voters to designate the candidates in the general election, and applied to both partisan and non-partisan offices (such as judgeships).

201 **The first state to elect a U.S. Senator by a vote of the people was Oregon in 1906.** In the Oregon General Election on June 1, 1908, an initiative petition instructing the legislature to vote for the people's choice for United States Senator was approved by a vote of 69,668 yes to 21,162 no. Prior to that time, each state's senators were elected by the Legislative Assembly. Eventually, a constitutional amendment provided for direct election of all U.S. Senators. **Jonathan Bourne was the first person elected U.S. Senator by a vote of Oregon voters.**

202 Oregon became the **first state to enact a minimum wage law and authorized labor commission** on February 17, 1913. This was the nation's first minimum wage and maximum hours worked law for women.

203 Oregon enacted **the nation's first effective real estate regulatory license law** on Valentine's Day in 1919 (House Bill 425). California passed a law the year before but it was deemed unconstitutional.

204 **In 1965, Oregon became the first state to offer an alternative to the mechanical voting machine by instituting voter tally machines,** which enabled votes to be counted more quickly and to be available for future recounts. The mechanical voting machine was outlawed by 1969 because of its unreliability, its poor ability to facilitate recounts, and the possibility of its being manipulated.

205 In 1887 a legislative bill declaring the Pacific Ocean beach a public highway was tabled. In 1899, the Oregon Legislature declared the thirty miles of beach south from the Columbia River to be a public highway forever open to the people. From 1902 to 1909, Progressive Governor Oswald West continued efforts to preserve public access to all coastal tidelands by declaring them public highways. Lacking a route along the coast, an act sponsored by Governor West and passed by the legislature in 1913 declared the Pacific Ocean beaches from the mouth of the Columbia to the California border a public highway.

In 1966 the Surfsand Motel owner in Cannon Beach raised a court challenge to this "unwritten" concept by claiming that all beach property in front of his motel was private property. After a lengthy legal case (Oregon Attorney General Thornton vs. Hay), the courts ruled that the "right of custom" use of the beaches by prior generations had established the all-public beaches concept in full. After this threat, Governor Tom McCall encouraged passage of the **1967 "Beach Bill"** (HB 1601), which was sponsored by Reps. Bazett and Ouderkirk and Senator Yturri. The law made **Oregon the first state to declare sovereignty to forever maintain and preserve all the ocean shore existing within its borders. Oregon is the first state to require free access and public use of all its ocean beaches** below the high tide line. Later, two citizen initiatives to strengthen public access to beaches were overwhelmingly outspent by the major oil companies, and as a result both measures were defeated.

206 In 1971, the Oregon Real Estate Division began requiring that brokers and salesmen complete continuing education activities to keep up-to-date on complex and constantly changing real estate practices. This was a first.

206• In 1977, Oregon became one of the first states to publish legislative agendas in three languages, Spanish, Russian, and Southeast Asian languages (Vietnamese and Laotian) when the House Committee on Aging and Minority Services did so.

207 **In 1971, the Oregon State Legislature became the first nationally to decriminalize possession and use of small quantities of marijuana** (with a maximum fine of $100 for possession of less than one ounce). Ten states enacted similar decriminalization laws, including California, Colorado, Maine, Minnesota, Ohio, South Dakota, and Vermont. The State of Alaska Supreme Court in 1976 went further when it determined it a constitutional right for Alaskans to grow marijuana in their own home for personal use. The 1989 Oregon Legislature increased fines for non-criminal violations (civil offenses). Alaska voters recriminalized it in 1990. Decriminalization prevented approximately 3,500 Oregonians per year from entering the criminal justice system, saving the state money and keeping productive wage earners paying taxes.

208 A 1958 constitutional amendment, the Home Rule Charter, was adopted as state law in 1973. County government in Oregon was recognized as having the **highest degree of local discretionary authority of any state by a national inter-governmental relations advisory commission.** Seven counties have adopted home rule charters, wherein voters have the power to adopt and amend their own county government organization. The counties of Lane and Washington were the first to adopt home rule in 1962, followed by Hood River (1964), Multnomah (1967), Benton (1972), Jackson (1978), and Josephine (1980).

209 **Oregon is the first state in the continental U.S. to adopt comprehensive statewide land use and conservation policies/laws.** The Oregon Legislature passed the **Oregon Land Use Act** (SB 100) in 1973, which established a growth management strategy to balance the objectives of development and conservation. Protections for agricultural and forestry lands are specified.

The State of Oregon doesn't write or adopt comprehensive plans or zone land; cities and counties do. A mosaic of 278 local land use plans covers the entire state.

The authors were Senator Hector MacPherson a farmer from Lebanon and Senator Ted Hallock of Portland. The impetus for the bill was to keep development off forest and farmland. Governor Tom McCall signed the **Oregon Land Use Act** into law. The repeal of statewide planning has been referred to Oregon's voters three times, each time without approval. Oregon's land-use planning standards are addressed in 19 mandatory goals. The first fourteen goals were adopted by the Land Conservation and Development Commission (LCDC) on December 27, 1974. Goal 15 for the Willamette River Greenway was adopted by the LCDC on December 6, 1975. The final four goals, for coastal resources, were adopted on December 19, 1976.

Soon after gaining statehood in 1959, Hawaii adopted a different form of land-use planning in 1961. Since 1984 many other states have enacted state-wide growth management, including Florida, New Jersey, Maine, Rhode Island, Vermont, Georgia, and Washington. Many of these states based at least part of their programs on the Oregon model.

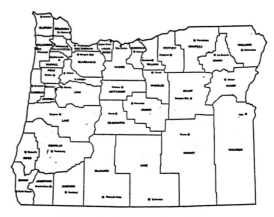

Map of Oregon Counties

Oregon's nineteen land use goals are in these areas:

Agricultural Lands
Air, Water, and Land Resources
Beaches and Dunes
Citizen Involvement
Coastal Shorelands
Economy
Energy
Estuarine Resources
Forest Lands
Housing
Land-Use Planning
Natural Disasters and Hazards
Ocean Resources
Open Spaces, Scenic and Historic Areas, and Natural Resources
Public Facilities and Services
Recreation Needs
Transportation
Urbanization
Willamette Greenway

210 In 1930, a joint effort by DuPont and General Motors resulted in creation of the synthetic compound trade-named **Freon**, which was put into refrigerators and air conditioners and later into aerosol cans as a propellant (hairspray, deodorant, industrial solvents, etc.).

Oregon was the first state to ban in-state sale of aerosol spray cans containing certain chlorofluorocarbon compounds (CFCs) as propellants (trichloro-monofluormethane, difluoro-dichloro-methane, or any other saturated chlorofluorocarbon compound containing hydrogen). The law (SB 771) prohibited such sales after March 1, 1977, to prevent further depletion of the earth's ozone layer.

CFCs are blamed for three-fourths of the depletion of atmospheric ozone. The ozone layer is vital protection to life on earth, preventing approximately 99% of the sun's mid-ultraviolet radiation from reaching the earth's surface.

Increased intensity of ultraviolet radiation poses a serious threat to life on earth, including increased occurrences of skin cancer, damage to food crops, damage to phytoplankton which is vital to the production of oxygen and to the food chain, and unpredictable and irreversible global climatic changes.

Representative Pat Whiting, Senator Walt Brown, and Senator Ted Hallock joined forces and were the main sponsors of Senate Bill 771. On June 16, 1975, Governor Robert Straub signed the bill into law, prohibiting the sale of that kind of aerosol spray can, saying, "If there is no hazard, the bill can be repealed. If fluorocarbons do threaten the earth's ozone layer — and earth's people — then they will be banned not only in Oregon, but throughout the world."

After the 1975 legislative session, Representative Pat Whiting of Tigard took the model legislation east, appearing on the national *Today* television show in a debate she won against a DuPont spokesman, and later before Congress. Congress wasn't moving fast enough on this issue, so the Executive Branch via **President Jimmy Carter's signature eliminated the use of Freon in aerosol cans nationally. By 1990, through international agreements, ninety countries had agreed to an accelerated phase-out of ozone-depleting chemicals.**

Atmospheric testing before 1980 showed that the invisible chlorofluorocarbons (CFCs) released into the environment were still in the atmosphere . . . and the concentrations were increasing about 5% annually.

The 1990 Federal Clean Air Act Amendments are based upon a 2% depletion of the ozone layer. Scientific studies have found the depletion to be already many times greater, with the largest hole in the ozone over Antarctica larger than the area of the U.S., and growing.

211 **The Metropolitan Service District (Metro) is the first directly elected regional government in the U.S.** (1979). Metro provides zoo, transportation, and solid-waste planning, and was responsible for construction of the twin-peaked Oregon Convention Center. Voters approved the present-day **Metro** in May of 1978 with a 55% approval; however, this support was mostly in Multnomah County, with only a slightly favorable edge in Washington County, and Clackamas County voters rejected the measure and unsuccessfully attempted to be removed from the jurisdiction. In November, 1992, voters approved the Metro charter, making it the nation's first regional government with a charter.

212 **Oregon is the first state to require wood stove certification** on the purchase of new stoves. In 1983, in the interest of the public health and welfare, it was declared Oregon's public policy to control, reduce, and prevent air pollution caused by emissions from new woodstoves.

213 **Oregon is the first and only state in the nation to continuously operate a lottery based upon the outcome of professional sports** (football and basketball). The Delaware lottery experimented with professional sports started in 1975, was sued by the NFL and won, but stopped that experiment. The Oregon State Lottery was approved by citizen initiative (1984) and started selling Sports Action tickets on April 25, 1985. Sports Action was approved by Legislature, and currently is offered only during the professional football season. Proposed federal legislation would make it illegal for state lotteries to offer games based on the outcome of sporting events. Delaware and Oregon were the only states with lotteries under consideration to be grand-fathered by Congress (1990).

214 **Oregon is the first state to encourage community service volunteerism** among high school students (16 to 19 years old inclusive). A post-secondary voucher program within the State Scholarship Commission provides one year of free tuition at state, private, or community college for up to 500 hours of volunteer work. The bill author is Jeannette Hamby, State Senator from Hillsboro. Since it started on October 3, 1989, **Volunteers in Service to Oregon (VISTO)** has been affected by a reduction in general state revenues.

215 At a special 1984 legislative session, Oregon became the first of twelve U.S. states with a unitary import tax to repeal it.

216 On January 1, 1991, Oregon became the first of the fifty states to raise the **minimum wage** above $4.25 and $4.50 per hour to $4.75 per hour. The District of Columbia has a vast array of minimum wages for different industries, a few of which are higher than $4.75 per hour.

217 The first major legislation approved in the U.S. to shift the environmental focus from pollution control to **pollution prevention** was passed in 1989 as Oregon's Toxic Use Reduction and Hazardous Waste Reduction Law. This law requires large toxic-compound users to evaluate their use of toxic chemicals and set specific goals for reducing their use of those chemicals. The law also provides technical assistance to industry in exploring safe alternatives. Sixteen states have followed Oregon's lead and passed similar pollution prevention laws between 1989 and 1991. Governor Neil Goldschmidt actually signed the law just a few hours after his counterpart in Massachusetts, Michael Dukakis, had signed similar legislation for the Bay State. (ORS 465-003 through 037 and OAR Chapter 340, Division 135.)

218 Over the years, the state government sterilized over 1,500 sex offenders. In 1983, the Oregon legislature passed a bill encouraging the use of Depo-Provera to reduce male sex drive for convicted sex offenders. Depo-Provera had been used for the treatment of sex offenders at Johns Hopkins University in Maryland since 1966, without state law. Depo-Provera is an option for police and the courts. Senator Jeannette Hamby of Hillsboro authored the bill.

220 Oregon is one of only two states in the U.S. with a flag that has symbols on both sides. The Massachusetts flag has a pine tree on its back. A beaver and state symbol appear on the Oregon flag.

Other progressive legislation includes workers' compensation and widows' pensions in 1913, compulsory education in 1921, and a system of public utility districts in 1930.

Oregon is one of the first U.S. states with legislation for a) restraining orders for battered spouses, b) gun control (extending waiting period for background checks; prohibition in public schools), and c) family employment leave following a birth or adoption. Oregon is the first state to totally revise its workers' compensation system (1990).

There are more legislative innovations described in chapters on
Citizen Initiatives,
Agriculture,
Education,
Energy,
Environment,
Forestry,
Human Services,
Health and Medicine,
Transportation,
Cities and Towns,
Utility Regulations, and
Future Firsts.

State Symbols Approved by the Legislature

State Bird (1927)	Western Meadowlark
State Song (1927)	"Oregon My Oregon"
State Tree (1939)	Douglas Fir
State Motto (1957)	"She Flies With Her Own Wings"
Father of Oregon (1957)	Dr. John McLoughlin
State Fish (1961)	The Chinook Salmon
State Rock (1965)	Thunderegg
State Animal (1969)	The American Beaver
Poet Laureate (1974)	William Stafford (appointed by Governor Tom McCall)
State Dance (1977)	Square Dance
State Insect (1979)	Oregon Swallowtail
Mother of Oregon (1987)	Tabitha Moffatt Brown
State Flower (1989)	Oregon Grape
State Gemstone (1989)	Oregon Sunstone
State Nut (1989)	Filbert (Hazelnut)
Historian Laureate (1989)	Thomas Vaughan

Citizen Initiatives or Direct Legislation

The voter initiative concept had origins in Switzerland. While Oregon was not the first state to adopt the Initiative Powers (South Dakota [1898] and Utah [1900] preceded it) Oregon voters were the first and have been the most frequent users of the initiative powers, approving dozens of initiatives addressing a wide variety of issues. This legislation is unique, and some has been replicated elsewhere.

William S. U'Ren
Advocate for Direct Legislation
(Oregon Historical Society Neg. # 018319)

221 On June 2, 1902, **Oregon voters overwhelmingly approved a constitutional amendment to adopt initiative and referendum powers** by an 11 to 1 majority vote (62,024 to 5,668). The 1903 Legislature passed an act (HB 23) making effective the initiative and referendum provisions of Article IV of the constitution of the State of Oregon. Since then, the people have used the initiative petition over 300 times, and the referendum has been utilized over 60 times.

The law, in effect, makes every citizen of the state a member of the state legislature. The law provides that a percentage of the citizens via petition signatures can place on the state ballot a proposed statutory act (with 6% of voters) or constitutional amendment (with 8% of voters) for approval or rejection by the voters at the next general election. Similarly, 4% of the citizens may invoke the referendum on a measure adopted by the legislature and give voters the opportunity to approve or veto the action.

In the 1880s, the Progressive Party dominated Oregon politics for many years. Progressive William U'Ren was leader of the Direct Legislation League **when the Oregon Legislature enacted the "Oregon System" of open government and direct citizen legislation based on initiative, referendum, and recall (a system now used by about two dozen states).**

222 The nation's first statewide citizen initiatives were approved by Oregon voters on June 6, 1904 for 1) the direct presidential primary process and 2) a local-option liquor law.

223 **Oregon is the first state to give voters power to recall elected officials.** Recall of public officials was the result of an initiative petition filed in January, 1908, and approved by the voters that year. The recall has had limited use in Oregon on the state level, with only three successful uses on local-government levels. Recall was first tried out in the City of Los Angeles, California.

Abigail Scott Duniway (center) casting her first official vote (1912). She fought 41 years to gain this privilege for women. (Photo courtesy of OHS Neg.Oreg. 4599)

224 On November 5, 1912, a constitutional amendment allowing women suffrage was finally passed 61,265 yes to 57,104 no, making Oregon the ninth state to allow women to vote. This was the sixth vote on this issue **of women's suffrage, the most votes on the issue by any state. Abigail Scott Duniway was the leader of the women's suffrage movement in Oregon.** Her brother, *The Oregonian* newspaper editor Harvey Scott, who opposed letting women vote, died in 1910.

225 In 1980, Oregon voters approved a ballot measure about nuclear plant licensing requiring voter approval and the existence of a nuclear waste facility. The vote was 608,412 for and 539,049 against. The initiative was sponsored by a coalition of non-profit organizations.

227 Legislated statewide Citizen Utility Boards started earlier in Wisconsin and Illinois. When the Oregon Legislature didn't move on the idea, an initiative petition was sponsored by the Oregon State Public Interest Research Group (OSPIRG), a statewide consumer organization. Oregon became the first state in the United States with a **voter-initiated and approved Citizens' Utility Board**.

In 1984, 637,968 Oregonians voted to establish the Citizens' Utility Board of Oregon (CUB) to represent the interests of utility consumers on telephone, electric, and natural gas matters before the Oregon Public Utility Commissioner and to insert educational information in monthly utility bills. In opposition to the initiative, the large utility monopolies outspent CUB supporters 100 to 1. A coalition of Oregon utilities fought the inserts, and the U.S. Supreme Court, in a decision pertaining to a similar California case, ruled in favor of the utilities so as not to "infringe their freedom of speech."

From 1985-1992, CUB participated in **34 regulatory cases in which Public Utility Commission decisions saved Oregon residential and business utility ratepayers over $200,000,000 dollars** in proposed rate increases annually statewide. CUB's biggest victories include Oregon's **first utility refund to customers**, when U. S. West Communications (legally Pacific NW Bell) was ordered to reduce rates $56 million in 1987, including a $14.55 cash refund per ratepayer, and $24 million annually thereafter.

--BUCKLE-UP-- --

228 A persistent initiative petition resulted in **approval of a safety belt law by voters for the first time in the U.S.** In a 1963 auto accident, a lap belt saved John Tongue's life. John Tongue served as President of the Oregon Lifebelt Committee, which placed an initiative on the ballot, but it failed, with 44% of the vote. In May, 1990, after Arizona and Alaska passed a seat belt law, Oregon was one of 15 states without a mandatory seat belt law, and the only western state without one. On July 6, 1990, over 80,000 signatures of registered voters qualified a ballot measure, which was approved by the voters. Passengers aged sixteen and under were already required to use a seat belt. According to Oregon Traffic Safety Commission observations, even before the law was passed by voters in November, 1990, Oregon had the highest seat belt usage of any non-law state.

229 Oregon's **1990 seat belt law, the strongest in the nation,** included primary enforcement, an average fine of $25 with a maximum fine of $50, and requirements for back seat passengers (all occupants). **The law reduced motor vehicle occupant deaths by 19.2%, saving 90 to 100 lives in the first year, and resulted in $242 million in savings for Oregon taxpayers in medical expenses for serious injuries**. Some insurance companies issued rebates to their Oregon customers. The National Highway Traffic Safety Administration estimates the cost of the average fatality at $700,000 based on the economic contribution of one life. Since the seat belt law went into effect on December 7, 1990, the number of deaths for 1992 was the lowest in twenty years.

$ No Sales Tax ¢

230 **Oregon is one of five states in the nation that does not have a general state sales tax;** the others are Alaska, Delaware, Montana, and New Hampshire. In 1989, Oregon ranked 23rd among states on the per capita state and local tax burden, 7% below the U.S. average.
Prior to the approval of the Property Tax Limitation by 53% of the 1990 voters, Oregon's tax system was considered one of the most progressive in the nation. After total implementation of the 1990 Property Tax Limitation, Oregon will have the third lowest per capita tax state and local tax burden in the nation, if it is not revised.

Oregon voters have rejected sales tax proposals nine times (1933, 1934, 1936, 1944, 1947, 1969, 1985, 1986, and 1993). The greatest support was 29% voter approval in 1934. In the November, 1938, general election, Oregonians voted down a sales tax plan which was intended to finance an extended old-age pension plan that had been approved in the preceding statewide primary. On November 9, 1993, 25% of the voters supported a sales tax.

231 The only state not allowing an emergency clause on a tax measure is Oregon.

First U.S. Post Office west of the Rocky
Mountains, Astoria, Oregon Territory, 1847
(OHS Negative 001875)

First U.S. Customs House west of Rocky
Mountains and on Pacific coast at Astoria,
Oregon Territory, 1849 *(OHS Negative 300-a)*

Admission to the United States in Chronological Order

1.	Delaware	December 7, 1787	26.	Michigan	December 6, 1837
2.	Pennsylvania	December 12, 1787	27	Florida	March 3, 1845
3.	New Jersey	December 18, 1787	28.	Texas	December 29, 1845
4.	Connecticut	January 9, 1788	29.	Iowa	December 28, 1846
5.	Georgia	January 12, 1788	30.	Wisconsin	May 29, 1848
6.	Massachusetts	February 6, 1788	31.	California	September 9, 1850
7.	Maryland	April 28, 1788	32	Minnesota	May 11, 1858
8.	South Carolina	May 23, 1788	**33.**	**Oregon**	**February 14, 1859**
9.	New Hampshire	June 21, 1788	34.	Kansas	January 19, 1861
10.	Virginia	June 25, 1788	35.	West Virginia	June 20, 1863
11.	New York	July 26, 1788	36.	Nevada	October 31, 1864
12.	North Carolina	November 21, 1789	37	Nebraska	March 1, 1867
13.	Rhode Island	May 29, 1790	38.	Colorado	August 1, 1876
14.	Vermont	March 4, 1791	39.	South Dakota	November, 2, 1889
15.	Kentucky	June 1, 1792	40.	North Dakota	November 2, 1889
16.	Tennessee	June 1, 1796	41.	Montana	November 8, 1889
17	Ohio	March 1, 1803	42.	Washington	November 11, 1889
18.	Louisiana	April 30, 1812	43.	Idaho	July 3, 1890
19.	Indiana	December 11, 1816	44.	Wyoming	July 10, 1890
20	Mississippi	December 10, 1817	45.	Utah	January 4, 1896
21.	Illinois	December 3, 1818	46.	Oklahoma	November 16, 1907
22.	Alabama	December 14, 1819	47.	New Mexico	January 6, 1912
23.	Maine	March 15, 1820	48	Arizona	February 14, 1912
24.	Missouri	August 10, 1821	49.	Alaska	January 3, 1959
25.	Arkansas	June 15, 1836	50.	Hawaii	August 21, 1959

Federal Legislation and Appointments

The Federal Government fulfilled a large role in the development of the Oregon Country from the Louisiana Purchase, Lewis and Clark's Corps of Discovery, and treaties with indigenous people to the present. Four countries had claims to the Oregon Country: Spain, Russia, Great Britain, and the U.S. No country could claim exclusive title to the entire region. International laws applied four tests to establish claim of title to land territories: discovery, exploration, settlement, and treaties.
The first law to recognize the equality of the sexes (Donation Land Claim Law) was passed by Congress in 1842.

History shows that in response to anti-alien feelings of the times, Congress enacted Chinese and Japanese exclusion laws in 1882 and 1924. The constitutional provision denying blacks, mulattoes, and Chinese the right of suffrage was not repealed until June 28, 1927.

232 The first U.S. official in the Oregon Territory was Dr. Elijah White, Indian sub agent. Anson Dart became the first full-time superintendent of Indian Affairs in 1851.

233 William T'Vault was appointed the first Provisional Postmaster General in 1845. (He was a newspaper editor too).

234 John M. Shively was the first Oregon Postmaster at the first post office west of the Rocky Mountains, at Astoria, Oregon Territory, 1847. Shively left for the California gold mines in 1849.

235 Colonel William Wing Loring was appointed the first U.S. Army Commander in the Oregon Territory in 1849.

236 John Adair was appointed first in charge of the first Customs House on the west coast in 1849 to collect duties on imports (photo, page 42). The Customs House Building in Astoria was completed in 1852 and was the first Federal building on the Pacific coast.

237 William Strong was appointed the first Oregon Territorial Judge in 1850.

238 The first Preliminary Survey of the Columbia River's mouth was in 1850.

239 John Evans was appointed first Geologist in the Oregon Territory in 1853.

240 One of the first women to receive a presidential appointment as a U.S. Postmaster was Elizabeth Millar Wilson. President Grant appointed her in 1874 and she served for 12 years at The Dalles, where high-topped stages carried the mail.

242 **Richard Lewis Neuberger**, first a State Senator then U.S. Senator from Oregon (from January 3, 1955, to March 9, 1960), was the person behind many important pieces of legislation. He was **author of the first Federal billboard legislation** that set standards for protection of beauty and scenery, and that encouraged states to ban placement of billboards next to existing Federal interstate highways.

Richard Neuberger was the first U.S. Senator to sponsor an increase in the Federal gasoline tax so that construction and maintenance of the U.S. highway network, instead of relying on deficit financing, would operate for motor vehicle drivers on a "pay-as-you-go" basis.

243 **A conservationist, U.S. Senator Richard Neuberger was co-author, first co-sponsor, and a leading advocate of the Wilderness Act. The Wilderness Act** (sponsored by Senator Hubert H. Humphrey of Minnesota) eventually passed in 1964, four years after Richard Neuberger's death.

244 Oregon Senator McNary was the author and an effective leader in sheperding through Congress in 1924 the Clarke-McNary Act. This was an innovative measure that **strengthened the fire protection alliance of Federal Forest Service, state government, and private timbermen.** The statute provided seedlings to states for reforestation. By the middle 1970s, via provisions of the Clarke-McNary Act, over 18 million acres had been reforested and 39 million acres received forest fire protection. McNary authored other conservation-oriented legislation for research, taxes, and expansion of federal forests.

In the 1930s, **Senator Charles L. McNary was the U.S. Senate minority leader.** McNary won nomination as Vice-Presidential candidate on the unsuccessful Republican ticket with Wendell Wilkie in 1940. He helped start the Bonneville Power Administration, and McNary Dam was dedicated by President Eisenhower (1954).

Oregon ranks high among the public-land states, with almost exactly one-half of the land within Oregon's borders owned by the U.S. Government. Most of it is managed by the U.S. Forest Service and Bureau of Land Management.

245 After the Royal College of Physicians in London brought forth the first report on the harmfulness of smoking, **U.S. Senator Maurine Neuberger of Oregon took action. She authored and introduced the first cigarette warning label legislative bill** at the Federal level in 1966. In spite of an intense lobbying effort against it, a similar law was eventually approved requiring cigarette packages to contain the following statement (or variations of it):

> **SURGEON GENERAL'S WARNING:**
> **Cigarette Smoking May Be Hazardous To Your Health**

Recent Warnings

> **SURGEON GENERAL'S WARNING:**
> Smoking Causes Lung Cancer, Heart Disease, Emphysema, And May Complicate Pregnancy.

> Stopping Smoking Now Greatly Reduces Health Risks

246 U.S. Senator Maurine Neuberger sponsored legislation for the coloration of margarine, at the state level first and then in the U.S. Senate. Maurine Neuberger also wrote the "baby-sitting bill," the first legislation introduced allowing tax credits for working mothers.

Precedent-Setting Supreme Court Decisions

247 **Fewer hours for working women.** Muller vs. Oregon, 208 US 412 (1908), sustained an Oregon law that "No female shall be employed in any factory more than ten hours in any one day." The "inherent difference between the sexes" justified "a difference in legislation" and "upholds that which is designed to compensate for some of the burdens which rest upon her." Prior to the Muller decision, courts had used "due process," designed to protect groups of people that were in a vulnerable position. This marked the first instance of a "Brandeis Brief" (named after Louis Brandeis, a reform lawyer and later Supreme Court justice) and the use of sociological, economic, and historical data to support a legal position, rather than just prior court cases.
(See #198)

248 Pacific States Telegraph and Telephone vs. Oregon, 223 US 118 (1912). The Supreme Court declined to invalidate Oregon's newly adopted right of popular initiative against a challenge that the initiative process violates the U.S. Constitutional provision guaranteeing a "republican form of government." (Article 4, Section 4, U.S. Constitution.)

249 **Pierce vs. Society of Sisters** (Sisters of the Holy Names), 268 U.S. 510 (1925), **constituted a landmark decision defining constitutional protections for religious freedom under the First Amendment. This was an anti-Catholic schools case.** Ku Klux Klan legislative control and hysteria in the state capital caused a wave of legislation against Catholics and religious freedom. In 1922, a citizen initiative calling for the closure of all religious and private schools passed by a vote of 115,000 to 103,000. The resulting court case pitted the Catholic Church versus Governor Walter M. Pierce of Oregon. Compulsory education in Oregon started in the 1920s. Since school was required, parents would have been criminally liable by fine and imprisonment for not sending their children between 8 and 16 years old to public schools. Before the private-school closing went into effect, the U.S. Supreme Court decision of June 1, 1925, voided the Oregon Public School Law, which would have abolished private and parochial schools.

250 **De Jonge vs. Oregon,** 299 US 353 (1937). **Dirk De Jonge** (a member of the Communist Party) **was arrested in Portland while speaking about labor issues during a Pacific Coast strike. Precedent was set on the right to free assembly.**

Dirk De Jonge was arrested by Portland police while he spoke about strike issues at a meeting during the peak of the Pacific Coast maritime strike in 1934. He was charged with criminally advocating the overthrow of the government. Irving Goodman was his attorney. De Jonge was convicted and sentenced to seven years. Gus Solomon (later to become a U.S. District Judge for Oregon) undertook to appeal the case before the Oregon Supreme Court, which reaffirmed the conviction. Osmond K. Frankel, on behalf of the main office of the American Civil Liberties Union in New York City, took the case to the U.S. Supreme Court. The U.S. Supreme Court reversed De Jonge's conviction with the opinion that De Jonge did not advocate overthrow of the government. The Court held that freedom of assembly is as basic a right as freedom of speech or freedom of the press. This decision has become a true **landmark in the field of First Amendment law.**

251 **Oregon vs. Mitchell,** 400 US 112 (1970). Congress could lower the voting age for Federal elections from 21 to 18 years, but was held to be without power to lower the voting age in state elections. This case led to passage of a state law that granted 18-year-olds the vote in Oregon in all elections.

252 **Oregon vs. Hass,** 4020 US 714 (1975). The U.S. Supreme Court said a state may not impose greater restrictions on public officers as a matter of Federal constitutional law when the U.S. Supreme Court has refrained from doing so. (Miranda Rights case)

253 **Oregon Employment Division vs. Smith,** (110 S.Ct. 1595) (1990). Alfred Smith of the Klamath Indian Tribe claimed First Amendment entitlement to unemployment compensation benefits after his discharge as a drug counselor because of using peyote in a ceremony of the Native American church. This 1990 decision fundamentally reshaped rights and protections of the **First Amendment's** free exercise of religion clause. The 1991 Oregon legislature enacted a law allowing religious use of peyote to be a defense to criminal charges of drug use.

254 The State of Oregon has been **a pioneer in interpreting provisions of its state constitution independently from identical or similar provisions of the U.S. Constitution.**

255 **Oregon is the only state that does not confer to the people the power of impeachment** (for any elected office).

256 **Oregon is the only state whose Bill of Rights confers the right to "reform or abolish the government."**

257 **U.S. vs. Exxon was the largest final civil judgment in the history of U.S. law**. Oregon Attorney General Dave Frohnmayer argued the appeal on behalf of all U.S. states, territories, and possessions. The $2.1 billion restitution judgement went to consumers, paid through state energy conservation measures. This affected other petroleum companies. Later, the $4 to $6 billion Stripper Well case was settled by Frohnmayer and other state attorneys general in the aftermath of the Exxon judgement.

258 **Namba vs. McCourt**, 185 Or 579 (1949). Prior Federal laws stated that a Japanese alien was not allowed to own or lease land for farming purposes. This was challenged when a young honorably discharged Japanese-American war veteran, Kenji Namba, and his father, Etsuo Namba, leased land near Gresham for growing berries. Oregon Supreme Court Justice Rossman had the courage of his convictions to go beyond existing U.S. Supreme Court precedents under the equal protection clause in order to restore the rights of 1,500 Japanese-Americans to farm land, allowing free access to ordinary occupation in whatever community in which s/he resides.

258• The **first spousal rape case** in the country was started by Greta Rideout in Marion County against her husband, John Rideout. The trial, which lasted a week, began December 19, 1978. The jury of eight women and four men reached a unanimous verdict acquitting John Rideout. Salem attorney Charles Burt received over 4,500 letters about the case.

258• Former State of Oregon Attorney General **Dave Frohnmayer won more cases before the U.S. Supreme Court than any current Attorney General in the nation** (1991-92) and any other attorney in Oregon. Oregon was fortunate and unique in that most state Attorneys General don't personally argue cases before the U.S. Supreme Court. From 1981 to 1991, Dave Frohnmayer lost only one of seven cases before the U.S. Supreme Court. Generally, only one in ten cases is argued by an Attorney General.

258• **Hewitt vs. SAIF** (State Accident Insurance Fund), 1982. The statutes had stated that only women were to receive death benefits in the event of an industrial accident. When a woman died in an industrial accident, the husband filed for benefits. The Oregon constitution states that all citizens regardless of gender have the same privileges, and hence equal rights (the state constitution is gender-neutral).

Counties

Oregon Counties	Date Created

Original Districts

1. Tuality   July 5, 1843
   (became Washington County September 3, 1849)
2. Yamhill   July 5, 1843
3. Clackamas   July 5, 1843
4. Champoeg   July 5, 1843
   (became Marion County September 3, 1849)

Districts established by Provisional
Government on July 5, 1843
(OHS Negative 8775)

Counties Formed from the Original Districts

5.	Clatsop	June 5, 1844
6.	Polk	December 19, 1845
7.	Benton	December 23, 1847
8.	Linn	December 28, 1847
9.	Douglas	January 24, 1851
10.	Lane	January 28, 1851
11.	Jackson	January 12, 1852
12.	Klamath	October 17, 1852
13.	Tillamook	December 15, 1853
14.	Coos	December 22, 1853
15.	Multnomah	December 22, 1854
16.	Wasco	January 11, 1855
17.	Curry	December 18, 1855
18.	Josephine	January 22, 1856
19.	Baker	September 22, 1862
20.	Umatilla	September 27, 1862
21.	Union	October 14, 1864
22.	Grant	October 14, 1864
23.	Columbia	January 16, 1871
24.	Lake	October 24, 1874
25.	Crook	October 24, 1882
26.	Morrow	February 16, 1885
27.	Gilliam	February 25, 1885
28.	Malheur	February 17, 1887
29.	Sherman	February 25, 1889
30.	Harney	February 25, 1889
31.	Wallowa	February 11, 1887
32.	Wheeler	February 17, 1889
33.	Lincoln	February 20, 1893
34.	Hood River	June 1, 1908
35.	Jefferson	December 12, 1914
36.	Deschutes	December 16, 1916

Oregon's 36 counties

Utility Regulation

Utilities such as electricity, telephone, gas, and transportation (trucks, buses, trains) are regulated at the state level. Regulatory issues include public safety, competition, monopolistic control, and public service.

259 **Until 1986, Oregon was the last (and hence only) state with a single-person Public Utility Commission.** Oregon had a three-member Public Service Commission (PSC) until 1930 when, at Governor Julius Meier's request, the legislature changed the PSC from a three-person commission to a single-person commission to reduce the budget and gain power. In 1986, more than 724,000 Oregonians approved a **citizen initiative to re-form a three-person Oregon Public Utility Commission.** Charles Davis was the last single-person statewide utility regulatory decision-maker in the U.S. Charles Davis was appointed to the same position twice in one year when he headed the expanded three-person PUC for a few months.

260 After 65 years transporting thousands of passengers and packages, the Oregon Utility Commissioner brought to a halt the lifetime of the **last interurban electric train running in the country at that time, when the Portland Traction Company stopped on January 26, 1958**.

261 Oregon was the first state to require a **railroad milepost inventory** of emergency response agency boundaries.

Weigh Station (photo courtesy of Oregon Department of Transportation)

262 In 1947, **Oregon became the first U.S. state with a weight-mileage tax on trucks** to pay for state highways. In 1992, a little more than $180 million was collected in Oregon from the weight-mileage tax on trucks.

263 Oregon became the first state to require that **Emergency Response Areas** be furnished with information on the types and quantities of hazardous materials moving through their districts by rail.

264 Oregon PUC actions were the first in the U.S. to use a **special formula to predict accident potential at railroad crossings.**

265 The first state to have a **base state agreement** to make it easier for motor carriers in another state to pay local user taxes was Oregon.

266 In 1989, Oregon was **one of the two first states** (Florida was the other) **with telemarketing abatement symbols next to subscribers' names in telephone directories.** Telephone customers can indicate if commercial solicitation calls are not desired. See the white pages of Oregon telephone directories. In Oregon, the • symbol costs 50¢ to 75¢/month, for an annual rate of $6 to $9.

• Commercial Solicitation Calls Prohibited

266• **Oregon had the nation's toughest telemarketing laws as of July 1992.**

  a) Telephone companies are encouraged to offer customers a "no solicitation calls" symbol (•) in telephone directories.
  b) Telephone solicitors are also prohibited from calling a person who has asked not to be called again.
  c) Telemarketers must register at the State Department of Justice.
  d) The use of automatic dialing and announcing devices (ADAD) for commercial solicitation is prohibited.
  e) A law in effect since 1979 requires telephone solicitors to identify themselves and provide other information within 30 seconds after beginning a conversation.

267 On March 9, 1990, Oregon became the **first state in the nation to inaugurate an electronic monitoring system** to keep truckers from cheating on their payloads. The system also cuts down on vehicle thievery while making it easier for trucking companies to keep track of their equipment. The system combines weighing trucks in motion with automatic vehicle identification.

268 Oregon was the first state to initiate cooperation among interstate truck inspections. The **Commercial Vehicle Safety Alliance** started in 1990.

Oregon is the first state in the U.S. with a **voter-approved Citizens' Utility Board** *(See #227).*

(For more *Utilities*, see *Communications, Energy, Supreme Court,* and *Citizen Initiatives* chapters.)

Peace and War

U.S. WARS

Estimates of American War Dead

Revolutionary War (England)	~ 4,435
War of 1812 (England)	~ 2,260
Mexico	~13,283
Spain	~ 2,446
Civil War	~510,332

(Union troops suffered about 350,000 deaths, and Confederate troops suffered about 160,000 deaths)

World War I	~116,708
World War II	~405,399
Korea	~54,246
Vietnam	~58,655
Panama	23

(estimates range from 2,000-5,000 Panamanian civilians killed)

Iraq-Kuwait	210

(est. 150,000-250,000+ Iraqi deaths)

269 **The U.S. War of 1812 with Great Britain led to the British Navy's brief wartime "military occupation" of the Oregon Country. The occupation occurred when the HMS (His Majesty's Sloop of War)** *Raccoon* **sailed into the mouth of the Columbia and seized American fur trading post Fort Astoria in December 1813.** Fort Astoria was already in English hands. Post-war negotiations demanded that Astoria be returned to the U.S. The Treaty of Ghent (1814) ended the War of 1812 and provided that "all territory, places, and possessions whatsoever taken by either party from the other during the war . . . shall be restored without delay." *(See also #79)*

270 Oregon's Provisional Government passed the **first militia law** of the Oregon Country on July 5, 1843. It authorized formation of a battalion of mounted riflemen, composed of the male inhabitants of Oregon between the ages of sixteen and sixty who wished to be recognized as citizens by the government.

271 Black measles killed 198 Cayuse Indians, mostly children, and instigated the Whitman Massacre on November 29, 1847. The **first militia of the Oregon Provisional Government was organized** after 14 settlers were killed at that massacre.

272 Asa Lovejoy was Oregon's first Adjutant General (December 27, 1847 to 1854).

Oregon Country Wars against people native to this land:
Cayuse War 1847-50
Rogue River War 1851-56

    (about 400 deaths)

Yakima War 1855-58
Modoc War 1872 (most costly war)
Bannock War 1878 (about 130 deaths)
These wars led to "peace and friendship" treaty making, which created the small Indian reservation as an institution, a place to reside in perpetuity. U.S. Superintendent of Indian Affairs Joel Palmer (1853-56) used the reservation system as a means for protecting the natives from the whites and to bring peace to the two races. Under the Joel Palmer negotiated treaties **the U.S. Government paid as little as 2.3¢/acre for hundreds of square miles of land,** e.g., the **first treaty approved by Congress (1854) with Indians in the Northwest** was the September 10, 1853, treaty with the Rogue River tribe.

272• The **Oregon Trail of Tears** refers to the 1856 round-up of coastal natives. Starting in midwinter, January 24, 1856, the U.S. military marched 30 to 40 bands of people (300 to 400 people) up the coast from Southern Oregon to the Siletz and Grande Ronde reservations. The people were not allowed to stop to bury their dead or tend to their sick, and half the people died on the trip.

In 1924, Oregon Indians were given full U.S. citizenship.

273 **Oregon's first veteran,** William Cannon (1755-1854), was 57 when he arrived in Oregon in 1812. William Cannon was a pioneer blacksmith who's believed to be the only U.S. Revolutionary War veteran to be buried in Oregon. He fought in at least two major battles of that war. He was recruited for the tortuous overland expedition led by Wilson Hunt Price that arrived at Astoria in 1812. This was **the first transcontinental trip after the Lewis and Clark Expedition.** He was one of the first blacksmiths at Fort Vancouver and the builder of the first flour mill in 1828. At age 73, William Cannon became part of a trapping party. He was apparently an influential elder among Oregon's pioneers, voting with the majority for organizing a government at the 1843 meeting at nearby Champoeg.

274 **Fort Clatsop was the first military post west of St. Louis.** In 1975, the Oregon Historical Society secured land so that a replica of Lewis and Clark's Fort Clatsop could be built on the site of the original fort.

275 Though only a U.S. state for a few years, Oregon was an exception to loyalty to the Union during the Civil War. It was widely debated, but Oregon chose to stay neutral. **The first military installation built at Fort Stevens was by the Union Army in 1863 during the Civil War** to guard the entrance to the Columbia River from Confederate attack. It was named for General Isaac Ingalls Stevens, the first governor of the Washington Territory.

276 **U.S. Senator Colonel Edward Dickinson Baker from Oregon was the first Northern officer and the only member of Congress to die during the Civil War.** He died while leading his troops at the Battle of Balls Bluff, Virginia. He's the only U.S. Senator to serve in a military action while a senator. His statue stands in the Capitol Rotunda in Washington, D.C. Baker City and Baker County are named for him.

277 Edward R. S. Canby became the first and only U.S. general killed in the Oregon Country Indian Wars when he died in the Modoc Indian War in northern California in 1872. General Canby was headquartered in the Department of the Columbia in Vancouver or Portland in 1874.

278 **The *Battleship Oregon* fired the first shots in the battle on Santiago in the Spanish-American War,** July 3, 1898. The *Battleship Oregon* also served in World Wars I and II.

279 In May, 1898, the Oregon Volunteer Group was part of the first military expedition sent to the Philippines in the

Spanish-American War. **Oregon troops were the first to enter the Walled City of Manila on August 13, to raise the U.S. flag. They received the surrender of 13,000 Spanish troops and officers.** The militia company from Salem was the nation's first to respond to the call, and the first to be inducted.

280 In 1912, Oregon's Naval Reserve was three ships, named *USS Marblehead, USS Boston,* and *USS Goldsboro.* Twenty-five percent of the enlistees for the First World War trained on these ships.

281 Oregon's Harry Lane was one of only six U.S. Senators to vote against U.S. entry into the First World War in 1917.

282 During World War I Oregon was known as the "Volunteer State" because Portland's National Guard was the **first national guard regiment in the country to be mobilized and ready for service.**

283 Oregonians supplied **more volunteer soldiers per capita in World War I** than any other state.

"Spruce for the Air" and **"Fir for the Sea"** were World War I slogans for wood war planes and ships.

284 Oregon received a "first" awarded by U.S. Surgeon General Rupert Blue for having the lowest venereal disease rate among enlistees in World War II.

285 With the U.S. entry into World War II, the Federal Government increased the shipbuilding effort. Portland became one of the few major shipbuilding centers in the nation. Henry Kaiser's Oregon Shipbuilding Corporation built three shipyards in St. John's, Swan Island, and Vancouver. Oregon Shipbuilding launched the area's first Liberty ship on September 27, 1942. In its first year, 76 additional ships were completed. **A national record for production of Liberty ships was established when the *Joseph N. Teal* was put together in less than two weeks.** Oregon Shipbuilding Corporation swiftly became the leader in production of Liberty ships, building 322 Liberty ships, 147 tankers, and 141 small aircraft carriers.

JUNE 21, 1942 FORT STEVENS, OREGON WAS ATTACKED BY A JAPANESE SUBMARINE (I-25), 17 ROUNDS FIRED. THE 249™ COAST ARTILLERY PREPARED TO RETURN FIRE, — NO ORDERS CAME — ? ? ? ?

WWII
JUNE 21, 1942

FIRST ATTACK ON U.S. MAINLAND SINCE 1812.

286 Fort Stevens received the distinction of being **the only mainland installation on the continental U.S. to be fired on since the War of 1812.** Less than seven months after the attack on Pearl Harbor, on the night of June 21, 1942, the fort saw its only action when a Japanese submarine, the I-25, fired seventeen shells in its vicinity. The shelling caused very little damage, and since the submarine was out of range, the command at Fort Stevens did not return fire. Fort Stevens has the longest history as an active military post in Oregon (1863-1947), through both World Wars.

287 Hood River-born Minoru Yasui was in solitary confinement for nine months in the Multnomah County jail in 1942. He was **the first person to deliberately defy wartime curfew regulations for Japanese-Americans** living on the west coast. On the night of March 28, 1942, Minoru Yasui walked through the streets in downtown Portland, twice telephoning the FBI, twice asking Portland police to arrest him, but all refused; so he walked into police headquarters. He was arrested, tried, and convicted, and the conviction was affirmed by the U.S. Supreme Court. He became the first University of Oregon Law School graduate of Japanese ancestry.

288 On August 15, 1942, a float plane launched by catapult from a Japanese submarine, flown by pilots Nubio Fujita and Shoji Okuda, dropped two 76-kg (170-pound) incendiary bombs in a densely wooded area east of Brookings.

289 Mrs. Walter Harris, whose husband won a drawing at the Portland shipyards, became the first black woman to launch a World War II ship.

290 Balloon bombs made of rice paper were launched from Japan into the eastern jet streams and took three days to reach Oregon.

291 The Grant-Smith-Porter Ship Company in Portland constructed 50 new ship hulls in record time for Uncle Sam.

293 Hazel Ying Lee (4th Class) was the first Chinese-American in the WWII WASPs (Women's Air Force Service Pilots).

294 **The only deaths on the American continent during World War II due to enemy actions occurred on Oregon soil** just a mile east of the Klamath-Lake county line at Salt Spring. On May 5, 1945, six people at a Sunday school picnic were killed by a **balloon bomb launched from Japan.** These were the only deaths attributed to thousands of Japanese balloon bombs. The balloon bombs also posed incendiary threats to the forests, particularly near Brookings. It was during the war, and the government hushed up the news of the "unexplained" blast completely for almost three weeks. The dead included Elsie Mitchell (26 years) and five children aged 11 to 14 yrs: Dick and Joan Patzke, Edward Engen, Jay Gifford, and Sherman Shoemaker. Rev. Mitchell was the Bly church group's only survivor.

295 The aluminum industry began in Oregon in 1945 for the war effort. One-hundred sixty thousand workers were drawn to the war industries, including Oregon's first substantial black population. Large numbers of Spanish-speaking immigrants came to work in Oregon's growing food industry. During the decade between 1940 and 1949, Oregon led all states with an increase in population of 36.9%.

296 U.S. Air Force Captain Clyde Curtain of Gresham is Oregon's only Jet Fighter Ace. Captain Curtain fought with the 335th Fighter Squadron in Korea from 1952-53 and had five aerial victories.

296• The **largest Navy Mothers' unit in the nation**, the Battleship Oregon Club of Portland, had 132 members in 1959.

Photo of Wayne Morse (courtesy of Oregon Historical Society Negative #73858)

297 **Wayne Morse of Oregon led the national protest as the first of only two U.S. Senators to oppose U.S. involvement in the Vietnam War** (the Gulf of Tonkin Resolution, August, 1964). The second senator was Ernest Gruening, D-Alaska. **A Wisconsin native, Oregon's Senator Morse voted against all Vietnam War military appropriation bills.** Senator Morse favored the United Nations. He opposed unilateral military action when war with China was threatened over Formosa (now Taiwan) in 1954.

298 In the 1960s, Oregon Governor Mark Hatfield was **the nation's only governor to oppose the war in Vietnam.**

299 In August, 1970, the "Governor's Ball" sponsored by Governor Tom McCall, was the **first state-sponsored rock music festival in the U.S. "Vortex"** was held in McIver Park near Estacada and cost less than $13,000. The rock music festival successfully distracted 35,000 young potential anti-war demonstrators away from the national convention of the American Legion, which was being held in downtown Portland. The "impeachable" Vice-President Spiro Agnew made a surprise visit to speak at the convention.

300 Jeanne Holm, who attended Sunnyside School, Washington High School, and Lewis and Clark College in Portland, became **the nation's first woman general** (1973). She retired as a Major-General.

301 In 1981, Oregon's Legislative Historian Cecil Edwards, with Salem librarian Hugh Morrow's help, recognized that the state was due monies for protecting travelers, miners and settlers on the Oregon Trail during the Civil War. The state sequestered a long-overdue payment of $100,000 from the Federal Government. With interest, the overdue bill would have totalled over $45 million.

302 **Oregon is the first place the U.S. Government's White Train for nuclear weapons transport was stopped by protestors**. After 37 years, the secret weapons White Train was stopped for the first time on northeast Portland tracks for about an hour on February 24, 1984. Thirty-three anti-nuclear and peace activists were arrested.

303 **Oregon was the first state with a Peace Check-off on state tax forms.** Oregonians could check off a contribution for the Oregon Peace Institute (OPI) on state income tax returns. Proceeds fund projects to teach peace to children and youth statewide. The Oregon Peace Institute, **the first peace center in a shopping mall in the U.S.,** contains peace education materials and peace products. Other peace centers are university-based. OPI was founded by Elizabeth Furse and Robert Gould in 1987. The Oregon Peace Institute is located at The Galleria, 921 SW Morrison, downstairs and Suite 520, Portland, Oregon 97204.

OREGON PEACE
INSTITUTE

304 In 1985, Oregon became the **first state to pass a resolution opposing U.S. aid to the Contras and supporting negotiations to end the Contra War in Nicaragua.** Resolution sponsors were Senators Margie Hendrickson and Jeannette Hamby for the Council for Human Rights in Latin America.

305 Benjamin Linder, a 27-year-old mechanical engineer from Portland, had finished one hydro-electric plant in El Cua, Nicaragua in 1986. On April 28, 1987, Ben Linder was in San Jose de Bocay, assisting Nicaraguans constructing a second hydro-electric system, when he was killed in the U.S. Government-backed Contra war against the Nicaraguan government. Ben Linder was the **first of two American citizens killed by the Contras.**

306 Mark Hatfield of Oregon was the **only U.S. Senator to voice official opposition to the U.S. Government invasion of Panama** in December, 1989.

307 **Portland is the first U.S. city to honor Japanese citizens with a memorial recognizing the internment of Japanese-Americans during World War II.** In 1942, nearly all persons of Japanese descent living in Oregon, Washington, and California were ordered by their Government to evacuate their homes and were confined to camps in isolated areas for three years. Over 110,000 men, women, and children were affected. Most Japanese-Americans lost everything they owned. The memorial along Portland's downtown waterfront was dedicated in 1990 to remember both the Japanese-American story and the Bill of Rights that protects the freedoms of the American people.

308 The Columbia River ecosystem is threatened by the production of weapons of war upriver at the Hanford Nuclear Reservation in the State of Washington. Since 1943, **more nuclear waste from nuclear weapons' production has been stored at the Hanford Nuclear Reservation than any place on earth.** Nuclear waste is the world's deadliest substance and it will be radioactive for thousands of years.

309 On January 12, 1991, Mark Odom Hatfield was the **only U.S. Senator to oppose both of the resolutions to go to war against Iraq.**

310 **On the** <u>day</u> **Congress approved war against Iraq** in support of United Nations' resolutions, **the largest peace demonstration in the U.S. was held on downtown Portland streets**. On Saturday, January 12, 1991, the Demonstration for Peace in the Middle East was attended by 12,000 to 15,000 people. This peaceful march was 23 blocks long.

311 **Oregon was the first state to** pass a resolution (SJR 1) "requesting the President and Congress **to seek a peaceful solution to the Persian Gulf crisis."** Tricia Smith, the only freshman Senator to take office for the 1991 Legislative session, on the <u>first</u> day, January 14, 1991, made her <u>first</u> <u>floor</u> <u>speech</u> proposing SJR 1, requesting **the President and Congress to seek to exhaust all reasonable alternatives to the use of force against Iraq. Senate Joint Resolution 1 was approved unanimously.**

Political Achievements

312 There was no constitutional amendment for an unelected governor. However, Mrs. Carolyn B. Shelton became the **first woman "acting" Governor in Oregon (and perhaps the first female acting Governor in the U.S.)** from 9:00 am Saturday, February 27, until 10:10 am Monday, March 1, 1909, when Secretary of State F. W. Benson (who'd been sick) was sworn in. The previous governor, George Chamberlain, had left for Washington, D.C. to be one of the first of the newly elected U.S. Senators to take office, and hence gain seniority. Mrs. Carolyn Shelton was his "Chief of Staff." A local Salem newspaper called Oregon's three governors in 50 hours a "world's record for changing rulers."

This was fifteen years before the first two women to be elected Governor of a state took office within five days of each other in January 1925, in Wyoming (Nellie Tayloe Ross) and Texas (Mariam Amanda Fergeson).

Mrs. Shelton's few days as acting governor are significant because her brief responsibility came before women had the right to vote in Oregon. Mrs. Shelton is quoted as saying, **"Filling his shoes was easy; filling his hat was another matter."**

Barbara Roberts became the first woman elected governor of Oregon 80 years later, in November, 1990.

313 The first legislation in Oregon to allow women to vote was proposed by David Logan. Abigail Scott Duniway organized the Oregon State Equal Suffrage Association in 1894. **Abigail Scott Duniway worked for 41 years to obtain for women the right to vote.** An initiative for women's suffrage was finally approved November 5, 1912. **Abigail Scott Duniway was the first legal voter in the first Oregon election open to women. It took six campaigns to gain women the right to vote.** *(See photo #224)*

The argument that women did not want to vote even if they had the right to vote was crushed at the first election in 1912 when the percentage of women voting was as high as that of men, if not higher, in the majority of towns and cities.
(According to legend, Charlie Parkhurst, a one-eyed stagecoach driver, voted in Baker County and it was after Charlie had died that the undertaker discovered Charlie was a woman!) This means ol' Charlie was apparently the **first woman in the nation to vote.**

314 President Ulysses S. Grant selected George H. Williams to serve as Attorney General in 1871, the **first Oregonian in the U.S. Cabinet.** Later, George Williams was the only Oregonian nominated to the Supreme Court. Informal opposition led President Grant to withdraw the nomination.

315 **George Henry Williams**, former U.S. Attorney General, was first elected mayor of Portland at the age of 79. He was **then the oldest mayor in the country** in 1902.

316 Walter M. Pierce in 1933 at 72 years old became **the oldest first-term representative in the history of Congress**.

317 Mark Odom Hatfield circulated the first petition in the nation for General Dwight Eisenhower's nomination by Republicans in 1952.

318 For the first time in the United States, on November 7, 1950, Dick and Maurine Neuberger became the **first husband-and-wife team simultaneously elected to both chambers of a state legislature.**

319 U.S. Senator Wayne Morse of Oregon held the record for **the most nonstop talking**. In 1953, Wayne Morse spoke in Congress on the Tidelands Oil Bill for 22 hours and 26 minutes. Senator Strom Thurmond broke this record when he spoke for 25 hours.

320 **Wisconsin native Wayne Morse (1900-1974) is the only person elected to the U.S. Senate twice as a Republican (1944, 1950) and twice as a Democrat (1956, 1962).** He also served in the U.S. Senate as an Independent (1952) between his Republican and Democratic affiliations. He served as one of Oregon's Senators from January 3, 1945 to January 3, 1969. (*See photo #297*)

321 **U.S. Senator Maurine Neuberger,** who served in the U.S. Senate from 1960-67, **was the first woman elected directly to the U.S. Senate by a vote of the people in her own right, without appointment and without first serving in the House of Representatives.**

322 Robert F. Kennedy's only defeat in his 1968 presidential primary campaign was when Oregon voters approved Eugene McCarthy.

323 The **first woman and first Oregonian in the history of the nation to win an electoral college vote is Theodora "Tonie" Nathan of Eugene.** Tonie Nathan ran as Vice-Presidential candidate of the Libertarian Party twelve years before Vice-Presidential Candidate Geraldine Ferraro won electoral votes. The State of Virginia gave the Libertarian Party ticket one electoral vote in 1972.

324 When Neil Goldschmidt became Mayor of Portland in 1973 at the age of 32 years, he was the **youngest mayor of a major city in the U.S.** He served as mayor of Portland until 1979, when he was appointed U.S. Secretary of Transportation by President Carter.

325 A larger percentage of Oregon voters (30%) **supported a minority candidate** (Jesse Jackson) in the 1984 U.S. presidential primary than had any other northern state in U.S. history.

325• On June 29, 1993, Oregon voters were the nation's first to participate in a statewide vote-by-mail election. Only 40% of the registered voters voted.

326 The Model Presidential Nominating Convention, which started in Portland in 1964 as both an educational and extracurricular event for students, is a unique and surprisingly accurate gauge of the political climate. An Aloha High School social studies teacher, James B. Barlow, is the chief coordinator and originator of the Model Presidential Nominating Convention. The students at the convention go through the procress of selecting presidential and vice-presidential running mates for the political party that is not in control of the White House. Personal appearances have included: Nelson Rockefeller (1964), Bobby Kennedy (1968), George McGovern (1972), Jimmy Carter (1976), Ronald Reagan and George Bush (1980), no one in 1984 (Gary Hart and Jesse Jackson made presentations via satellite), Jesse Jackson and Michael Dukakis (1988), and Bill Clinton and Jerry Brown (1992). Geraldine Ferraro was chosen as the vice-presidential candidate in 1984. The 1992 Model Presidential Nominating Convention was attended by over 3,500 students from Oregon, California, New York, and Washington State. Some colleges hold mock nominating conventions, but none on the same scale.

326• The first all-woman city council took office at Yoncalla on November 2, 1929. The mayor was Mary Burt, a Pacific University graduate (1873). Other council members were Bernice Wilson, Nettie Hannan, librarian Jennie Laswell, and Edith Thompson.

327 In 25 consecutive presidential elections from 1892-1988, Crook County in central Oregon was the **only one of the nation's over 3,100 counties in which the majority voted for the winner of every presidential election. Crook County was a "bellwether" during a period of 100 years**. Crook County's overall record as a **"bellwether"** would have been perfect except in 1888 it went for Grover Cleveland, who won the popular vote but lost the Electoral College vote to Benjamin Harrison. Crook County lost its "bellwether" status on election day, 1992. Prineville is that county's only incorporated city.

327• The nation's first Voter Infomation Hotline, Vote Smart, started in Corvallis during the 1992 election campaign. Their toll-free number received over 200,000 telephone calls in five months. Vote Smart is a starting point allowing citizens to obtain basic, factual, nonpartisan information. Community volunteers (200) and college students (130) provided facts to callers from every state on the policies, experience, and financial supporters of the presidential, congressional, senate, and governor candidates. Vote Smart services reached the media and distributed printed information. Vote Smart is a project of the Center for National Independence in Politics and was funded by 28,000 members nationwide. Richard Kimball is Vote Smart Board President.

(The Vote Smart address is: 129 NW 4th St., Suite 204, Corvallis, Oregon 97330; telephone 1-800-786-6885.)

Governor Tom McCall was an effective spokesperson, supporter, and the signer of many legislative innovations, e.g., public beaches, beverage container deposits, land-use planning, and others. Tom McCall spoke often about the "Oregon Story," and he welcomed visitors. Photo of Governor signing some Oregon business papers courtesy of Audrey McCall.

Business Achievements

Less than half of one percent of all patents issued by the U.S. Patent Office in the past twenty years were to Oregonians. However, some Oregon products are nearly ubiquitous.

Creativity, communication, and personal service will help Oregon meet its vision of the future. Business advancements, achievements, and inventions are classified as follows:

Agriculture (rankings, Beer and Wine)
Animals (including Marine Animals)
Architecture
Art
Communication
Education
Energy
Environment
Forestry and Big Trees
Health and Medicine
Human Services
Transportation, Trade, and Bridges
Unclassified Business Advancements (including Inventors, Textiles, and Technology)
In-State Firsts

Agriculture

The abundance of trees made the land expensive to clear. Agriculture is Oregon's #1 industry. Oregon is a leader in production of many crops because of its varied climate, long growing season, and geography. Oregon has over 200 different crops and state crop production totaled $1.96 billion in 1990. Nationally, only California ranks ahead of Oregon in crop diversity. The Willamette Valley is one of the most fertile agricultural lands.

Rankings

The following Oregon agricultural crops all ranked first in the nation in 1989:

328 **Peppermint** (oil from Oregon-grown peppermint is the **highest quality in the world** and is used every day in toothpaste by people **worldwide**. Malheur County is the state's leading producer of peppermint.)
329 **Rye Grass Seed**
330 **Fescue Grass Seed**
331 **Orchards Grass Seed**
332 **Kentucky Blue Grass Seed**
333 **Blackberries** (approximately 85% of the total harvested in the U.S.)
334 **Boysenberries**
335 **Youngberries**
336 **Red Raspberries**
337 **Filberts** (Oregon provides 98% of the domestic filbert, or "improved hazelnut" market, with Germany being the largest importer.)
338 **Prunes**
339 **Red Clover**
340 **Rhubarb**

341 Oregon is the nation's largest **grower and seller of Christmas trees,** especially Douglas Fir Christmas trees and clones.

342 One crop, **grass seed,** has over 1,000 varieties. There are over 700 grass seed growers in Oregon, and these farmers produce **most (60%) of the grass seed in the world** (including fodder grass and ornamental grass).

343 **Kohlrabi seed** (Oregon grows 80% of the world's supply, making it the #1 producer in the world.)

344 **Sugar beet seeds** (98% of the sugar beet seeds grown in the U.S. are from Oregon, the #1 producer in the world.)

345 **Oregon grows most of the grass seed for golf greens in the world.** The Willamette Valley is the U.S. leader in many grass seed varieties, such as orchard grasses, rye grasses, bent grass, and fine-leaf fescues.

346 In 1992, ornamental agriculture was Oregon's largest income-producing independent agricultural business. Oregon is also the leading supplier of **cut English holly.**

347 Oregon ranked first in the Northwest and third nationally (after California and Florida) in **wholesale production of nursery crops** in 1991.

348 Oregon in 1991 lead the nation in production of **liner stock of fruit, flowering, and shade trees.** Seedlings, rooted cuttings, and grafted trees grow as much as six to nine feet in nurseries in a single season. Over 90% of all nursery crops are exported.

349 **Oregon leads the nation in the growth of bearded iris, with the two largest retailers,** Shreiner's Iris Gardens and Cooley's Iris Gardens. **Irises are usually** in bloom from mid-May to mid-June only, and acres are visible west of Interstate 5, north of Salem.

350 Farmers in the Willamette Valley produce the highest percentage of supersweet corn in the U.S. and quality blue lake green beans.

351 The first white people to cultivate **seeds** in the Oregon Country were the crew of *The Ruby*, captained by Charles Bishop, in January, 1796. Seeds were planted that spring on an island (near Ilwaco, Washington). That fall, after returning from a voyage, they harvested potatoes and several beans.

352 The **Oregon Country's initial relatively large-scale farming** was operated by the Hudson's Bay Company in 1825, with the following regional firsts:

353 The **first fruit trees** grew from seeds transported from London about 1825 to Vancouver. The first orchard was planted by William Bruce, Dr. John McLoughlin's Scottish gardener.

354 The **first wheat grown** in the Oregon Country was in 1826 near Fort Vancouver from one bushel of seed ordered from Canada by Dr. McLoughlin in 1825.

355 The **first planting** of potatoes, peas, and beans began in 1825.

356 The **first formal garden of flowers** was planted, with the first dahlia planted by William Fraser Tolmie.

357 The **first field crops** were planted in 1826, with 12 bushels of spring wheat harvested.

358 The first seeds from England arrived on the *William and Ann* in 1827, one of the first seagoing vessels to reach Fort Vancouver.

359 Dr. John McLoughlin grew two bushels of barley and commenced the first brewing.

360 **One of the first apple trees** was planted at Fort Vancouver about 1829.

361 **Strawberry planting and harvesting** started at Fort Vancouver in 1831.

362 Representing the Royal Horticultural Society, David Douglas (1799-1834), a Scottish-born botanist, made two lengthy trips to the Northwest to collect specimens and seeds for the gardens of Europe. He **discovered and introduced hundreds of plants and more than fifty species of trees** (including the Douglas fir and sugar pine). In 1792, Archibald Menzies did the first classification of the botanical name, *Pinus taxifolia*, known commonly as the Douglas fir. David Douglas is credited with the first recorded use of the name Cascade Mountain Range.

363 John Ball was **the region's first school teacher, first lawyer, and first American farmer.** With help from settlers in the spring of 1833, he and a friend planted, raised, and harvested a crop of wheat on French Prairie.

364 Asa Lovejoy canned the first fruits, berries, and vegetables in the Pacific Northwest near Oregon City in 1870.

365 **The Oregon Nursery Company in Orenco claimed to be the largest exporter of nursery stock in the world in 1908.**

366 The first filbert tree in Oregon was planted at Scottsburg by Sam Strictland, a British sailor and former Hudson's Bay Company employees in 1858. The first large filbert orchard in the west was 200 trees planted by George Dorris in Springfield in 1900.

367 **The first production of frozen fruits and vegetables for the commercial retail market came from Hillsboro.** A. J. Ray and Bertrand E. Maling helped start the gigantic frozen food industry when they received a contract from General Foods Corporation in 1929. Previously, the only quick-frozen food that was packed for retail outlets was fish, on the east coast. The canning plant of Ray-Maling Co., Inc. was converted for the production of frozen foods. The processing method was one devised by Clarence Birdseye, the pioneer of the quick-frozen industry. **The first frozen strawberries were shipped east by refrigerated rail in 1929.** The company became part of General Foods in 1934, and in 1945 the name was changed to Birdseye Snyder Division of General Foods. When the plant closed in 1975 it had almost 700 employees.

368 Oregon became the first state to start an **overseas agricultural marketing office** when Eastern Oregon farmers opened one for wheat in Japan in 1946.

369 With the establishment of the Oregon Wheat Commission in 1947, **Oregon became the first state in the nation to organize producer-supported commodity commissions.** Numerous producer-supported commissions operate in Oregon now.

370 **The nation's first and only export service center** opened in the Alber Mill building in NW Portland (October 30, 1990). The Oregon Department of Agriculture operates a one-stop, full-range Export Service Center, including product evaluation, certification of food exports, quality control, food certification, and labeling. Since it opened in Salem in 1987, the Oregon Department of Agriculture has certified well over 1,000 food products for export to Japan.

371 The **marionberry**, produced in Marion County, combined the loganberry with the boysenberry.

372 The **maraschino cherry** is a product of a new method developed by Oregon State University researcher Ed Wiegand in 1925.

373 **Easter lily bulbs** grown on a marine terrace that extends from Brookings south into Del Norte County in northern California account for more than 80% of the world's supply.

374 One farmer west of Portland supplied most of the purple ink, stamped by the U.S. Department of Agriculture on graded meat, from 15 acres of black raspberries.

375 Corvallis is the home of the National Clonal Germplasm Repository, built in 1981 by the Agricultural Research Service of the U.S. Department of Agriculture. It is the **first and largest of nine such repositories, where germplasm for wild and cultivated crop plants is maintained** and evaluated so that it will be preserved for use by scientists around the world.

376 The **first successful eradication of a major gypsy moth infestation** in the U.S. using only a safe biological insecticide was in Lane County (1985-89). The Oregon Department of Agriculture pioneered the moth eradication.

377 The J A S Testing Lab in Salem is the first **laboratory in the U.S. to test foods for meeting Japanese agriculture requirements.** In 1987 Oregon earned the privilege of exhibiting the premiere food symbol of Japan, the Japanese Acceptance Symbol. The J A S mark assists sales and exports by guaranteeing quality Oregon products to major markets such as Korea, Japan, and Taiwan.

378 Since 1976, the Oregon Miniature Rose Co. in Aloha has cultivated many new roses, including the Maurine Neuberger, the "best" red miniature.

379 In 1989 the Oregon legislature passed the **first Organic Food Labeling Law** in a consumer's right-to-know approach. "Organic food" was defined; products couldn't be sold as "organic" if they were grown with any pesticides.

380 In 1930, the Josephine County Growers and O.S.U.'s Extension Service built the **nation's first movable cannery built by a county** for field use.

381 Steinfeld's sauerkraut facility in Scappoose is the **only sauerkraut plant west of the Mississippi River.** The Steinfeld's plant in Portland processes over a million pounds of cucumbers a day during harvest season.

382 Peter McIntosh, a Canadian cheesemaker, and T. S. Townsend established the first commercial cheese factory in Tillamook County in 1894. Tillamook was the **first community in the U.S. to brand its cheese.** This happened in 1918. The Tillamook County Creamery Association was organized in 1909 as a quality control organization for 25 cheese factories operating in Tillamook County.

382• Oregon was the first state with agricultural rules in 1974. Other states developed agricultural rules also. Oregon was the first with a legislative agricultural law. Oregon Tilth was the first to do soil analysis, and it's the only organic certifier in the state.

382• Wholesome and Hearty Foods, Inc. of Portland makes the **Gardenburger**™, **the first meatless burger**, and has sold over 49 million of them. Wholesome and Hearty Foods is the first company to get the name of a trademarked product, **Gardenburger**™, on menus at restaurants, hospitals, colleges, the military, etc. It's the first company to make a non-cholesterol, nonfat milk out of almonds.

383 Oregon was "at the top" nationally in **strawberry acreage** in 1957.

384 Though precise statistics aren't available, some say Oregon is **one of the top three producers of marijuana** in the nation, and others say it's been Oregon's biggest crop.

385 Oregon has the largest number of producers of **elephant garlic** in the U.S.

386 Oregon has the **nation's largest harvest and sales of wild mushrooms** (Morels, Chantrelles, Ceps), totalling $29 million in sales, with 76% going to international markets.

387 Tillamook Country Smoker is the largest producer of beef jerky west of the Mississippi River.

387• A fully mature sunflower 2.2 inches tall was grown by Michael Lenke of Lake Oswego, Oregon in 1985, using a bonsai technique, and was listed in the Guinness Book of World Records as the **World's Smallest Sunflower**.

388 Mercedes Bates, an Oregon State University graduate who did extensive research in food technology, is the person who fabricated the character **Betty Crocker** for marketing.

388• AGRITOPE, Inc.'s ethylene control program has identified a gene whose insertion into vegetables, fruits, flowers, and other plants permits longer storage.

Beer

389   There was a public vote for prohibition of alcohol in the Oregon Territory in 1844, and in 1849 it was repealed.

390   Henry Saxer's Liberty Brewery (Davis at First Avenue in Portland) was the first commercial beer-brewing plant in the Pacific Northwest (1852). It was purchased by Henry Weinhard in 1862.

391   **The Blitz-Weinhard Brewery is the oldest continuously-operating brewery west of the Mississippi River.** A brewery was established by John Muench in 1856 in Fort Vancouver, Oregon Territory. Henry Weinhard worked for John Muench in 1857 and in 1859 acquired the brewery from him. Weinhard moved that brewery to Portland, sold it in 1862 and that same year bought Henry Saxer's Liberty Brewery. Henry Weinhard's brewery has been in the present building (1133 NW Burnside Street in NW Portland) since 1904. During the alcohol prohibition era, soda pop and ice were manufactured there.

392   **Oregon became the first state in the nation to become "dry."** On January 1, 1916, the law prohibiting alcohol took effect, three years before it did in the rest of the states. In 1913-14 Governor Oswald West's adamant opposition to alcohol led to voter approval of statewide prohibition during his last year in office. Later, in 1919, Oregon ratified the Federal Prohibition law.

393   One-quarter of the hops grown in the world come from Oregon. In 1926, the largest hops ranch in the U.S. was in Salem. From 1865 to 1910, more hops were grown on Oregon farms than anywhere else in the nation. Oregon led the nation in harvests, producing many varieties.

394   The **first and only national microbrewery festival in the country** is held at Tom McCall Waterfront Park in Portland in August. The Oregon Microbrewers Festival started in 1988 has grown to an attendance of over 15,000 Oregonians. In 1993, 60 microbrewers from 26 states and Canada participated in the festival.

395   Portland has **more brewing activity per capita** than any other metropolitan area in the nation.

396   Oregon is the first state to require **educational classes for all alcohol servers who serve by the drink** (Oregon Liquor Control Commission administered).

397   Oregon is **one of the first and few states to regulate beer kegs by requiring keg tags.** These tags state the purchaser name, location where to be used, and seller. Oregon's legal drinking age has been 21 years since Oregon Territory Days, except of course during Prohibition.

Wine Industry

398 In 1985, Oregon became the **first state with an official state wine cellar.** Located at Oregon Department of Agriculture headquarters in Salem, the wine cellar contained about 30 cases of Oregon wines in 1991.

399 **Oregon has the nation's strictest wine-labeling regulations.** Oregon's appellation laws go beyond Federal requirements in percentage of varietal grape content (90%) and true vintage year. Labels can't use geographical names, e.g., Champagne, Burgundy, Chablis (OAR 845-10-915).

400 The **first publicly-owned common stock vineyard in the Northwest** is Willamette Valley Vineyards and winery. Started by a large group of wine consumers, Willamette Valley Vineyards made a public share offering and raised over $900,000, with over 1,600 families or 2,620 consumers owning the company. Willamette Valley Vineyards, which is located south of Salem, released its first wine on May 30, 1990.

401 Oregon **harvests of pinot gris grapes rank #1 nationally in volume.** Oregon is the **first region** to emphasize pinot gris.

402 Oregon is **the first state where a wine with true gamay noir is produced.** Beaujolais-style red wines are usually produced from grapes grown in the Beaujolais region of France.

403 The only places in the U.S. growing pinot meunier grapes are near McMinnville, in the vineyards of Panther Creek Cellars and Eyrie Vineyards.

404 The Oregon Winegrowers' Association initiated passage (i.e., drafted first law) of reciprocal wine shipment laws to allow purchase in one state and shipment to home state. Some good ideas travel north to south; for example, the State of California passed a similar reciprocal wine shipment law four years before the Oregon legislature finally passed the law.

405 Scott Henry of Henry Estate Winery developed a unique trellising system that is named after him.

406 AGRITOPE, Inc. of Beaverton is a pioneer in biotechnological firsts in micropropagation for vineyards.

Public Ports to and from Oregon

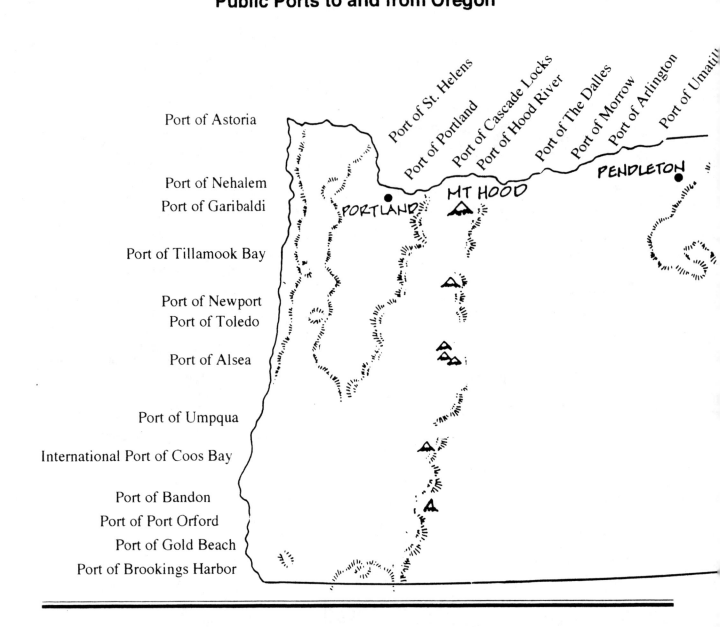

Port of Astoria

Port of Nehalem
Port of Garibaldi

Port of Tillamook Bay

Port of Newport
Port of Toledo

Port of Alsea

Port of Umpqua

International Port of Coos Bay

Port of Bandon
Port of Port Orford
Port of Gold Beach
Port of Brookings Harbor

Port of St. Helens
Port of Portland
Port of Cascade Locks
Port of Hood River
Port of The Dalles
Port of Morrow
Port of Arlington
Port of Umatilla

PENDLETON

MT HOOD

PORTLAND

Lighthouses in Oregon

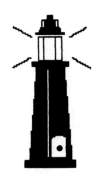

Tillamook Rock Lighthouse (built 1881, used until 1957)
Cape Meares Lighthouse (built 1890)
Yaquina Head Lighthouse - active (built 1873)
Old Yaquina Bay Lighthouse (1871, used until 1874)
Cleft-of-the-Rock Lighthouse (1 mile south of
    Yachats) - active (built 1976)
Heceta Head Lighthouse - active (built 1894)
Umpqua River Lighthouse - active (built 1894)
Cape Arago Lighthouse - active (built 1866, 1909, 1934)
Coquille River Lighthouse (built 1896, used until 1939)
Cape Blanco Lighthouse - active (built 1870)

Animals

Millions of years ago, crocodiles, dinosaurs, rhinos, and tigers inhabited Oregon. Wolves created special hardships for settlers. Currently, Oregon has one of the largest expanses of wildlife refuges in the U.S. There are 250 rare or endangered species of plants and 60 rare or endangered species of animals in the state. The pileated woodpecker, salmon, northern spotted owl, and marbled murrelet are a few of the endangered species of animals.

408 Oregon's state animal is **the beaver, the "dam builder." Second only to humans, the beaver is the animal that can most change the environment.**

409 **Oregon Furs!** The following fur-bearing animals were also in abundance in the Oregon Country in the early 1800s: otter, lynx, fox, raccoon, marten, skunk, muskrat, mink, bear, and others. Beaver hats were popular. Fur and trapping firsts were accomplished by the Hudson's Bay Company, the Pacific Fur Company, the North West Company, and the Russian American Fur Company.

410 Trapping expeditions were begun by Donald McKenzie to trap beaver and make pelts, rather than relying on barter for furs from Indians.

411 Hudson's Bay Company achieved successful commercial exploitation of the region by fur trading on a large scale. Before settlers migrated, beavers were the big builders in the valleys. In a four-year period (1834-37), the Hudson's Bay Company annually received an average of 100,000 beaver skins from trappers and Indians. As the human population grew, the beaver population declined, due to overtrapping, and now beavers are legally protected and more abundant.

412 The **first farm animals** in the Oregon Country were the hogs and sheep with the Astor party aboard the ship *Tonquin* in 1811.

413 A ship from California brought the **region's first livestock** in 1814.

414 The **first dairy cattle** were shipped by the Hudson's Bay Company from the Sandwich Islands (Hawaii) and grazed on acreage next to Fort Vancouver in the latter 1820s.

415 In 1834, the **first remains of a mastadon discovered** in Oregon were sent to London by Dr. John McLoughlin.

416 John Minto imported the best pedigreed merino sheep in the U.S. into Oregon from Wales in 1858.

417 **The Washington Park Zoo is the oldest in the West.** Richard B. Knight, a pioneer Portland druggist, founded the first zoo, a place where sea captains would leave pet bears and parakeets. The City of Portland took over ownership, making the zoo public in 1887. The zoo is now home for over 700 animals in 215 species, of which 56 are endangered or threatened.

418 Jack Edwards founded the Hay Creek Ranch, the largest Merino sheep-breeding ranch in the world, starting in 1898. There were over 50,000 sheep at that ranch in Jefferson County.

419 The **"Wonder Cow,"** Viva La France, a jersey cow, **held three world records** at one time for milk and butter fat production. This cow, which produced 5,332 pounds of fat in a six-year period, belonged to Pickard Brothers of Marion. (Average: 2.4 lbs/day.)

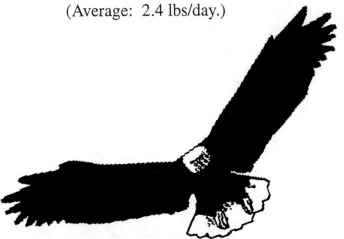

420 Klamath Forest National Refuge and the Upper Klamath and Lower Klamath Wildlife Refuges contain the **largest concentration of wintering bald eagles in the U.S.** (Bear Valley). More than 500 species of wildlife have been identified in the Klamath Basin with 50 species of mammals, 30 different types of reptiles, and 32 species of fish. There are 255 bird types.

Over 400 species of birds have been recognized in Oregon.

421 There's a 270,000-acre refuge on Hart Mountain protecting **one of the continent's largest herds of pronghorn antelopes,** 800 to 1,000 mule deer, and about 500 bighorn sheep.

422 The pronghorn antelope is the world's fastest land animal over distances greater than 1,000 yards. Pronghorn antelopes can run 55 to 60 miles per hour for a half-mile, and average 35 mph for four miles.

423 Oregon has had one of the densest concentrations of slugs in the world.

424 The National Fish and Wildlife Forensics Laboratory on the campus of Southern Oregon State College in Ashland is the **world's first crime lab for animals.** The crime laboratory uses new technologies to help catch poachers and traders in illegal wildlife products internationally.

425 Some of the largest llama herds and ranches in the U.S. are in Oregon.

426 **The largest amount (45%) of the 216 million board feet affected by U.S. Fish & Wildlife Service proposals to save the spotted owl are in Oregon.** There are at least 900 owl nesting sites on private lands.

427 The Malheur Wildlife Refuge is one of the nation's largest bird sanctuaries, with over 300 species of birds and 58 species of mammals.

427• Animal Aid is a nonprofit organization in Portland which provides services that included the first regional computerized animal lost and found matching in the greater Northwest. Their system matched over 20,000 lost companion animals and their people from 1983 to 1993. Their cost-effective computerized-matching system started in 1987. Animal Aid saved local governments a substantial part of the costs of shelter and euthanasia for stray animals. Animal Aid's Lost and Found had to close due to lack of funds (in spring, 1993).

Elephants

428 **The Washington Park Zoo had the most prolific elephant breeding program in the world,** and is still one of the most successful elephant breeding programs.

429 Packy, the elephant born on April 14, 1962, at the west's oldest zoo, the Washington Park Zoo, is unique in that he was the **first elephant born in the western hemisphere in 44 years.** Packy weighed about six and a half tons in 1993.

430 The **Washington Park Zoo had the largest captive elephant herd in the world,** and, in 1993, it had 12 elephants.

431 With 23 Asian elephants sired at the Washington Park Zoo, it holds the **world record** for the number of births (25) of elephant offspring in a zoo. The Zoo has the **first second-generation elephants born in captivity.**

431• The veterinarians, curators, and elephant keepers at the Washington Park Zoo, with help from CH2MHill, designed the first "Elephant Restraint Chute" (May, 1980) to control elephants during medical treatments and maintenance. "**Zoo Doo**" sales raised funds to build it.

432 Tusko at the old Lotus Isle amusement park in North Portland was the "largest elephant in captivity."

Marine Animals

433 The Pacific Ocean is **the world's largest ocean,** with about 64 million square miles. Approximately 27 species of marine mammals inhabit or migrate through Pacific Ocean waves off Oregon shores, with over 300 varieties of fish. Gray whales migrate over 16,000 miles in their round trip south from Alaska.

434 **Sea otter** were plentiful from lower California to Alaska's Aleutian Islands when early seagoing explorers arrived.

435 During the 1820s, the **first commercial salmon packing** in the Oregon Country occurred at the Hudson's Bay Company. Oregon's first factory for canning salmon was built in 1864 in Astoria.

436 The **only wildlife refuge in Oregon where people are totally prohibited is Oregon's coastal Wildlife Refuge of 1,400 island rocks and reefs.** Oregon's largest seabird colonies nest at Three Arch Rocks National Wildlife Refuge.

437 The Oregon **Sea Lion Caves** are some of the largest in the U.S., and contain hundreds of sea lions.

438 The **largest anadromous salmon runs were in the Columbia River,** but slowed as dams were constructed for hydroelectric power and flood control. Technological innovations such as seine and drift nets aided fishermen, but not fish.

440 President Roosevelt dedicated Lower Klamath National Wildlife Refuge as the **first U.S. waterfowl refuge** in 1908.

442 At Bonneville, 42 miles east of Portland, is **the largest salmon hatchery in the world**. The State of Oregon had fish hatcheries in the early 1900s. There are 33 State fish hatcheries and two Federal fish hatcheries in Oregon. **The State of Oregon had the first salmon enhancement program.** The salmon population was low and headed down in 1992.

443 The **only known places worldwide** where a unique form of calcite crystal grows in marine mud are in Clatsop County, Oregon, and Pacific County, Washington. These single-celled fossils, found July 14, 1941, are called the Astoria formation of foraminifera.

444 **A freshwater jelly fish was discovered for the first time on the Pacific Coast** in a stream running through the Eastmoreland Golf Links by Dr. L. E. Griffin and his assistant at Reed College. Freshwater varieties of this jelly fish have formerly been found in Philadelphia and Europe.

445 The **first estuarine sanctuary in the U.S.** is the South Slough National Estuarine Sanctuary where the rivers meet the sea in Charleston. It was established by Congress in 1972.

446 **The first U.S. ocean port state body to claim jurisdiction over marine fisheries reaching 50 miles off its shore was the Oregon legislature.** Governor Tom McCall considered the measure unenforceable and an infringement of Federal jurisdiction, so he vetoed the bill. In spite of the Governor's veto, it was repassed in 1974. Subsequently, Congressional action expanded U.S. jurisdiction off all U.S. coastlines to 200 miles into the Pacific Ocean.

447 Weyerhauser started the nation's first private salmon venture in 1977 with a fish ladder and counting station at a hatchery, Oregon Aqua Foods, off Yaquina Bay. Sea-fresh coho began climbing the ladder in 1977.

448 The first **microbe** to be named after a state is *Methanohalophilus oregonese*, Latin for salt-loving methanogen, a one-celled organism that hates oxygen and lives in Alkali Lake north of Lakeview.

449 Charged by the legislature to do so, the Oregon Land Conservation and Development Commission on November 8, 1990, adopted the **nation's first state plan for managing ocean resources.**

450 The white sturgeon is the **largest freshwater, stream-ascending fish** of North American coastal waters. White sturgeon are found in the Umpqua, Columbia, Snake, Willamette, and Rogue rivers. The largest Columbia River sturgeon caught was 12 feet 6 inches long and weighed over 1,200 pounds.

451 One of the largest squids and one of the the largest spineless animals caught in the world was a giant squid caught off the Oregon coastline by fisherman Gary Steffensmier in 1978. This giant squid had a five-foot-long body, weighed 225 pounds, and measured 24 feet between outspread armtips.

Architecture

*Buildings over 100 years old
are regarded as antique.*

452 Joseph, a Sister of the Sacred Heart (born in Quebec, 1823), knew carpentry, was handy with tools, and became **the region's first female architect** (1856). "Mother Joseph" built the first hospital, Catholic school, mission, and orphanage in Vancouver, Oregon Territory. She was honored in 1953 by the American Institute of Architects as the Northwest's first architect.

453 Horace and Jane Baker constructed the only cantilevered pioneer log cabin in the Oregon Territory in Carver in Clackamas County in 1856.

454 **Pioneer Courthouse in Portland is the oldest Federal structure still standing in the Northwest,** and is one of the oldest active courthouses in the country. Construction of Pioneer Courthouse, which occupies a full block, started in 1869, ten years after statehood was attained.

455 **The largest log cabin in the world** was built in 1905 for the Lewis & Clark Exposition from hand-picked, horse-logged trees from many sites, including the Clatskanie-Delena area of Columbia County. The Forestry Building in northwest Portland on 25th between Vaughn and Upshur was 209 feet long, 102 feet wide, and 72 feet high. There were fifty-two log pillars six feet in diameter. The interior resembled a church, with tree trunk columns setting off balconies and exhibition galleries along both sides. The floors of the largest log cabin were portions of great logs nine or ten feet in diameter. One million board feet of logs went into its construction.
(See photo page 105)

456 Ladd's Addition is one of the first platted subdivisions west of the Mississippi River. Ladd's Addition, which was begun in southeast Portland in the early 1900s, used to be a 125-acre farm. William Ladd's design is similar to the criss-cross layout of Washington, D.C., with diagonal boulevards, traffic circles, and a park system. Ladd's Addition is among the oldest planned communities in the west. **Ladd's Addition** is the site of the **only Baptist church owned by the deaf.** Ladd's Addition includes the oldest house in Portland, the 1860 farmhouse of the original land claim holder, James Stephens.

457 Simon Benson gave Portland $10,000 in 1912 to install its first 20 drinking fountains. The first fountain was installed at Fifth and Washington streets. Today there are forty Benson fountains in Portland and one in Sapporo, Japan, Portland's long-time sister-city.

458 When built in 1924 and 1925, the ten-story Lithia Springs Hotel in Ashland was the tallest building from Salem to Sacramento. The hotel was renamed the Marc Anthony in 1962.

459 **The Astor Column is the first and only large memorial structure of reinforced concrete finished with a pictorial frieze in sgraffito work.** The 535-foot-long frieze commemorates all the events which led to the establishment of American claims to the Northwest Territory. The Astor Column is 125 feet high with 165 steps, and stands atop Coxcomb Hill in Astoria 700 feet above the sea. The monolith was funded by the Astor family, designed by New York architect Electus D. Litchfield and erected in 1926. The monument's decorations were painted by Italian artist Attilio Pusterla. It was modeled after the famous Italian Trajan Column built in Rome, Italy, by Emperor Trajan in 114 A.D.

460 The Owyhee Box Canyon in Malheur County is spanned by a dam 405 feet in height. It was the **highest dam completed in the world through 1935**.

461 Timberline Lodge National Historic Landmark was built in 1937 at 6,100 feet above sea level, facing west. **It's the highest National Historic Landmark and was the first building in a Federal Government program for visitors to public recreation areas.** Indigenous wood used in construction of the building and furniture included Port Orford cedar, Douglas fir, Ponderosa pine, oak, red cedar, hemlock, and western juniper.

462 Within the City of Portland there's a greater concentration of buildings fronted by cast iron (or plastic facsimiles) than in any other U.S. city west of New York City's SoHo District.

463 Oregon may be the only state to have had two capitols burn to the ground. Oregon's fifth Territorial Assembly convened in the **first official Territorial Capitol**. The first capitol burned to the ground in 1855. The second capitol was constructed on the original site in 1876, but fire destroyed it in 1935.

464 A contest was held to select a design for the new statehouse, and the winning design was submitted by architects from Trowbridge and Livingston of New York. The capitol was dedicated and opened to the public in 1938. The gold pioneer was mounted atop the building. A fund-raising drive among Oregon schoolchildren in 1984 raised lots of dimes and nickels, with a total collection of about $40,000 to regild the gold pioneer.
(See front cover photo of pioneer)

465 Two large blimp hangars south of Tillamook were built in 1942 during World War II at the Naval Air Station. From the Tillamook Naval Air Station a fleet of lighter-than-air blimps used for coastal surveillance searched out and sank enemy submarines. The hangars, 1,072 feet long, 192 feet high (about 20 stories), and 296 feet wide, were the **two largest wooden structures in the world until one burned** on August 22, 1992. The Tillamook Blimp Station was one of five on the west coast and the only one remaining not currently owned by the U.S. Government. The owner is the Port of Tillamook Bay. The hangars housed 251-foot-long blimps with helium-filled gas bags. The hangars were later used as a base for the world's first helo-blimp, which was used to do heavy industrial and forestry lifting. One hangar could hold six football games at one time.
(see photo page 105)

First Oregon Territorial Capitol
(Courtesy of OHS Negative 015963)

First Oregon State Capitol, Salem
(Courtesy of OHS Negative 006366)

Equitable Building, 1948
(courtesy of OHS Negative 53455)

466 **The 12-story building completed in 1948 for Equitable Savings and Loan offices utilized innovations which influenced skyscraper designs throughout the world**. Designed by Portland architect Pietro Belluschi (born in Ancona, Italy, 1899), the Equitable Building was built on the southwest corner of SW Sixth Avenue and Washington Street in Portland.

Congress had passed a law prohibiting construction of any private buildings so that all resources would go towards winning the war. **The Equitable Building was one of the first commercial office buildings built after World War II.**

467 **Innovations in the Equitable Building included:**
The windows were designed not to open and had to be washed from the outside.

468 The building had no exposed light fixtures inside or outside.

469 Pietro Belluschi was probably the first architect to use a flush aluminum-covered concrete exterior wall skin in which the structural frame, spandrels, and glass are virtually in the same plane.

470 The plate glass was doubled and sealed in a fixed frame.

471 An early application of the heat pump principle utilized water from three underground wells to exchange heat.

472 The Equitable Savings and Loan Building was the West Coast's largest air-conditioned commercial office building, and it had the most modern design.

473 It was the nation's first office block in the "International" style to be erected.

(See photo on back cover)

474 Lloyd Center construction started in 1958, and it opened August 2, 1960, becoming the **first and largest covered shopping mall in the world.** In the early 1970s it became **one of the most successful shopping malls in the U. S.** By 1993, Lloyd Center had 175 stores.

476 Dedicated in Portland in 1982, the Portland Building is the **first post-modern building.** The architect is Michael Graves, a designer from Princeton, N.J.

477 The KGON-FM tower (603 feet tall) atop Healy Heights in southwest Portland is **the tallest structure from San Francisco to Seattle.** The tower is unique and a first in its construction style, with a varandeel truss space frame. The reinforced tower has three steel legs filled with high-strength concrete designed to withstand wind and earthquakes.

478 The Willow Creek Dam in Heppner is a unique 165-foot-high, 1,780-foot-long flood control dam built by the U.S. Army Corps of Engineers entirely with a roller-compacted structure. It's a first in the world. Roller-compacted concrete is made with sand, rock, cement, and water spread into one-foot layers and compressed. Leaks have sprung from the dam.

479 The Montgomery Park building in northwest Portland is one of the largest private rehabilitation projects this side of the Mississippi River. Montgomery Park was also one of the largest historic rehabilitations on the west coast in the 1980s.

480 When it was built in 1978, Clackamas Town Center was the largest shopping center in the Northwest.

481 The **largest ball-bearing dance floor in the U.S.** was at the Crystal Ballroom on West Burnside and 14th in Portland. Generations of people listened and danced as musicians made music at the Crystal Ballroom, including the Woody Hite band, the Grateful Dead, and Buffalo Springfield. Part of the floor burned in 1988.

481• The longest raised, covered skybridge in the U.S. is a 660-foot pedestrian walkway between the Oregon Health Sciences University and Veterans Affairs Medical Center in Portland. The skybridge is 150 feet above street level, it's resistant to thermal expansion and seismic movement, and 12,000 bolts were used in its construction. The skybridge opened in November, 1992.

Art

Pacific Northwest Indians produced unique artistry. Some Indian totems depicted transformations between animals and humans. The nature of art is its uniqueness. Can you visualize every column of text as a totem pole? Where does creativity come from?

482 The Oregon Country's first amateur theatrical performances were a series of three plays, *Love in a Village, The Mayor,* and *Three Weeks after Marriage.* The acting was by crew members of the *Modeste,* a British sloop anchored off Fort Vancouver during the spring of 1846.

483 Portland's first symphonic concert occurred in Oro Fino Hall, June 15, 1866, and the first orchestral society was formed by 1875. The Oregon Symphony is the **first orchestra west of the Mississippi River, and one of only six major orchestras established in America prior to 1900.** It started as the Portland Symphony Orchestra in 1896, with W.H. Kinross conducting the initial concert at Marquam Grand Theater on October 30th. It became the Oregon Symphony Orchestra in 1967. And it's now simply the Oregon Symphony.

483• **Current Oregon Symphony conductor James DePriest is the only African-American conductor of a major (top 30) orchestra in the nation.** James DePriest came to Portland in 1980 from the Quebec Symphony, Canada's oldest. The Oregon Sym-

phony Orchestra's first recording, *Bravura,* was released as a compact disc (1987). In 1993, the Oregon Symphony had the highest paid subscription attendance per capita of any orchestra in the nation.

484 The Portland Art Museum opened in Portland in 1905, making it the greater **Northwest's first public art museum.**

485 The Oregon School of Arts and Crafts was founded by Julia Hoffman in 1906 and is **America's oldest continuously operating craft school.** It's the nation's largest school for craft disciplines. It is the only accredited crafts school in the nation that directs all its resources to professional education.

487 The Skidmore Fountain on Southwest First Avenue in Portland was dedicated on September 22, 1888, to honor druggist Stephen G. Skidmore. Its architect was J. M. Wells and the sculptor was Olin L. W

The "Harney County Sagebrush Symphony," Burns, on the largest wooden violin before musical tour of the Willamette Valley (1915). The youth ensemble performed throughout central Oregon. *(Photo by Rufus Heck courtesy of OHS Neg. 14287, #118-A, see front and back cover)*

488 Oregon's first youth ensemble began in Burns, in 1912. Mary V. Dodge, a violinist who trained in Boston, formed a group of children that came to be known as the **"Sagebrush Symphony."** The above "Harney County Sagebrush Symphony Orchestra" photo was taken before the group came to the Willamette Valley in 1915 to make music.

488• The **Portland Junior Symphony** was also formed by Mary V. Dodge with Jacques Gershkovitch in 1924; it was renamed the Portland Youth Philharmonic (PYP) in 1967. **The Portland Youth Philharmonic is the oldest group of youth musicians in the U.S. The PYP is the nation's first youth orchestra with a full-time conductor**, and it's the first commissioning orchestra, with six commissioned conductors since 1959. PYP is **the first recording orchestra in the Northwest** (1961). The orchestra has no tuition and is open to all qualified student of all races, creeds, and colors.

The PYP has had just two conductors, Jacques Gershkovitch and Jacob Avshalomov. PYP had completed five international tours by 1993.

489 On the front of the Portland Building is **the statue Portlandia, the largest hammered-copper sculpture made in the U.S.** Portlandia's sculptor is Raymond Kaskey. The Statue of Liberty in New York City is taller (151 feet) than Portlandia, but was a gift from France to the U.S. in 1886.

490 The Britt Festival in Jacksonville is the **oldest outdoor music festival in the Northwest.** The festival founder and first musical director, John Trudeau, started with a classical music program in 1963.

491 **The "world's first 24-hour coin-operated art gallery" was opened in 1985.** The gallery and the Church of Elvis are located near Skidmore Fountain in Old Town, Portland. (Elvis Presley died on August 16, 1977.)

492 The Contemporary Crafts Gallery, the **nation's oldest non-profit art gallery, has displayed many first showings.** The CCG has always been located in a building in SW Portland built by the Federal Works Progress Administration in 1937 (3934 SW Corbett).

493 The Oregon Shakespeare Festival Association, which started in Ashland, is **one of the largest non-profit theatres in the U.S., and it's the oldest authentic reproduction of an Elizabethan theatre in the western hemisphere.** Credit for the idea and effort belongs to Angus Bowmer, who wanted to celebrate the Fourth of July in 1935 with William Shakespeare's plays. The first Shakespeare Festival had two plays, *Twelfth Night* and *The Merchant of Venice*. The festival grew and now attracts actors, directors, critics, and audiences from all over the U.S. and many foreign countries.

494 The **first calligraphy society** in the U.S. was started in Portland by Lloyd Reynolds in 1967 and incorporated in 1974. Governor Tom McCall appointed Lloyd Reynolds as the state's (and possibly the world's) **first Calligrapher Laureate.** Portland has the only public school district where *italic handwriting* is taught. A society-prepared textbook is used.

495 Stanford Conroy Wood of the Latin jazz band Upepo in 1970s invented the vibraband, made of latex rubber, the first flexible reed instrument.

496 The Eugene Saturday Market is the **oldest open-air crafts market in the U.S.** It started in May, 1970. It was an idea brought back from Central America by Lotte Streisinger, a local artist, who saw similar markets while she was in Central America. The market is open outdoors every Saturday from April to October and indoors at the Lane County Fairgrounds from Thanksgiving to Christmas.

496• Portland Saturday Market, located under the Burnside Bridge, is the **largest continuously operating open-air crafts market in the U.S.** Sheri Teasdale and Andrea Scharf started Portland Saturday Market with the help of businessman Bill Naito, a bank, and a $1,000 loan from the Metropolitan Arts Commission in 1974. Saturday Market has 280 to 400 craft booths open every weekend day from April to Christmas.

497 **The first International Museum of Carousel Art** has over 50 carousel horses. The museum has the **largest collection of carousel art in the world,** with 19 machines and over 700 animals. The museum has some of the oldest carousel animals operating in the U.S. It was established in 1984 by Duane and Carol Perron.

498 The world's largest portable carousel has been located at the World Forestry Center in Southwest Portland during summer months.

498• Started in 1969, the Oregon Country Fair is the largest and longest running annual counter-culture festival.

expose yourself to art

499 The timeless poster *Expose Yourself To Art* was the most widely sold poster made in the Northwest. From 1987-88, the poster sold more copies (legitimate and counterfeit) than any other poster in the U.S. Over 430,000 copies have been sold since it was published in 1978, not counting lots of counterfeit copies. It's been seen in Europe and South America. In 1977, Mike Ryerson took a photo of his friend J. E. "Bud" Clark on the downtown transit mall in front of a sculpture. The photo became a poster in 1978 after NW Portland's *The Neighbor* newspaper conducted a contest to name it.

J. E. "Bud" Clark was elected mayor of the City of Portland in 1984, and proceeds from signed copies of *Expose Yourself To Art* helped retire the popular official's campaign debt.

(courtesy Heineman Graphics, 609 SW Sixth Ave, Portland,)

499• The Portland Music Association and Mayor Bud Clark put on eight large-scale annual musical events at the Memorial Coliseum for local charities. Over the eight years more than $250,000 was distributed to various Portland charities. The six-hour Bud Ball #8 in 1992 was billed as **"the largest collection of musical talent (77 bands) in one indoor location in the nation."**

500 The largest free jazz festival in the Northwest was started in 1980 to honor community activist Howard Galbraith. The Cathedral Park Jazz Festival is held the third weekend in July under North Portland's St. John's bridge.

500• The Mt. Hood Festival of Jazz is the **largest jazz music festival in the Pacific Northwest** (attendence is about 30,000 over the three-day event). The jazz festival started in 1982 in Gresham.

Title: Art 87 J1   © Daria

501 ABACI Gallery of Computer Art is **the first computer fine-art gallery in the world.** ABACI features the largest private collection of local, national, and international computer fine art. Above is owner and entrepreneur Daria Barclay's first piece of computer fine art, which was displayed at the first opening of the gallery in Portland in April, 1988. ABACI Gallery is located in the Pearl arts district of Northwest Portland.

Communication

Original Indian language and artwork sufficed for early communications. Now, during the Information Age, Native American tribes have been using facsimile machines for years. Oregon creates print and electronic media, builds some of the fastest computers, and produces interactive television.

502 The *Flumgudgeon Gazette and Bumble Bee Budget* was the **first news sheet in the West.** The satirical semiweekly was handwritten and first read during the 1845 legislative session at Oregon City.

502• The Oregon Spectator, the **first newspaper in the West**, started publishing on February 5, 1846.

502• **The first U.S. Post Office west of the Rocky Mountains was located in Astoria, Oregon Territory, 1847.** Postal regulations stated that for 40¢ a letter could be sent "to or from Astoria or any other post office on the Pacific coast within the U.S. territory."

503 The **first telegraph message** in the Northwest was sent March 5, 1864, giving the region a communications link to the east. Simeon Reed was involved in the company formed to build this first telegraph line to California.

504 The **smallest original newspaper page in the world** was the 3" by 3.5" *Daily Banner* of Roseburg. Editions dated February 1 and 2, 1876, still survive.

505 Just two years after Alexander Graham Bell's invention of it, the **first telephone demonstration in the Northwest was in Portland**, March 28, 1878. The American Telephone and District Telegraph Company was incorporated May 15, 1878, and by August 2, 1878, this company started the state's first telephone exchange service with 33 subscribers at No. 3 First Avenue in the back room of the Western Union building. The first phone conversation probably included one of its incorporators, Dr. O. P.Plummer, F. H. Lamb, and D. F. Leahy. The first coast-to-coast telephone call was in 1915 between Alexander Graham Bell in New York and Thomas Watson in San Francisco.

506 Samuel Grant Hughes started a tiny telephone company (Independent Telephone Co. of Forest Grove) in 1888. His was the **first telephone network in any area now served by GTE-NW.** The original switchboard is a General Telephone Co. of the Northwest souvenir that's been displayed in many parts of the U.S.

507 **"Where Cowboy Is King,"** about the Pendleton Round-Up, was the first film with Life O'graph, and was the first film produced in Oregon and successfully distributed nationally and internationally (1914).

508 Benson Polytechnic High School's KYG radio station began broadcasting in Portland on March 23, 1923, as the **first AM radio station in the nation licensed to a school district.** It's now KBPS 1450 AM.

510 The first **radio network broadcast on the Pacific Coast** was by KGW on October 23, 1924.

511 In 1932, **the first police radio transmitter in the nation** was installed by the Portland Police Bureau; and it could only transmit one-way to police cars.

512 **The first community antenna television in the U.S. was started in 1947** on the roof of the Astor Hotel in Astoria. Ed Parsons picked up television signals broadcast from the only television station in the Northwest, KING-TV in Seattle, over 200 miles away. Originally, there were only three subscribers.

513 Dozens of U.S. cities had broadcast television before it came to Oregon. KPTV became the **first ultra-high frequency (UHF) commercial television station in the world** when it started broadcasting on September 20, 1952, on Channel 27. KPTV was owned by Empire Coil Company of New Rochelle New York, and went on the air with a test pattern September 18, 1952. The first programming was a speech by Herbert Mayer, the owner of Empire Coil Company. It was followed by a documentary about the UHF transmitter. At 5:00 pm that day, KPTV received and broadcast NBC's *All Star Revue* with Margaret Truman and Jimmy Durante. Beginning October 1, the 1952 World Series, in which the New York Yankees beat the Brooklyn Dodgers four games to three, was seen on the first full-scale television programming seen in Oregon. KPTV viewers needed a special band modification to receive the UHF signals. 1952 programming included *I Love Lucy, Hopalong Cassidy,* and *Love*

of Life. KPTV has operated as independent Channel 12 since March 8, 1955, after merging with KLOR Channel 12. Results of studies indicated that two-thirds of the viewers read less and visited friends less. There was no videotape in the 1950s and early 1960s, so television's excitement included *live* commercials.

514 KPTV in Portland had **one of the oldest and longest-used mobile television production vans** (from 1955-56 to 1990). The beam in studio A is one of the largest. KPTV's "Ramblin' Rod" is one of the nation's oldest (1964) continuous kids' shows.

514• The rural Harney County telephone exchange is one of the nation's largest at about 5,200 square miles. A U.S. Postal Service carrier route in isolated Harney County can be about 300 miles per day.

515 The **west coast's first drive-up telephone** was installed at the Gateway Shopping Center in east Portland (1959).

516 One of the **first community access cable television productions** west of the Mississippi River used videotape recorders at a Hillsdale garage on June 6, 1974. It was made possible by a grant from the Oregon Educational Coordinating Commission. John Platt was the producer.

517 The most viewed public affairs program in Oregon, *Town Hall*, started September 12, 1976, debating a nuclear energy initiative, with Tom McCall, moderator.

517• On November 10, 1981, the **first organized NO TV Day** encouraged people to **pledge not to watch television** at all for a full day. It was sponsored by The

Video Access Project, Bob Flug, Director. There was a hotline for people to call if they needed help to not watch television, and games were played at the Northwest Service Center in Portland to show alternatives to television.

518 Oregonians are outnumbered by new local phone books each year. The community Blue Pages concept for telephone directories, centralizing and classifying government offices and schools listings with resource information, was begun by the author (January, 1977). He spent most of the following five years evaluating the concept for the Federal government and persuading the telephone industry to implement it. The Blue Pages concept is partially implemented in over 360 million books internationally.

519 The City of Portland and its citizens went through an extensive process in the 1970s to determine what they wanted from a cable television franchise. In 1982, **East Portland had state-of-the-art cable television with a total of nine different local-origination channels.** From 1982 to 1984, Cablesystems Pacific (later known as Rogers Cablesystems) had one of the **largest numbers of community programming channels (with nine local-origination channels, Arts, Education, Environment, Seniors, City TV, Kids, Government, Sports, an Interactive channel** [Telidon], **and five public access channels)** of all cable television systems in the U.S. Cablesystems Pacific also operated one of the earliest remote-control pay-per-view movies/events menus in the western U.S. One of the local-origination channels started by the

initial cable franchisee, Cablesystems Pacific, has become the longest continuously-operating, city-mandated Black community television channel (BCTV) in the U.S. (since 1982). Art Alexander was the first producer on the channel.

Interactive Cable Television Channel 44

519• Another local-origination channel started by Cablesystems Pacific in April, 1982, was **the first interactive residential cable television channel in the Northwest, and one of the first in North America**. Users at home interacted with an educational color graphics and text database via touch-tone telephones. The national award-winning, interactive, computer graphics-based electronic magazine, "Interesting Facts About Portland," was produced under contract for Cablesystems Pacific (and later Rogers Cablesystems) by the author. The graphics database of over one million pixels reached 40,000 homes in east Portland 24 hours per day for over two and a half years. Similar systems operate in other North American cities. *(For more black and white versions of 1982-84 color graphics, see #10, #428, #487, #574, #826, #1028, and #1125).*

520 Open since June 25, 1986, the American Advertising Museum is the **first museum in the universe devoted solely to**

Oregon Firsts

advertising. The museum is located at the former site of Erickson's Saloon (NW 2nd + Burnside).

522 According to the national A.C. Nielsen Company ratings, Oregon Public Broadcasting's KOAP-TV rated first in prime-time viewing hours for the 1991-92 season among metered markets. *Oregon Field Guide* was the most popular program.

523 The husband-and-wife team of computer consultants Peter and Trudy Johnson-Lenz of Lake Oswego have a number of firsts to their credit. As part of a National Science Foundation study, Trudy and Peter became early participants in the New Jersey Institute of Technology Electronic Information Exchange (EIES) System. The Johnson-Lenz duo did innovative work on EIES including a "hypertext" tour of alternative futures in collaboration with Robert Theobald. Peter and Trudy Johnson-Lenz started the first online **"electronic chapel,"** ATUNNE, in 1980. The computer screen reads, *"Close your eyes, pause quietly for a few moments and be here now."* Trudy and Peter coined the term "groupware" in 1981, and they wrote the first software to integrate word processing, database management, remote information retrieval, and electronic mail. The Johnson-Lenzes started via computers connected to their electronic cottage the first interactive self-development seminars in 1988.

523• On May 3, 1993, in Salem and May 4 in Portland, two individuals, "Private" and "Anonymous," distributed the world's **first Data Donor Cards.** These cards were passed out to acknowledge valid

and legitimate privacy needs and the change in privacy expectations for both male and female telephone callers resulting from new switches the telephone company first began using to switch **all telephone calls** for automatic "Caller Identification" and related services in Portland, Salem, Milwaukie, Oregon City, and Lake Oswego on May 4, 1993.

Higher Education

524 In 1870, Oregon State College in Corvallis granted the first academic degrees in the West by a state-assisted college or university.

524• The nation's first Technology Department was established at Oregon State University in 1919.
524• The *Acona*, the nation's first oceanographic research vessel designed specifically for university-sponsored research, was acquired by Oregon State University.

524• OSU and Western Oregon State College established the nation's only jointly administered School of Education (1982) and the first teacher warranty program (1986).

524• The nation's first marine experiment station is the Hatfield Marine Science Center in Newport established in 1988.

524• The nation's largest indoor rock-climbing facility opened at Oregon State University beneath Parker Stadium in 1990.

524• The only organization with written permission from Walt Disney Studios to use the Donald Duck character without paying royalties is the University of Oregon.

Education

If adequately funded, current educational reforms may become Oregon's most significant contribution.

525 The first school in the Oregon Country started when John Ball was hired by John McLoughlin to teach children in exchange for his shelter at Fort Vancouver in the winter of 1832-33.

525• **The Oregon Country's first library** was at the Red River settlement in 1816. The Fort George (Astoria) library with 50 books in 1821 was moved to Fort Vancouver. The Multnomah Circulating Library started in Oregon City (1842) with 300 volumes.

526 The Pacific NW's first Catholic boys' school, St. Joseph's College in St. Paul, started with 30 resident students on its first day, October 17, 1843.

527 Willamette University in Salem is the **first school organized in the Pacific Northwest which became an institution of higher learning**. Trustees of the Oregon Institute, an elementary school for Methodists founded by Jason Lee, bought a two-year-old Indian Manual Labor school which opened August 13, 1844, and started sessions for five white children. **Willamette University was chartered by the Territorial Legislature in 1853**, and it later established the NW's first college of law, and the West's first Methodist theology school.

528 Tabitha Moffat "Grandma" Brown came out the Oregon Trail with her son Orus in 1846 when she was 66 years old. She settled at West Tualatin Plains and gathered 15 to 20 immigrant orphans in a school in a log

church on what later became the west campus of Pacific University. **This was the West's first orphanage.** Tabitha Moffat Brown is referred to as the **Mother of Oregon.**

(photo courtesy of Pacific University)

529 In the Act establishing the Oregon Territory in 1848, Congress established a **territorial library** with the primary function to serve officers of the territorial government.

530 Pacific University in Forest Grove received the first charter granted by the territorial government on September 29, 1849.

531 The **oldest educational building continuously in use west of the Rockies** is Old College Hall, built in 1850 on the campus of Pacific University.

532 The first public schools were opened at Portland, West Union, and Cornelius in 1851. Legislation in 1855 created the office of County School Superintendent.

533 St. Mary's Academy, the Pacific Northwest's first girls' Catholic institution of learning, was started on October 21, 1859, by the Sisters of the Holy Names from French Canada.

534 **Chemawa in Salem is the nation's oldest surviving off-reservation Native American boarding school.** Chemawa is the largest Federally-supported institution for basic education and training of Indian boys and girls from the Pacific Northwest. Originally in Forest Grove, it re-opened in 1886 in Salem with 207 students.

535 In 1898, Marylhurst College, the Pacific Northwest's first liberal arts college for women, opened in Clackamas County.

Carnegie Library for Umatilla County at Pendleton (photo courtesy of State Library)

536 **Oregon is the only state in the U.S. in which every community that was offered funds to build a library from Andrew Carnegie's foundation actually met the commitment with matching funds.** There is great social significance to the movement for free libraries. From 1901 to 1915, the following 24 Oregon communities built Carnegie Libraries: Albany, Ashland, Baker City, Dallas, Enterprise, Eugene, Grants Pass, Hermiston, Hillsboro, Hood River, Klamath Falls, La Grande, McMinnville, Marshfield, Medford, Milton, Ontario, Oregon City, Pendleton, Portland, Salem, The Dalles, Union, and Woodburn.

536• Pacific University operated the first academic library west of the Rocky Mountains to receive any Carnegie Library funds ($20,000; April 5, 1905).

537 The nation's first mail order library service was begun in 1911 by the Oregon State Library in Salem.

538 On five Sundays in January, February, and March, 1965, Portland State College's team won NBC television's academic *College Bowl* game, and **retired as undefeated champions.** The team consisted of Jim Westwood (captain), Larry Smith, Robin Freeman, and Mike Smith. The coach was Ben Padrow. They broke the existing *College Bowl* scoring record and held the new record for several weeks.

539 The Harney County Union High School District in Eastern Oregon operates the last **public boarding high school**. Crane High School near Burns is the **only tax-supported boarding school in the U.S.** The sparsely populated area has one of the largest consolidated school districts in the U.S.

540 **The longest-running alternative public school (grades K-12) in the United States** is the Metropolitan Learning Center (MLC) in NW Portland (since September, 1969). MLC's unique curriculum is enhanced through use of no letter grades, written evaluations, cooperative learning, a non-competitive atmosphere, self-paced learning, and electives in grades 1-12. MLC was co-founded by Emil Abramovic and Abe Bialstoski for "social change through education."

541 Oregon college students began the **first student-funded Public Interest Research Group in the United States,** now called OSPIRG. This was in 1970, during the Vietnam War, and morale had declined on U.S. campuses after the Kent State University killings in Ohio.

542 In 1971, Tigard High School became the first high school in the Northwest and one of the first high schools nationally to provide **academic credit for community-based career education.**

543 Single mother Barbara Roberts, a resident of the Parkrose School District, initiated and successfully lobbied at the state level for the **first law in the U.S. that required educational rights for handicapped students in 1971.** Just over a year later, the Federal Government adopted a similar law. Oregon Trail pioneer descendant Barbara Roberts became governor (1991).

544 The Oregon Institute of Technology in Klamath Falls is the **only polytechnic institute** in the entire Pacific Northwest. Oregon Institute of Technology is the first school or university in the U.S. with its internal temperature controlled by geothermal energy.

545 In 1976 Eagle Point School District became one of the nation's first school districts to shut down because of a lack of money. The closure came after local voters rejected a million-dollar levy five times. The North Bend schools' closure in 1986-87 led to the "safety net" referred by the legislature and approved by voters in 1988.

546 Portland Community College is the **Northwest's largest institution of higher learning**.

547 Reed College is the only undergraduate school on the continent with an **experimental nuclear reactor.**

Among liberal arts colleges, Reed College (founded in 1909) has the nation's highest percentage of graduates who are Rhodes Scholars.

548 Colegio Cesar Chavez in Mt. Angel (1973-1983) was **the first independent Chicano college with an accreditation candidacy in the United States.** Accreditation was first received from the Northwest Association of Schools and Colleges in Seattle, Washington, in 1975.

549 The average 1990-1991 Scholastic Aptitude Test (SAT) scores **rank Oregon students first** of the 23 states where at least 40 percent of high school seniors took the test. Oregon had ranked second for the previous four years.

550 In 1965, the Oregon State Library in Salem became the **first state library in this nation to publish a master book catalog.**

551 The Oregon construction library at Multnomah County Library is unique as the "first Public Library of construction publications in the country."

552 The Oregon State Library is the first **"Center for the Book"** west of the Mississippi River, as designated in 1990 by the Library of Congress.

553 Published in Oregon from 1983-1990, the *Young American* newspaper was the "only national newspaper" for kids. Up to 4.6 million copies of the newspaper were distributed nationally. (It's out-of-print now.)

554 "Uncle Sam in the Oregon Country," the **first exhibit in a series** by the Library of Congress entitled "States of the Nation," opened at the Oregon State Library in October, 1990.

555 The **Portland Public Schools System (PPS) is the first in the nation to decide to fully implement a multi-cultural/multi-ethnic curriculum** (1989). The change was started when PPS added an Afro-American emphasis in third, fourth, and fifth grades. Eventually, the curriculum will be expanded to all grades, including kindergarten, and will also include the contributions of Hispanic, American Indian, and Pacific Island cultures. PPS was the first school district in the nation to move toward inclusion of all geocultural groups in human history.

556 Oregon is one of the first states to sell baccalaureate bonds for post-secondary educational needs, and is the **only state selling baccalaureate bonds in-state only**. The first sale of State of Oregon baccalaureate bonds in May, 1988-89, was very popular, with $15 million sold out in three hours. The largest group of purchasers was grandparents, buying bonds for their grandchildren. The state's second sale sold $41.5 million.

557 Pursuing an idea of Norman Eder, the Oregon Graduate Institute of Science and Technology in Hillsboro printed and issued the **first scientist trading cards in the United States** in 1991.

558 **The Oregon Educational Act for the 21st Century adopted by the 1991 Legislature represents the most fundamental restructuring of the educational and training system adopted in the U.S.** After a planning period, this **Act** would, if funded, do many things, e.g.: **1)** expand the Head Start preschool program; **2)** combine classrooms of students in kindergarten through third grade; **3)** extend the current 175-day school year to 185 days by 1995 and to 220 days by 2010; **4)** require basic academic training by age 16 or 10th grade; **5)** separate students into two groups—college preparatory and academic technical—after the tenth grade; **6)** allow parents to move students to new schools if academic progress is unsatisfactory; **7)** give dropouts assistance in mastering basic skills; **8)** test academic and technical skills in grades three, five, eight, and ten; **9)** allow talented teachers and administrators to help train teachers to help schools meet standards. The **Oregon Educational Act for the 21st Century** was sponsored by Representative Vera Katz of Portland. New York-born Vera Katz was elected mayor of the City of Portland and was sworn in on January 4, 1993.

(For more, see
In-State Firsts
Education #1272-1276
and *Schools #1439-1446*.)

Energy

Wind energy has blown boats both to and from distant shores.

Archaeology and carbon dating provide evidence that fire has been used in Oregon for energy and clearing land by people native to the area over 13,200 years Before Present.

Today, we are faced with diminishing energy sources. Alternative and sustainable energy sources are needed. Some energy sources, including hydroelectric power, affect natural resources, especially salmon. Trees are a renewable resource that take decades to grow.

559 Long before non-Indians settled in Oregon, geothermal resources were used by Native Americans. Citizens in Ashland, Klamath Falls, Lakeview, and Vale use geothermal energy now. The City of Klamath Falls straddles an area that is **one of the largest underground geothermal resources in the world.**

559• Portland was first lighted by gas starting on June 5, 1866.

560 The first electrified ship to come up the Columbia and Willamette rivers, the *Columbia*, used an Edison dynamo.

561 **The first municipal electric system in the Pacific Northwest** started at McMinnville (1889).

Light bulb drawn from photo of early Edison bulb (courtesy of BPA)

562 A sailor who'd just sailed from New Jersey where he'd seen Thomas A. Edison demonstrate the incandescent light arrived in Portland in early September, 1880. He brought with him one of the first incandescent bulbs. It was hooked up with bare copper wires to the Edison dynamo that powered the ship *SS Columbia* to light **the first electrical incandescent light in the Northwest!** The single light was lit for three days and thousands of people came to see the light and the boat. (The wire was strung from the Clarendon Hotel porch, and the light hung over First Avenue near NW Flanders Street in Portland.)

563 Willamette Falls Electric on June 3, 1889, **introduced to the world the first long-distance (13 miles) commercial transmission of direct-current hydroelectric "high-tension" power,** from Oregon City/West Linn to Portland. Two 300-horsepower water wheels were belted to single-phase generators rated at 720 kilowatts.

564 In 1890, Willamette Falls Electric also achieved the **first long-distance transmission of alternating electrical current in the world** along the same route, from Oregon City/West Linn to Portland. Alternating current was chosen over direct current because it was more adaptable to the complexity of expanding electric systems, and it could be transmitted farther with less energy than direct current.

565 Oregon was the **first state in the Union to levy a tax on motor fuels** when in 1919 the legislature passed a law providing for a tax of one cent per gallon of gasoline and one-half cent per gallon on all distillate sold or distributed within the state. **This was the nation's first tax on gasoline for road improvements.** Other than the Columbia River Highway, there were only a few paved roads except within some larger cities. The dirt roads were inches deep in dust during summer and a foot deep in mud during winter.

566 Newly-elected state representatives Loyal Graham of Forest Grove and W. B. Devon of Carlton favored "good roads" and met in Forest Grove to try to solve road problems. **The question they asked was, "Couldn't we levy a tax on gasoline?"**
Rep. Loyal Graham received many requests for copies of the law from officials of several states. Within a few years, the Oregon gasoline tax was replicated and became the main source of highway revenue for every state in the Union and the District of Columbia. Most countries in the world now tax gas, amounting to billions of dollars, though some governments use the revenues for more than just roads. When the tax began, it brought $404,000 into the Oregon highway fund. As gasoline sales increased, more roads could be built. In 1932 the Federal Government first levied a gas tax. In 1992, the tax (risen to 22¢ a gallon) was producing more than $292 million annually in Oregon. From 1919 to 1992 Oregon motorists paid $4.1 billion in gasoline taxes.

567 **The Bonneville Dam is the first major Federal hydropower dam on the Columbia River.** The Bonneville Dam, which is 4,100 feet across, was started in 1933 and completed in 1938 at a cost of $32.5 million. Bonneville Dam had an initial capacity of 115,250 horsepower, which later was increased to over 500,000 horsepower.

568 Bonneville Dam was constructed with special features unused previously. The dam provided passageways and ladders for migrating salmon. Its navigation locks lifted ships higher (30 to 70 feet) than any other lock.

569 The Columbia River system is the **largest single force of hydroelectric power** in North America. The river serves one of the nation's largest irrigation systems. Oregon ranked first in percentage of energy use from hydroelectric power in 1954. More of the largest hydroelectric plants in 1964 were powered by the Columbia River than any other river in the world.

570 **BPA was the first Federal agency with a branch office in the the nation's capital.** The Bonneville Power Administration (BPA) headquartered in Portland is the **first Federal power-marketing agency.**

571 Energized in 1970, the **Celilo Converter Station controls all the electric power** generated by the Columbia River system's thirty major dams (from British Columbia to Montana to Oregon), plus that produced by coal, oil, nuclear, and the other facilities in the Pacific Northwest. It is the only

facility in North America that distributes energy via the Intertie from the Northwest to the Southwest and vice-versa. Every day alternating current is converted to direct current for transmission.

572 The BPA constructed high and very long electrical power lines to connect the Pacific Northwest and the southwestern U.S. These are the first very high power **direct current lines to be built in the nation and the world's longest,** stretching 846 miles non-stop to the Sylmar Converter Station in Los Angeles. Four lines carry electricity as both alternating current at 500,000 volts and direct current (two) at 750,000 volts. Oregon State College engineer Eugene Starr in 1945 established the conceptual basis for long distance transmission of high-voltage direct current.

574 In the 1950s, the State of Vermont passed a law banning non-returnable glass containers, but it did not include cans. The law was allowed to expire.

Oregon is the first state to require a deposit (5¢) on beverage containers (1971). Essentially the "Oregon Bottle Bill" "prohibits the sale of non-returnable beverage bottles and cans" in the state and outlaws beverage containers with a detachable metal pull tab opener. The plastic rings that keep six-packs together must decompose within four months of disposal.

Beverage containers comprised between 49% to 82% of all non-degradable litter in Oregon. **Since 1972, by re-using containers, over 1.4 trillion BTUs of energy have been saved annually compared to using throwaway bottles.** Litter has been reduced and space has been saved in many landfills, and jobs have been created. The **"Oregon Bottle Bill"** (HB 1036) was written by Rep. Paul Hanneman of Cloverdale, with seven co-sponsors. It was enacted July 2, 1971, and effective October 1, 1972.

Former Governor Tom McCall, who signed the "Oregon Bottle Bill," received an award in Japan for Oregon's efforts.

Oregon in 1990 had a 93% to 94% return rate for cans and bottles, according to the Oregon Liquor Control Commission.

From 1972-83 bottle and can deposit laws were adopted in ten states: Vermont ('72), Maine, Michigan ('76), Massachusetts ('79), Connecticut, Iowa ('79), New York ('76), California ('87, modified scrap value), Delaware ('82, just bottles), and Maryland, as well as the District of Columbia.

Energy

575 Oregon was the **first state in the continental U.S. to adopt comprehensive statewide land use and conservation policies/laws.** The land-use goals encourage planning to save energy in urban, suburban, and rural areas. *(See #209)*

576 Oregon was the **first state with a wind energy tax credit** for installing wind-powered electric generators. It included the world's first state anemometer (windspeed meter) loan program. Wind turbine buyers had to prove they would actually generate power onsite before receiving a tax credit that reduced Oregon's revenue. The wind energy tax credit and anemometer loan program were conceived and lobbied by Lee Johnson of *RAIN: Journal of Appropriate Technology* in the 1970s.

577 In 1973, the Oregon **Public Utility Commissioner office became the first in the nation to adopt energy curtailment plans.** These plans were designed for voluntary and mandatory curtailment of energy use (e.g., in worst-case scenarios of low water at Columbia River hydroelectric dams).

578 During the 1973-74 petroleum crisis, **the odd/even calendar day gasoline rationing policy using license plate numbers instituted by Oregon Governor Tom McCall was a first in the nation.** This plan became a model other states adopted quickly to deal with gas shortages. The Oregon Energy Information Officer, Don Jarvi, and Wayne Bowlby deserve credit for developing and implementing the idea.

579 The 1973 Legislative Assembly approved an energy research study. The 1975 Transition document was produced by the Office of Research and Planning of Governor Tom McCall's office, Joel Schatz, Director.

580 The nation's first Consumer's Guide to Woodstoves was written by Bill Day of Anchor Tools and Woodstoves in 1975. It was the first guide to woodstove quality in the U.S. It rated the workmanship, parts availability, and materials by manufacturer, specific brand name, and price.

581 The **first solar sub-division in the Pacific Northwest** consisted of 15 houses and a community building in the West Hills of Portland straddling the Multnomah-Washington County border and was initiated and designed by Bill and Barbara Church, Dorothy Dixon, and six families in 1977. This solar sub-division was constructed nine years before the City of Portland passed comprehensive solar-access ordinances. The homes in the planned development were so energy conserving that thermal heat storage of heat from south-facing greenhouses was found to be unnecessary. *(For more information contact Bill Church, 6454 SW Barnes Road, Portland, OR 97221.)*

581• The U.S. Federal Energy Regulatory Commission issued the first license to an Indian tribe when it gave the Confederated Tribes of the Warm Springs Reservation of Oregon approval for constructing the Pelton Reregulating Hydroelectric Project. The dam dedication was on July 16, 1992.

582 The Oregon State Parks System was **the nation's first to provide solar-heated public showers in campgrounds** (1977). This project lowered the cost of providing hot-water showers by efficiently using solar power.

583 **The City of Portland developed the first municipal energy plan of any city of any size in 1979. Portland's Home Energy Conservation Policies** included specific programs to weatherize low-income rental homes.

584 The Hood River Conservation Project made Hood River **the most energy efficient community in the West** and probably in the U.S. in the 1980s. It's a model of weatherization cooperation. This massive research project monitored energy usage before and after weatherization of 85% of the homes with electric heat. The Bonneville Power Administration provided most of the funds for the project, which showed that energy conservation could save the expense of building power plants. **This marked the first time a whole community was weatherized.**

586 The Oregon Department of Energy in 1980 became the nation's first to have resident State inspectors working in a nuclear plant (eight hours/day).

We Serve

587 **Oregon and New Jersey are the only two U.S. states without self-service gasoline** and that require the employment of gasoline attendants to pump gas. An initiative measure to permit **self-service dispensing of motor vehicle fuel** at the retail level was defeated in 1982 with 440,824 yes votes to 597,970 opposed.

588 After a 15-year effort by the Wood Energy Institute of Oregon, in 1985 the state Building Codes Agency was persuaded to adopt the first state **solid-fuel chimney regulations**. The regulations required products to meet or exceed the actual maximum chimney fire temperature of 2100° Fahrenheit. The previous standard was 1700° F.

589 **Portland was the largest major US. city with comprehensive solar-access ordinances** when they were approved in 1986. The City of Portland combined and modified solar-access ordinances from the cities of Ashland, Bend, Eugene, and Woodburn as well as Deschutes County. The solar-access ordinances established property rights so people who wish to use sunlight (e.g., southern exposure, active solar water heater) can't be blocked.

590 In 1974, Oregon adopted the Northwest's first energy code for new buildings, and it has since been strengthened. A home built in 1993 to standard energy efficiency specifications uses 50% the heating energy as a home built in 1979.

591 The Oil Heat Commission was established by the 1989 Oregon Legislature to increase energy efficiency, conservation, and environmental protection via landmark legislation which established a national precedent. Its environmental protection program established a trust fund to finance **clean-up of heating oil tank release**. This commission is financed by monthly assessments of heating oil dealers.

592 In 1989, **Oregon became the first state to include external costs in its power plan.** The PUC's 20-year least-cost plan includes environmental costs (fish, wildlife, and conservation).

593 In 1977, Oregon became the first state to authorize expenses by utilities to provide **consumer conservation measures**. In 1974, a tariff filed by Portland General Electric for thermal insulation started consideration of the expenses.

594 The idea for an interstate energy council came from Portland Mayor Neil Goldschmidt's office, 1977-78. The Pacific Northwest Power Planning and Conservation Act was signed into law by President Carter (Public Law 96-510) in 1980. This Northwest Power Act is the **first time committed in Federal statutes that energy conservation was deemed legally to be a resource. The Pacific Northwest now ranks on top nationally in terms of conservation.** The Northwest Power Act could be a model for a national energy plan.

595 The Emerald Public Utility District in Lane County became the first public utility district in the Northwest to generate energy from a landfill (1992).

596 Bonneville Power Administration (BPA) has developed a number of the high-voltage technologies used throughout the world.

597 The nation's first comprehensive utility programs for homeowners was mandated by Oregon in 1977. More than 130,000 homes were made more energy efficient via the help of program loans and grants. More than 220,000 energy audits were completed through the programs.

597• Oregon started the first Small Scale Energy Loan Program, where the state sells general obligation bonds to finance energy conservation and production.

597• Oregon is the first state with computerized energy code compliance forms for new commercial construction. This automates and expedites the work of architects and engineers.

(See also these related chapters: *Legislative Innovations, Bridges, Communications, Environment, and Transportation.*)

Environmental Actions

Prior to the arrival of the first Europeans, fire was used for millenia by Indians, the original landlords, as the most effective way to manage the environment and improve hunting and crops.

Oregonians learned early that environmental degradation can and must be cleaned up eventually. The state is definitely a leader in some environmental protections both nationally and internationally, but there is much yet to be done. Oregon trails some states in pollution prevention and clean-up.

Many environmental firsts have been previously detailed in the section on laws and other chapters, and they are worthy of repetition.

* The 1967 Oregon **Beach Bill** requires free access to and public use of all ocean beaches. (See #205)
* Oregon was the first state in the continental U.S. to adopt comprehensive statewide **land-use and conservation policies** or laws. Hawaii had land-use laws in 1961. (See #209)
* Oregon was the first state to **ban in-state sale of aerosol cans containing specific chlorofluorocarbon (CFC) compounds** as propellants. This law led to a national ban and international actions to protect the atmospheric ozone. (See #210)
* Oregon was the first state to require wood-stove testing and certification as **"clean-burning" stoves**. (See #212)

* Oregon's **Toxic Use Reduction and Hazardous Waste Reduction** Law is innovative. (See #217)
* In 1974 Oregon became the first U.S. state to extend its jurisdiction over marine fisheries to 50 miles. (See #446)
* Oregon enacted the nation's first **gas tax** (1919) for maintenance of roads. (See #565, #566)
* In 1971 Oregon became the first state to earmark state funds for the construction of **bicycle paths**. (See #862•)
* Oregon is the first state to encourage recycling by requiring **deposits on beverage containers** (1971). (See #574)

598 In the 1920s, water in the Willamette River wasn't suitable for swimming or drinking and fish died within minutes of contact. The **nation's first pollution control laws** were enacted when Oregonians became concerned and outraged. In 1938, the voting citizens overwhelmingly supported (247,685 **yes** to 72,295 no) an initiative petition creating a State Sanitary Authority to clean the river and control water pollution statewide.

The Willamette River clean-up went into low gear after World War II. The first municipal sewage treatment plants began operating in 1948 at Junction City and Newberg. Every city on the Willamette River had "primary" treatment (removal of at least one-third of the organic waste from sewage effluent) by 1958. Despite these efforts, pollution from pulp and paper mills continued to deplete oxygen from the river. The fall salmon run in 1965 was counted at a meager 79 fish.

Over an eight-month period in 1967, Governor Tom McCall headed the Oregon Sanitary Authority to give an emphasis to the importance of water pollution control programs. The 1967 state legislature required polluters to have pollution control permits, and gave tax credits to ease pollution control equipment installation expenses. Industries along the river and its tributaries installed equipment to control the release of pollution. The Willamette River was restored to cleanliness safe for swimming and other activities by 1972. Oregon's standards were among the first five in the nation to receive Federal approval. The fall salmon run in 1973 had increased to 22,000.

599 In April, 1950, Governor Douglas McKay appointed a subcommittee on air pollution to his Natural Resources Advisory Committee to study fluorides from aluminum reduction plants and gases from pulp and paper mills. Rather than legislating correction of the effects of air pollution from industrial sources, the 1951 Oregon Legislature established **the nation's first Air Pollution Control Act** (effective August, 1951) for control and prevention of air pollution.

600 **Stop Oregon Litter and Vandalism** (SOLV) is a registered nonprofit corporation founded by Governor Tom McCall and other business and community leaders in 1969. SOLV assists with more than 150 community cleanups in Oregon each year. SOLV was the catalyst in developing another volunteer program, **SOLV Oil Spill** (S.O.S.), the first time in the nation that corporations, environmental organizations, and government joined together to train citizens in oil spill remediation efforts <u>before</u> a major spill which could affect coastal areas or inland waterways occurred.

In 1984, **Oregon voters approved the most stringent radioactive-waste disposal laws in the United States (1984).** This measure was sponsored by the incorporated Portland organization Forelaws on Board. (Elaine Kelly, Treasurer, John Arum, and Lloyd Knox Marbet)

601 For over fifteen years Oregon had and may still have one of the **highest per capita recycling rates in the U.S.** Some states define recycling differently and comparable statistics have not been compiled. According to the Oregon Liquor Control Commission 92% to 94% of bottles and cans are returned for recycling.

602 The **first "most livable city" study** commissioned by the U.S. Environmental Protection Agency (EPA) utilized 1970 data and **ranked Portland as "America's most livable large city."** The criteria categories were economic, political, environmental, health, education, and social. This was the very first such EPA ranking.

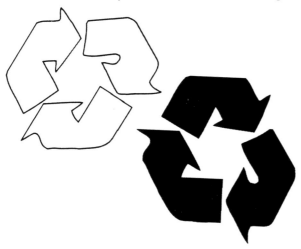

603 **Oregon is widely recognized for leadership in solid-waste recycling. Oregon is the first state to adopt an Opportunity to Recycle Act, which requires communities to provide drop-off centers or curbside programs, though it does not require individuals to recycle. The state focuses on market development and encourages recycling and procurement of recycled products through its comprehensive tax credit policies.** A bill (SB 405, 1983, Ch. 729) by the Senate Committee on Energy and the Environment requires those using disposal sites to provide customers (in cities of over 4,000 people) with the opportunity to recycle. The law includes promotion, education, curbside collection, and policies for the disposition of materials. It's cheaper to recycle than to deposit in a landfill.

604 Denton Plastics, Inc., in NE Portland was first to implement a post-consumer collection program for polystyrene foam containers. Denton Plastics' pioneers were the first to have a reprocessed resin certified with the "green cross." Denton Plastics is the first to trademark a program to **"recycle by the numbers."**

605 The **nation's first municipal garbage composting plant using rotating drums with static pile aeration** was dedicated on March 28, 1991, in NE Portland. Funded via Metro-issued bonds, the 18-acre, $28 million plant was capable of handling 600 tons of garbage per day. The composting plant used two 100-ton rotating drums to turn waste into compost. The composting plant, built by Reidel Environmental Technologies, Inc., and Resource Systems Corporation of Portland, used Dano MSW composting technology, which originated in Denmark. This project terminated in 1992 for reasons including bad odors.

606 CH2M Hill was founded in 1947 at Corvallis by Oregon State College engineering professor Fred Merryfield and three of his former students: Holly Cornell, Jim Howland, and Burke Hayes in Corvallis. CH2M Hill is now the Northwest's largest engineering design and consulting firm in the environmental services field. In 1992, CH2M Hill was the U.S. Environmental Protection Agency's largest contractor, frequently regarding toxic waste. CH2M Hill ranks on top for billings among U.S.-based engineering firms that do not double as construction companies.

607 **Starting in 1984, Oregon became the first state with an organized Volunteer Statewide Beach Clean-up**. This environmental concept ("**Adopt A Beach**") was originated by Judie Neilson, who worked at Oregon's Fish & Wildlife Department. Judie was the catalyst for first a statewide, then a nationwide, and now an international effort to clean plastics and litter from the world's ocean beaches. **More than 142 tons of debris have been collected by thousands of volunteers on Oregon's 400-mile coastline since 1984. In 1989, 900 tons of garbage was collected on beaches worldwide**, including 22 U.S. states, nearly all the U.S. coastal states. In Oregon in 1988, for example, plastics comprised 63% of the debris collected, including 141 tires and 3,800 cigarette butts. In March, 1992, a record 5,000 volunteers picked up more than 26 tons of trash. The clean-up occurs twice a year. Oregon's Department of Fish and Wildlife sponsors the fall beach clean-up; the state parks office sponsors the spring beach clean-up.

607• The **Ocean Resources Protections Act** is a planning compact among the states of Hawaii, California, Oregon, and Washington, the Pacific Islands, and the province of British Columbia, Canada. Oregon Senator Bill Bradbury sponsored Senate Bill 500 in 1991 in response to concerns about hazardous substances and gas and oil drilling off Oregon's coastline.

608 Three Northwest tribes (the Yakima Indian Nation, the Nez Perce Tribes, and the Confederated Tribes of the Umatilla Indian Reservation) were the only Indian tribes specified in the Nuclear Waste Policy Act of 1982 as **"Affected Tribes."**

609 The 1991 Legislature passed two bills which were progressive environmentally. One of the most comprehensive recycling laws in the nation, requiring 50% of solid waste to be recycled by the year 2000, was Senate Bill 66, sponsored by Senator Dick Springer of Portland. Oregon became the **first state to set a minimum content rate for plastic of 25% recycled or recyclable content.**

610 The 1991 Legislature passed the most restrictive heap leach mining laws (HB 2244) on the use of toxic cyanide to dissolve microscopic gold out of ore. The rules establish a permit process for companies seeking to establish heap leach mining operations, particularly for open-pit cyanide heap leach processing. The law requires special liners, leak detection equipment, and protections for wildlife and waterfowl.

611 The Port of Portland's International Airport in 1991 became the first major airport in the U.S. to implement a total recycling program. The recycling program was expected to save approximately $16,000 in its first full year (1992) of integrated airport-wide operation by recycling more than 280 tons of glass, cardboard, and office paper.

Forestry, Logging, and Wood Products

Trees are Oregon's greatest natural resource. Trees provide multiple benefits, such as improved air quality (using carbon dioxide and giving off oxygen), soil stability, shade, lumber, compost material, wind breaks, fuel, and beauty. Few places on earth have old-growth forests. The old-growth forests of western North America are among the most diverse in the world. Overshadowed by some of the **largest, tallest, oldest conifers** (cone-bearing evergreens), these forests have evolved over the centuries by withstanding natural and human disturbances. A few enormous trees still standing today were already centuries old when Columbus landed in America. After U.S. explorer Robert Gray, sailing the *Columbia Rediviva, discovered the Columbia River, he landed and found an ancient forest. However, "old growth" is generally younger than this.*

Currently, about 10% of original old-growth or ancient forest remains intact, and virtually all old-growth forests are on Federal lands. Ancient forests are being destroyed at a rate of about 75,000 acres/year. Less than 40% of current old-growth forest lands are currently proposed for protection for future generations.
Oregon's old-growth trees have greater potential for storing carbon than younger trees. This is one reason it's important to reduce the cutting of old trees and increase planting of young trees.

Oregon Firs!

This book is made of recycled paper. Trees are beautiful and serve many purposes essential to human life. Because of the early laborious and dangerous harvests, numerous lumbering techniques and ways to transport logs were developed in Oregon.

Oregon legislation in 1983 dedicated the first full week of April each year as Arbor Week (for planting trees).

612 The **first shipment of lumber from the Northwest** is credited to Captain John Meares. The English explorer and trader took spars from trees along with furs on a return trip to China in 1788-89.

613 **The first sawmill in the Pacific Northwest** was built by the Hudson's Bay Company in 1827 on the north side of the Columbia River not far from Fort Vancouver.

614 **More than four dozen species of trees were discovered in Oregon by** Scottish-born **David Douglas**. The **Douglas fir**, the world's largest non-sequoia tree, is named after him. *(See #352)*

615 The **first power-driven sawmill in the Oregon Country** was constructed just north of Champoeg in 1836 by Thomas McKay.

616 The **first paper mill in the Pacific Northwest** started in Oregon City in 1866, making paper from rags.

617 The first steam-driven circular saw began operation in Portland in 1850.

618 **The first timberland reserve in Oregon was the Bull Run Reserve on June 1, 1892,** which included the mountains and forested foothills of the Cascade Range from the Columbia River south to California. The first forest ranger was Adolf Aschoff.

619 The Crown Zellerbach's Clatsop County property was one of the first in the U.S. to be certified as a **tree farm**. Crown Zellerbach pledged to keep the land growing continuous crops of trees under the best forestry practices possible. The first purchase of forest land by the Crown Zellerbach Corporation on the Clatsop Tree Farm was on January 13, 1893.

619• **The largest log cabin in the World was built for the Lewis & Clark Exposition in 1905.** It was built from hand-picked, horse-logged trees from the Clatskanie-Delena area of Columbia County. The big log cabin, using tree-column architecture, housed the **Forestry Center** until late on a dry Monday afternoon, August 17, 1964, when it burned in a quick blaze. The Forestry Building in northwest Portland on 25th between Vaughn and Upshur was 200 feet long, 102 feet wide, and 72 feet high. It was enormous in size, with fifty-two log pillars six feet in diameter. Floor sections were great logs nine or ten feet in diameter. One million board feet of logs went into its construction. Approximately ten million people visited the Forestry Center.(*See photo page 105*)

620 Invention of the **first commercial production of Douglas fir plywood** was in St. John's, Oregon, by the Autzen family, owner of Portland Manufacturing Company, in 1904. The glue was applied by hand. Hand screws on wooden presses held the ply boards until the glue set. The wood boards were dried in standard lumber kilns. It was displayed for the first time at the large log Forestry Center during the Lewis & Clark Exposition in 1905.

621 The Plylock Corporation was the oldest Douglas fir plywood plant in the Northwest and used the nation's largest resin press.

622 Gigantic ocean-going rafts made of from one to five million board feet of logs were products of the ingenious Simon Benson and his engineers. By overlapping chains to cradle and keep logs together, in 1906 Simon Benson initiated the shipment of logs to southern California for wood products manufacturing and home building. A large log raft contained enough lumber to construct more than 200 large houses.

623 The C. A. Smith Lumber and Manufacturing Company built the largest sawmill in the U.S. in Marshfield (now Coos Bay) on February 29, 1908. It was operated by the Smith-Powers Logging Company, the Coos Bay Lumber Company, and later by the Georgia-Pacific Corporation.

624 The first transit-type fire finder was invented by forester William Bushnell Osborne in 1911-12.

625 William B. Osborne also invented the photo survey transit which takes photographic images of the entire horizon (1929-30).

626 A 1914 U.S. Bureau of Corporations Study found that there was **"more privately held timber in Oregon than any state in the Union."**

627 The **largest private timber holder in Oregon and in the U.S.** that same year, 1914, was the Southern Pacific Railroad.

628 **The nation's largest Ponderosa Pine forest grows** in Grant and Harney counties.

629 Oregon has **more National Forests** than any other state in the Northwest, and receives the largest amount of money from the U.S. Government for timber sales.

630 **To harvest spruce trees for airplane manufacture during World War I, the U.S. Government built the world's largest spruce sawmill in Toledo.** The sawmill was later purchase by C. D. Johnson Lumber Co. (now Georgia-Pacific). Throughout the war, the Spruce Division's roughly 1,500 men were headquartered nearby in Yaquina City.

631 Simon Benson (born in Norway) was the first person in the Pacific Northwest to **use a steam-powered donkey engine and rail locomotive equipment for transport of logs and wood harvesting in rainforests.**

632 John R. Porter was the first person to bring giant Sequoia tree seeds the northwest.

633 Charlie Wolf invented the Wolf electric drive saw while he worked at Peninsula Iron Works in Portland in 1920. The Wolf electric drive saw was powered by an electric motor off a portable generator with cutting-chain action able to move in either direction.

634 Wes Lematta developed the idea and his brother Jim, along with Bob Brown, were the pilots in 1971 when Columbia Heliocopters (Portland) pioneered use of heli-logging near Greenville, California.

635 **The world's largest lumber sawmill was built in 1926-27 along the Klamath River near Klamath Falls.** It's owned and operated by Weyerhauser Timber Company primarily for use with Ponderosa pine. It was called the world's largest pine lumber factory.

636 Norm Williams of Myrtle Point was the inventor of the first vacuum valve for log truck air brakes. He moved to Portland to start his own company, Williams Air Controls, in the 1930s.

637 In 1937, Tillamook's H. Clay Meyers II patented "straddle-mounting" which improved truck load stability and capacity.

638 Oregon surpassed its neighbor, Washington State, in 1938, and since has ranked first nationally, in producing softwood saw timber. Oregon had 23% of the national total then and had 18% of the total by 1992.

639 The Douglas Fir tree ranks as the **most important and prolific single timber species in North America, and was designated the state tree by the 1939 legislature.**

640 For decades and today, **one-fifth of all lumber products in the U.S. came and come from Oregon.**

641 The Oregon Forest Conservation Act of 1941 was **progressive legislation requiring reforestation on both state and private lands on a continuous-yield basis.**

642 In 1941, Albany Plylock Division built and installed the **world's largest high-frequency "thermal,"** allowing plywood up to seven inches thick to be produced. Twenty-seven Douglas fir plywood plants produced an output of 1,865 million board feet in 1949.

643 The nation's **first production plant for the processing of ethyl alcohol from sawdust and wood waste** was built in 1945 at Springfield.

644 **Weyerhauser Company (Springfield) was the largest forest products complex in the world (1945).** Forest products accounted for 80% of Lane County's exports.

645 Most states have no reforestation laws. **Oregon's Forest Practices Act (1971) is the first of its kind in the nation and is recognized throughout the world.** It set up state control over logging operations to ensure enforcement of progressive forest practices. The law requires landowners to reforest after harvest and to protect adjacent forest areas. This law has served as a model for other states and countries (e.g., Australia, Canada). The Oregon Forest Practices Act was amended in 1971 and 1987 and continues to be one of the most effective among states with similar regulations.

646 **Oregon is a leader in reforestation, with the largest number of trees planted.** In the 1988-89 planting season, an estimated 200,000 acres were planted with 100 million seedlings, or 37 seedlings per Oregon resident.

647 **Oregon is the nation's #1 producer of lumber and plywood.** About 43% of 1988 housing starts could have been built with Oregon wood. The average house uses 11,000 board feet of lumber and 5,000 square feet of plywood. Every American uses the equivalent of a 100-foot tree each year in the form of paper, etc. The average log truck on Oregon highways carries 5,000 board feet of timber. U.S. demand for timber is expected to increase 1.6 times by 2030.

647• Adaptation of the kraft process was developed to produce pulp from the residues of non-white trees, e.g., Ponderosa Pine, which is the most dominant forest type east of the Cascades.

648 **Oregon ranks first nationally in the manufacture of engineered wood products,** utlizing wood from 12 main tree species. **Oregon is the largest producer of lumber and panels.**

649 **The single most important invention affecting logging was the chainsaw in 1935.** The chainsaw allowed loggers to cut nearer the ground, and it became a necessary tool in fighting forest fires. Some later chainsaw innovations came from Omark Industries.

650 In 1947, lumberjack Joseph B. Cox invented **saw chain teeth**, based on ideas he developed watching Timber beetles, with two cutters on each turn. The chains were originally produced with hand-fitted linkage. Joe Cox received a patent for his invention on May 23, 1950. He sold the lucrative invention to Oregon Chain Saw, a company which had tremendous growth. Oregon Chain Saw changed its name to Omark (the O for Oregon, the mark for trademark).

651 The first modern **14-ply heavy-duty log truck tire** was one invention of Lloyd Christensen in 1934.

652 In 1934, Lloyd Christensen had Portland's Wentworth & Irwin Co. manufacture **some of the first dual-axle trailers in the logging industry** for him.

653 The **first Civilian Conservation Corps (CCC) camp in the Pacific Northwest was built in 1933 at Camp Applegate** on the Applegate Ranger District, Rogue River National Forest.

The Civilian Conservation Corps was started by President Roosevelt to build trails and roads, for reforestation, etc.

655 The Tillamook Burn in 1933 destroyed 240,000 acres, killing 13.5 billion feet of prime timber in **one of the continent's most devastating forest fires in modern history. Subsequent fires in the Tillamook Forest burned and reburned in six-year cycles in 1939, 1945, and 1951, for a combined total of 350,000 acres burned.** The big 11-day blaze was started August 14, 1933, by a fire from a logging operation in Gales Creek Canyon west of Forest Grove. Smoke could be seen as far away as Montana. This was the nation's largest fire until the Yellowstone National Park fire in Wyoming in 1988.

Wood fibre lost in the Tillamook Burn could have built one million homes and employed 13,000 people for 20 years.

Be aware. Help prevent forest fires KEEP OREGON GREEN!

656 **Oregon is the first state to reforest a major area.** In 1948 Oregon voters approved a constitutional amendment to finance reforestation of the Tillamook Burn and other state lands. **It is still the most massive reforestation ever undertaken by a state.**

(See #1426)

657 Prineville, Oregon, has five lumber mills and three molding plants in operation. Two of these molding mills were the **largest and second largest in the United States.**

658 Bohemia, Inc., of Eugene was the **largest manufacturer of structural glue-laminated beams and timbers**, in terms of volume, with production plants in Saginaw and Vaughn.

659 **Oregon has more softwood of harvestable size than all 13 southern states combined.** The southern U.S. states do not have reforestation laws.

660 **Over 80% of the nation's demand for Port Orford cedar is Oregon-supplied.** Port Orford cedar comes from the Siskiyou National Forest, and most of it resides in the Powers Ranger District. Acid-proof Port Orford cedar is used in the manufacture of battery separators.

661 **Of all the softwood in the U.S., Port Orford cedar is the most valuable. It is the only species that can be exported from Federal timber land as a log.** It resembles a ceremonial cedar no longer available in Japan, making it highly prized in that nation.

662 The **first solar-powered U.S. Forest Service radio** was used on Rustler Peak Lookout in Butte Falls Ranger District in the 1970s.

663 The **World Forestry Center** is the only institution dedicated solely to forest resources. The World Forestry Center is a private nonprofit corporation with an international Board of Directors that provides programs which all relate to forestry.

664 The first **all-woman tree-planting crew** in Oregon and probably in the U.S. consisted of six women working to plant trees, dig fire lines, and fight fires from 1967 until 1975 in Rigdon Ranger District near Oakridge.

665 The **Hoedads**, based in Lane County, are the **first and largest worker-owned, cooperative tree-planting crew in the U.S.**

666 The first **Federal timber sale** in Oregon (and possibly for the whole Forest Service) took place in what is now the Klamath Ranger District, Winema National Forest, in south central Oregon.

667 **Coos Bay has been the largest lumber-exporting port in the world.**

667• The town of Gilchrist in Klamath County is one of the nation's last "company-owned lumber towns."

667• The nation's largest collection of logging equipment is located at the open-air Collier Logging Museum about 30 miles north of Klamath Falls along U.S. Hwy 97.

The Forestry Center with visitors at the Lewis & Clark Exposition in 1905-06. It was the largest log cabin in the world until August, 1964, when it burned in a quick blaze. *OHS Neg. OrHi 39201*

This blimp hangar at Tillamook Naval Station is the world's largest clear-span wooden structure. A similarly large hangar a short distance away burned the night of August 22, 1992, in the largest fire in a single wooden building.
Aerial photo courtesy of U.S. Naval Archives, OHS Negative Number OrHi 86134

Oregon Firsts

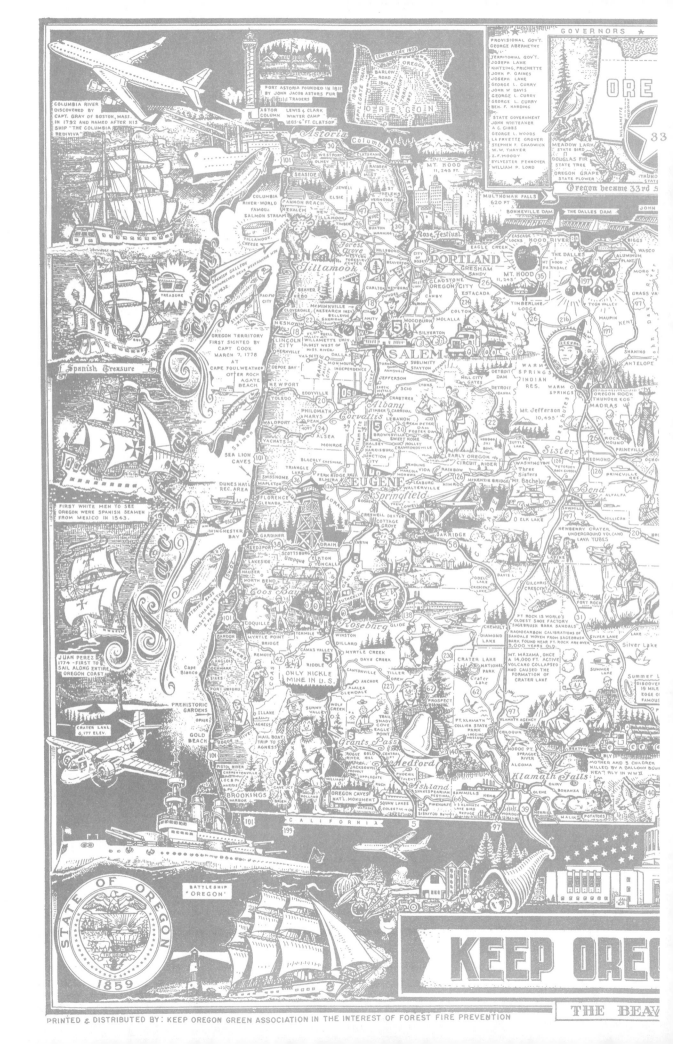

668 The Weyerhauser Company's Klamath lumber sander was the **largest sanding unit** ever designed, constructed, and operated in the United States at the time it began in 1977.

669 In the summer of 1983, Sherrill King became the first woman smoke jumper fighting forest fires.

670 The large beam in Camp 18 Restaurant in Columbia County is an 85-foot ridge pole, which is claimed to be the "largest known beam in the U.S."

671 The bark and needles of the Pacific yew tree produce taxol, which helps fight ovarian and breast cancer. Taxol has been approved for this use by the U.S. Food and Drug Administration.

671• Louisiana Pacific was incorporated in 1973 as an innovative spin-off from Georgia-Pacific. The Federal Trade Commission charged that Georgia-Pacific controlled too much of the production of Southern Pine plywood.

671• Both Keep Oregon Green and Keep Washington Green began in 1940. Keep Oregon Green started the first-ever forest fire school in 1983. The school graduated 1,000 students in the spring of 1992.

672 **More of the old-growth forests** under consideration for preservation by the U.S. Government to protect the endangered northern spotted owl are **in Oregon than any other state**.

672• The day before the Forest Summit, the First of April, 1993, at Tom McCall Waterfront Park, from 50,000 to 70,000 people attended an **Ancient Forests Celebration** and rally despite the rainfall. They heard music and speakers. Portland police said it was **the most peaceful large gathering** they'd ever seen. A coalition of over two dozen organizations sponsored the event.

672• At the Oregon Convention Center in Portland on April 2, 1993, President Bill Clinton, Vice President Al Gore, and four cabinet members (Interior, Agriculture, Labor, and Commerce) convened **the first Forest Summit. This was the first time so many high-ranking Federal officials were in Oregon at the same time.** After seven hours of input, President Clinton promised **a first draft** of a coordinated, integrated Federal plan within 60 days. On the **First** of July, 1993, the President unveiled a controversial plan to protect the endangered species, harvest Federal forest lands, retrain workers, and address whole-log exports.

If 100,000 average Americans stopped their junk mail, approximately 150,000 trees would be saved. SAVE **TREES !**
To have your name removed from many direct mail lists, simply send a written request to: Mail Preference Service
Direct Marketing Association
P.O. Box 3861
New York City, N.Y.
10163-3861

National Champion BIG TREES in Oregon

The Big Tree program recognizes 850-plus native and natuaralized species across America. There are currently 49 national champion and co-champion trees in Oregon. The Big Tree program started in 1940, and is operated by the American Forests in Washington, D.C. Trees are compared in overall size by using a combination of three measurements. A tree's trunk <u>circumference</u> *in inches is added to its* <u>height</u> *in feet plus one quarter of its* <u>crown spread</u> *in feet. Co-champions are signified by *. The number of champions changes as trees are "dethroned" when new trees are discovered and others fall.*

The list below for Oregon combines American Forests National Register of Big Trees (1992 Edition) and Oregon Forestry Department information on directions. For free information on how to measure and nominate a tree to the National Register, contact: AMERICAN FORESTS, National Register of Big Trees, P.O. Box 2000, Washington, DC 20013 **Global Releaf!** *How do you spell relief?* **R·E·L·E·A·F!**

	SPECIES	Circumference	Height	Spread	County
673	**Red Alder**	20'5"	104'	49'	**Clatsop**

Directions: Go 15 miles southeast of Astoria on Hwy 202, then via Longview Fibre Road (easement) across the Simmons Ranch, then along the Klaskanine River for about half mile along south bank. Landowner is Longview Fibre. Nominator: Ron Simon.

674	**Sitka Alder**	1'9"	30'	—	**Clatsop**

Directions: Off U.S. Hwy 26, eight miles NE near Necanicum Junction. Walk one mile up Saddle Mountain Trail in State Park. Nominator: Maynard Drawson.

675	**Oregon Ash**	21'11"	59'	45'	**Columbia**

Directions: Located on Sauvie Island approximately 10 miles NW of Portland off U.S. Hwy. 30. Cross bridge and go north on Sauvie Island Road about 2 miles turning right on Reeder Road. Follow this road 13 miles to north end of island and end of pavement. A narrow, unimproved dirt road proceeds about one and one-half miles to the tree this side of Cunningham Slough near the end of the road. The road branches twice. Take first left-hand road then the next right-hand road around the west edge of Ruby Lake. (This road is too wet to drive most of the year.)
Landowner is Oregon Fish & Wildlife Commission. Nominators: Eldon Boge and Robert Heilman.

676	**Pacific Bayberry**	4'4"	38'	34'	**Douglas**

Directions: Travel to Tahkenitch Creek 9 miles north of Reedsport. Follow the creek until you reach power lines (50 to 100 yards from ocean beach), turn south under power lines for 200 yards. Tree is 50 feet on left. Landowner is Siuslaw National Forest (Corvallis office). Nominators: B. Lewis, M. Clark, and R. Spray.

677	**Northwestern Paper Birch***	3'10"	66'	30'	**Wallowa**

Directions and landowner: State property on Minam River, 1 mile from confluence with the Wallowa River. Nominator: Frank Callahan.

678	**Water Birch**	9'3"	53'	42'	**Wallowa**

Directions: 0.75 miles past milepost 11 on the Little Sheep Creek Highway between Joseph and Imnaha. SE of Little Sheep Creek at the corner of a garden. Accessible by foot crossing the creek. Tree is visible from the highway. Landowner is Everett Talbot of Joseph (503-432-2622). Nominator: Maynard Drawson.

679	**Blue Myrtle/Blueblossom**	2'8"	41'	20'	**Curry**

Directions: Curry County Nominator: Frank Callahan

Please get permission from owner if you go on private property

NATIONAL CHAMPION TREES FOUND IN OREGON

	SPECIES	Circumference	Height	Spread	County
680	**Cascara Buckthorn*** (1975)	**8'3"**	**35'**	**54'**	**Coos**

Directions & Nominator: backyard of Mr. Vernon D. Ellis, 2112 Broadway, North Bend, OR 97459.

	SPECIES	Circumference	Height	Spread	County
681	**Cascara Buckthorn*** (1977)	**8'3"**	**37'**	**50'**	**Clatsop**

Directions: Seaside; 1982 + 1988 co-champion.   Nominator: Steve Ferguson.

	SPECIES	Circumference	Height	Spread	County
682	**Cascara Buckthorn***	**9'1"**	**27'**	**43'**	**Lane**

Directions: Siuslaw National Forest, Big Creek Drainage. Take road No. 1059 off Hwy. 101 at Devil's Elbow. Go 5 miles to end of pavement, turn left and go one-half mile, turn right and go one-quarter mile to switchback. Take trail east down hill.   Nominator: Ray Cross.

	SPECIES	Circumference	Height	Spread	County
683	**Silver Buffaloberry**	**6'6"**	**22'**	**20'**	**Malheur**

Directions-Landowner: In Oregon on property of Bob Campbell (Box 79, McDermitt, Nevada 89421) in Malheur County, approximately one mile north of the Oregon-Nevada line. Nominator: Frank Callahan.

	SPECIES	Circumference	Height	Spread	County
684	**Butternut**	**18'7"**	**88'**	**103'**	**Lane**

Directions: North side of 11th Avenue, one block west of Willamette Street in front yard. House is now apartment house; owner lives there and is manager. Landowner is George Wingard, 465 E. 11th, Eugene. Nominator: Robert Van Pelt

	SPECIES	Circumference	Height	Spread	County
685	**Oregon Myrtle** (California-laurel)	**41'9"**	**88'**	**70'**	**Curry**

Directions: Travel ten miles up south bank of Rogue River to Lobster Creek Picnic Ground. Cross bridge, travel one-quarter mile east on Road 3533. Tree is approximately 100 yards up hill.   Landowner is USFS Siskiyou National Forest.   Nominator: Ken Bigelow.

	SPECIES	Circumference	Height	Spread	County
686	**Port Orford Cedar**	**37'7"**	**219'**	**39'**	**Coos**

Directions: Elk Creek near Powers. Travel 43 miles from Powers on Forest Route #321 up the S. Fork Coquille River; turn left on Coal Creek Road #3145 and travel 20 miles then turn right on Elk Creek Road #3242; 33 miles further take the spur on the right; one-tenth mile further take another spur to the right; road ends one-tenth mile further. Here a platform has been constructed for viewing tree at Big Tree picnic area. Landowner is Siskiyou National Forest.   Nominator: Donald Denniston.

	SPECIES	Circumference	Height	Spread	County
687	**Birchleaf Cercocarpus**	**3'8"**	**34'**	**29'**	**Jackson**

Directions: West of Central Point about 3 miles on Ray Mitchell farm off Foley Lane. Landowner is Ray Mitchell, 6035 Foley Lane, Central Point, OR 97501. Nominator: Frank Callahan.

	SPECIES	Circumference	Height	Spread	County
688	**Giant Chinkapin**	**11'3"**	**115'**	**37'**	**Lane**

Directions: Lane Co. W. of Junction City on Hwy 36. Go to Wayne Leiburg House, 25644 Hwy 36. Go through back gate and follow Blue Ribbon up hill (on foot) to top of ridge. Stay on old logging road in southwest direction. Leiburg House to last blue ribbon on old road is approximately 57 chains. From last blue ribbon on road go due west 5 chains following blue ribbon to tree with blue ribbon around trunk. Legal description: T16S - R5W - 30 about center of NWNE. Landowner is International Paper Co. Nominator: Robert Soleman.

Please get permission from owner if you go on private property

NATIONAL CHAMPION TREES FOUND IN OREGON

SPECIES	Circumference	Height	Spread	County

689   Black Cottonwood   26'3"   155'   110'   **Marion**
Directions: Willamette Mission State Park; past champion (1984,1988) Estimated to be 256 years old. **World's largest black cottonwood.** Nominator: Maynard Drawson.

690   Narrowleaf Cottonwood   26'2"   79'   80'   **Malheur**
Directions: In Ironsides near Hwy. 26 in Malheur County.   Nominator: Donald Oakes.

691   Baker Cypress (or Modoc)   10'9"   129'   29'   **Josephine**
Directions: Steve Peak region, Range 5 W, Township 40 South, NW corner of the SW one-quarter section of section 22. Park at wide road cut and walk uphill to hillcrest above roadcut. Tree is visible from road. Landowner is Rogue River Nat. Forest USFS   (Medford). Nominator: Frank Callahan.

692   Monterey Cypress   27'9"   97'   106'   **Curry**
Directions: The "Harbor" tree is located in the front yard of the Chetco Valley Museum on U.S. Hwy. 101 (tree can be seen from highway; there's a sign on the highway). Landowner is Mr. Muncy, Box 936, Brookings.   Nominator: Frank Callahan.

693   Pacific Dogwood   14'1"   60'   58'   **Columbia**
Directions: North on Hwy. 30 from City of Clatskanie to Mayger Rd. to junction of Mayger Road and Rutter Road. Tree is in 'V' of junction, across Rutters Rd. from Old Quincy Grade School. Tree is growing on edge of Rutters Rd. Landowner is J. M. Tomberg. Nominator: J. E. Makela.

694   Western Dogwood *   1'8"   16'   28'   **Polk**
Directions: 10 mi. NW of Dallas, 1/2 mi. downstream from mill Creek Park. Nominator: Barbara Rupers.

695   Coast Douglas Fir   33'7"   329'   60'   **Coos**
Directions: Travel west from Roseburg to Burnt Mtn., stay on Burnt Mtn. Road till you reach (gravel) road. Travel to the end of this gravel road until road stops (water bar). You're on foot from there. Trail is flagged but not very accessible. Road is Middle Fork of Brummet Creek Road: 27-9-17.0. Landowner: B.L.M. Coos District, Coos Bay. Nominator: Hank Williams.

696   Rocky Mountain Douglas Fir 23'6"   158'   55'   **Harney**
Directions: Ochoco National Forest.   Nominator: Gordon Anderson.

697   Blackbead Elder   3'3"   42'   30'   **Columbia**
Directions: Lower Columbia River Highway,   U.S. 30 near Prescott, Columbia County. Contact: Columbia City State Forestry office.   Nominator: Oliver Matthews.

698   Pacific Red Elder   7'6"   30'   44'   **Lincoln**
Directions: Seven miles north of Gold Beach turn east off Hwy. 101 at N. Nesiles Beach. Go south on Frontage Road approximately one-quarter mile, then east up Adams Road to house number 94786 Adams Road. (This is the house on the south side of the road below the watertank.) The tree is in the creek behind the house near the west end of the lot. Landowner is Jim Rogers, 95187 Elk Road, Port Orford, OR 97465. Nominator: Tom Morgan.

699   Shasta Red Fir (1988 champ) **20'5"**   228'   32'   **Jackson**
Directions: Rogue River National Forest.   Nominator: Jack James.

Please get permission from owner if you go on private property

NATIONAL CHAMPION TREES FOUND IN OREGON

	SPECIES	Circumference	Height	Spread	County
700	**Black Hawthorn**	9'6"	33'	45'	**Multnomah**

Directions: Ten miles north of Portland out U.S. 30, cross bridge and go north on Sauvie Island Road. After two miles take Reeder Road to right and follow it 8 miles. The tree is along an east-west fence line about 150 feet west of road.   Landowner is Earl Reeder. Nominator: Frank Callahan.

701	**Columbia Hawthorn**	2'2"	18'	12'	**Wallowa**

Directions: On Imnaha River on road right-of-way approximately six miles upstream from the town of Imnaha.   Nominator: Frank Callahan.

702	**Oneseed Hawthorn***	6'7"	43'	37'	**Lake**

Directions: Tree is in the front yard of Mrs. Helen Proctor, 233 North G Street, Lakeview. Nominator: Frank Callahan.

703	**Silver Variegated Holly**	6'3"	40'	22'	**Tillamook**

Nominators: Frank Lockyear and Ernest Kolbe.

704	**Bigleaf Maple**	34'11"	101'	90'	**Clatsop**

Directions: One block south of Jewell on Highway 103 (west side) near road. Landowner is George Foster of Elsie.   Nominator: Maynard Drawson.

705	**Rocky Mountain Maple**	6'6"	63'	26'3"	**Hood River**

Directions: From Hood River proceed south on Highway 35 approximately six miles. Take a left on Fir Mountain Road traveling approximately eight miles until reaching a road that forks to the right (Old Jaymar Road).   Proceed down this road approximately one-eighth mile to tree. Landowner is Hood River County, 918 18th St., Hood River, OR 97031.   Nominator: David Foley.

706	**Sitka Mountain Ash**	1'7"	50'	18'	**Coos**

Directions: Off Highway 42, 1 mile east on Fairview Road to walking path north. NE 1/4, NE1/4, Section 25, T27S, R13W. Landowner is International Paper, PO Box 43, Gardiner, OR 97411.   Nominator: Lance Morgan.

707	**California Black Oak**	28'2"	124'	115'	**Curry**

("**Largest oak tree in the world**" *Courier* newspaper) Directions: On the side of a hill 62 miles (by road) northwest of Grants Pass far above Winkle Bar, the site of Zane Grey's cabin on the Rogue River. Landowner: Siskiyou National Forest/Cumming Ranch, Santa Rosa, California. Nominator: Ralph King.

708	**Lodgepole Pine***	12'4"	125'	53'	**Klamath**

Co-champion with tree in Valley County, Idaho.   Directions: Winema National Forest. Nominator: Robert L. Brackett.

709	**Ponderosa Pine***	28'	178'	45'	**Deschutes**

Directions: Located in La Pine State Park, near Deschutes River. Nominator: Frank Callahan.

709•	**Garden Plum**	7'7"	45'	41'	**Multnomah**

Directions: On Reed College Campus in SE Portland, on east end of main building. Nominator: Frank Callahan.

710	**Klamath Plum**	3'6"	28'	19'	**Klamath**

Directions: South end of Klamath Lake. Landowner is Kit Johnson, 1141 Lake Shore Drive in Klamath Falls.   Nominator: Frank Callahan.

Please get permission from owner if you go on private property

NATIONAL CHAMPION TREES FOUND IN OREGON

SPECIES	Circumference	Height	Spread	County

711 Western Serviceberry 3'9" 27' 22' **Douglas**
Directions: Fifty (50) feet from Interstate 5 and 2 miles south of Lane County line (in Douglas County). East side of highway within 56 feet of edge of roadway. Sets on edge of hill next to road cut, north side of slope. In small draw which has been filled. Landowner is Oregon State Highway Department. Nominator: Frank Callahan.

712 Wavyleaf Silktassel 2'4" 29' 22' **Curry**
Directions: In Azalea Park at Brookings. Nominator: Frank Callahan.

713 Brewer Spruce 13'8" 170' 39' **Josephine**
Directions and Landowner: In Siskiyou National Forest. The Miller Lake area can be reached from State Hwy. 238 out of either Grants Pass or Medford. At the town of Ruch take the road leading south to the Star Ranger Station where you can get a map and further directions.
Nominators: Robert J. Boston & J. Elwin Keatley.

714 Sitka Spruce* 56'1" 206' 93' **Clatsop**
Directions: Off U.S. Hwy 26, six miles southeast of Seaside at Crown Zellerbach's Klootchy Creek Park on Big Tree Road. It is co-champion with a tree in Olympic National Forest in Washington.
* With its 56-foot circumference, this is the largest tree of any species in Oregon. This sitka spruce is more than 700 years old. This one tree has enough wood for two six-bedroom houses.
Nominator: Maynard Drawson.

715 Black Walnut 23'2" 130' 140' **Multnomah**
Directions: Sauvie Island. Nominator: Dan Tillman.

716 Arroyo Willow 3'7" 27' 20' **Wallowa**
Directions: Located near Sheep Creek near 8.226 USGC marker.
Nominator: Frank Callahan.

717 Bonpland Willow 10'7" 37' 45' **Klamath**
Directions: Ask at Flowers Brothers Ranch (owners) in Midland, OR, south of Klamath Falls.
Nominator: Frank Callahan.

718 Hinds Willow 4'10" 50' 32' **Jackson**
Directions: Located on Parker Ranch in Jackson County, one-quarter mile south of gravel pit on north side of Bear Creek.
Landowner is Mr. Parker. Nominator: Frank Callahan.

719 Hooker Willow 4'3" 32' 27' **Clatsop**
Directions: Located on the Florence S. Warren Estate, outside Warrenton. Tree stands in horse pasture on flat land east of main house, which is abandoned. Several trees including Hooker and Scouler willows. Distinguishable only when catkins present.
Landowner is Dana Cheryl Larson. Nominator: Frank Callahan.

720 Scouler Willow 19'5" 53' 45' **Yamhill**
Directions: 12 miles northwest of Sheridan and 15 miles west near old cabin site. Willamina Section 28 of T 4 S., R7W, Willamette Meridian, SE 1/4, SW1/4, McMinnville. Nominator: John Reinstra.

721 Tracy Willow 3'0" 20' 15' **Jackson**
Directions: 75 Dean Drive (Off Old Stage Coach Road) in Central Point.
Landowner is Bob Schipper. Nominator: Frank Callahan.

Please get permission from owner if you go on private property

The "*Largest Tideland Sitka Spruce Tree in the World.*" 1903 Clatsop County, Oregon April 5, 1915
Diameter two feet from ground: 30 feet, 11 inches
Diameter six feet off the ground: 20 feet 4.5 inches;   Diameter
OHS Negative OrHi 8311

Health and Medicine

Advances, particularly in the health field, have always built upon previous achievements and can be qualified in detail.

722 The first autopsy in the U.S. by a woman physician on a male corpse was performed by Bethenia A. Owens-Adair in Roseburg, 1878. She studied in Philadelphia, Pennsylvania, at the Eclectic School of Medicine. She earned her M.D. in 1880 and was the first educated woman physician in Oregon.

723 Oregon's first hospital, St. Vincent Hospital, opened the country's first school of anesthesiology in 1909.

724 In 1912 St. Vincent Hospital opened the region's first pathology laboratory.

725 The first children's hospital in the Pacific Northwest was opened by Oregon Health Sciences University (OHSU) in 1926.

726 Linus Pauling, who was born in Portland, is the only person to receive double unshared Nobel Prizes, one for chemistry and one for peace efforts. He's best known for his research on and promotion of health through use of **vitamin C.** *(See also #1093)*

727 Oregon Health Sciences University established the first Cystic Fibrosis Center in the Northwest in 1963.

728 Oregon Health Sciences University was the first to offer at-home kidney dialysis in the nation and performed the state's first kidney transplant (1959).

729 Newton K. Wesley, a first generation Oregonian with Japanese parents, was one of the people who developed the **contact lens.** Newton K. Wesley graduated from North Pacific College of Optometry in Portland and had optometry practices in Beaverton and Portland. Newton K. Wesley and George Jessen developed the contact lens at the Illinois College of Optometry in the 1940s.

730 Oregon Health Sciences University developed the first ocular microscope, which greatly improved the safety of eye surgery, in 1948.

731 The **first woman president of a state medical society**, Dr. Leslie S. Kent of Eugene, Oregon, was elected on September 18, 1948.

732 Oregon Health Sciences University opened the nation's first university-centered children's eye clinic (1949) and the first ophthalmology research lab in the Northwest (1950).

733 The Starr-Edwards valve is **the first artificial heart valve.** Dr. Albert Starr developed the heart valve in August, 1960, at Oregon Health Sciences University with now-retired engineer Miles Lowell Edwards. This first device was surgically implanted into Phillip Amundson on September 21, 1960. It is significant because it marked the beginning of a modern method of surgery on heart valves. The Starr-Edwards valve has been the **most-used heart valve replacement in the world** with over 137,000 implants. It's an elegantly simple replacement part for a damaged heart.

734 The world's first cardiac telemetry station opened at St. Vincent Hospital in 1963.

735 The first **three-dimensional** (stereo) **fluoroscopic X-ray** system was developed by P. J. Kuhn. The first unit was installed at the Oregon Health Sciences University in Portland, April 15, 1966.

736 Since 1969, Oregon has been leading the nation in **out-of-hospital births** (deliveries in clinics, at home with a midwife, grandmother's home, etc.).

737 A-DEC, Inc. (Newberg), is one of the largest manufacturers of dental equipment in the world. The company began in 1969 when Ken Austin replaced the larger, hard-to-service motor-driven dental equipment with a small air-operated vacuum system. A-DEC, Inc., was the first to develop equipment for sit-down dentistry.

738 Oregon Health Sciences University developed the nation's first regional **newborn screening program** in 1975.

739 The Virginia Garcia Memorial Health Center opened in 1975 at Cornelius and is the first migrant health clinic funded by a major health system (Sisters of Providence). The clinic is the **first unionized migrant health clinic in the Northwest and one of the first in the U.S.** All workers (from physicians to clerks) except administrators are part of the bargaining unit.

740 **DMSO** (dimethyl sulfoxide), a chemical compound derived from wood processing, was developed by Dr. Stanley Jacobs, chemist Robert Herschler, and an OHSU research team in 1963. DMSO became prescriptive in the U.S. in 1978 for interstitial cystitis. DMSO (also called the Wonder Drug) has been used by 500 to 600 million people worldwide. DMSO is used mostly topically to relieve pain, reduce swelling, and improve blood supply.

741 **The first rural health district in the U.S.** was created by voters in 1980 (South Gilliam County Health District).

742 Dr. Charles Dotter is called the "father of interventional radiology" or transluminal angioplasty. **Dr. Dotter pioneered the use of catheters to open blocked vessels** (done under X-ray guidance). This method led to an era of non-surgical health care techniques. OHSU's Dotter Institute for Interventional Therapy is unique in the world.

743 Dr. Olivier Civelli, a brain work researcher at OHSU, **cloned key brain chemicals** (several dopamine receptors in the brain) for the first time. They are implicated in numerous neurological disorders.

744 The OHSU Biomedical Information and Communication Center contains the **largest health information database in the Northwest**, and is a national model using the latest technology. **ORHION** (Oregon Health Information On-Line) database provides access to the growing field of medical knowledge via telephone and computer.

745 The Oregon Health Sciences University Center for Research on Occupational and Environmental Toxicology is unique in the U.S.

746 Dr. Roy Swank has received seven patents for developing **blood filters** and methods that are widely used in operations. Dr. Swank has also been a leader in showing the close relationship between consumption of saturated animal fat and the ravages of multiple sclerosis.

747 One of the world's first centers to focus on the molecular biology of the brain is Portland's OHSU's Vollum Institute of Advanced Biomedical Research.

748 Oregon became the first state to stop public financing of heart, liver, and bone marrow transplants in 1987.

749 Janet Adkins of Portland was **the first person to use the suicide machine** (June 4, 1990) built by Dr. Jack Kevorkian, a pathologist from Oakland County, Michigan.

750 St. Vincent Hospital and Medical Center in 1991 became the first center worldwide to use a **thrombolytic laser**. The first **muscle wrap surgery** (dynamic cardiomyoplasty) was performed at St. Vincent on July 11, 1991.

751 Oregon became the first state to establish an **Heirloom Birth Certificate** to fund programs to prevent child abuse and neglect (1985). Personalized birth certificates (9" wide by 20" long) are signed by the Governor and cost $25.00.

752 In 1986, St. Vincent Hospital sponsored the region's first large-scale, free cholesterol screening, serving 4,000 people.

752• In 1987, St. Vincent Hospital and Medical Center became the first West Coast clinical test site for **laser-assisted angioplasty**.

753 Precision Castparts Corp. of Milwaukie makes unique prosthetic devices for implanting into human hips and knees.

754 Oregon Health Sciences University operates the **nation's largest neurological clinical research program**, including multiple sclerosis, stroke, epilepsy, movement disorders and Alzheimer's disease (1990s).

754• The leading preventable cause of death in Oregon is tobacco consumption. Beginning in 1989, the Oregon Health Division became the **first to ask on death certificates:**

"Was tobacco a contributing factor to the cause of death?"

In 1989 there were 6,276 deaths in Oregon attributable, at least in part, to tobacco use, including infant deaths and passive smoking. In 1990, there were 6,580 similar deaths in Oregon.

755 Epitope, Inc. of Beaverton developed a saliva collection device (OraSure) which could be used for AIDS testing as well as other testing. OraSure is used in Europe but is not yet approved by the U.S. Food and Drug Administration.

755• The bark and leaves of the Pacific yew tree are the source of a powerful new cancer drug called **taxol**. Hauser Northwest, Inc., of Cottage Grove has been selected by Bristol-Myers Squibb as the authorized supplier of yew bark and taxol for this effort. Yew bark is peeled from logs, dried, and sent to Boulder, Colorado, where the taxol is extracted.

756 **The first state with a specific policy decision to meet the problems posed by limited health care availability and rationing** is Oregon. Over twenty states and countries have started a similar public process, including Vermont, California, Georgia, Massachusetts, North Carolina, Colorado, Hawaii, Missouri, Tennessee, Japan, Australia, and England.

Oregon Health Decisions, a grassroots movement in bioethics, was started in 1983 by Dr. Ralph Crawshaw, Brian Hines, and Michael Garland because of the Federal Government's failure to permit significant decision-making at the state and local levels. The citizen-based Oregon Health Decisions is directed at promoting education and actions surrounding ethical issues in health care.

National attention focused on Oregon in 1987, when the State denied a leukemia patient, seven-year old Adam Jacoby ("Coby") Howard an expensive bone marrow transplant he needed to survive. Oregon Health Decisions held over 300 meetings thoughout the state in a process to discuss pressing needs and to address and resolve problems associated with personal autonomy, equity of access, prevention of illness, and cost containment. In February, 1988, the first open forum for Oregon Health Decisions was held in Bend. It focused on funding for organ transplants and broader health care financing. Organ transplants had a low priority compared to funding for more wide-reaching health services.

The results of this decision-making process were assembled into a people's parliament. The public came, was in-formed, and said, "Let's ration health care, logically." Since then, six significant laws have been passed by the Oregon Legislature without significant opposition. The next steps include health promotion and disease prevention. American Health Decisions is a coalition of citizen groups concerned about health care ethics.
(Oregon Health Decisions, 921 SW Washington, #713, Portland, OR 97205; (503) 241-0744)

757 Oregon is a leader in trying to provide health care to poor people (Medicaid recipients) and control health care costs. In 1987, Oregon became the **first state to discontinue most very costly transplants for a few people on Medicaid so that a variety of health services, including basic preventive care, could be provided to many more people.**

Oregon is the **first state to base subsidy decisions on the relative value of specific components of health care (rationing)**. It's trying to extend coverage by prioritizing services on the basis of 1) effectiveness, 2) cost, and 3) public health values. The appointed Oregon Health Commission developed priorities for hundreds of medical procedures and ranked 709 medical treatments (diagnoses/procedures) including placing mental health and chemical dependency equally with other medical services. Both clinical input about what procedures work (effectiveness) and community input on importance of the medical treatments were considered in the prioritization of the medical treatments. The Health Coverage Bill was written by Senate President John Kitzhaber to ensure everyone access to those defined health services that are most important and effective and are worth providing with adequate compensation.

The Oregon Basic Health Services Act was adopted in 1989. On March 19, 1993, the State of Oregon received a waiver granted by the Clinton Administration allowing the state to redesign and implement the current Medicaid package of medical benefits for the Oregon Health Plan.

An estimated 450,000 Oregonians don't have health insurance. The Oregon Health Plan is a comprehensive program to assure the vast majority of Oregonians have access to good health care. Though the Medicaid portion has received the most publicity, the plan's requirements for employers would affect the most people.

The Oregon Health Plan has three basic components to expand access:
• Medicaid coverage was extended to all Oregonians below the official poverty level, using a prioritization of health services. (Senate Bill 27)
• Senate Bill 534 establishes a high-risk pool for uninsurable citizens who because of pre-existing conditions were denied insurance.
• Senate Bill 935 established a special insurance pool by mandating that employers provide health insurance coverage for all "permanent" workers and their dependents by July 1, 1996 or 1997, or pay into a special insurance pool. This mandate will be eliminated if certain conditions are met. (A "permanent" employee is defined as working 17.5 or more hours a week.)

Numerous states and many countries (e.g., Japan, Canada, Great Britain, Sweden, Finland, Australia, New Zealand, Germany) have contacted the State of Oregon about the health plan. The countries are interested in how to set explicit priorities as the basis for developing a benefit package.

The Health Resources Commission was established to control costs. The Oregon Health Plan was a topic of debate by candidates in the 1992 Presidential campaign.

758 The 1991 Oregon Legislature adopted a widely posted educational warning graphic (above) regarding pregnancy and alcohol (SB 502). Every senator signed on in support of this bill, which requires all retail premises with valid liquor licenses to post signs informing the public of the effects of alcohol on pregnant women. This supports one goal of the Oregon Benchmarks. (Senator Jeannette Hamby, author)

758• Oregon Congressman Ron Wyden announced on April 30, 1993, that the French abortion pill RU-486 will be clinically tested on 2,000 women nationwide in an effort coordinated by the Oregon Health Sciences University. This is the first time the drug has been tested in the U.S. RU-486 has been used legally in France, Britain, and Sweden by over 150,000 women.

Human Services

The "human services delivery system" can be broadly defined to include social, health, education, government and other services that meet individual and collective needs and improve the communities' well-being.

Oregon has taken steps to become a leader nationally in its attempts to develop its human resources by setting benchmarks for evaluating problem-solving efforts.

A brief summary of the Oregon Human Investment Strategy is included in Future Firsts. (See #1542)

Human investment makes sense.

By the late 1800s, Portland reportedly had more homeless persons per capita than any other U.S. city. People were arriving in wagons, boats, trains, and on foot.

759 **Oregon's first home for the elderly** was the Patton Home for the Friendless, founded by the Ladies' Union Relief Society on December 9, 1887. It was named for Mathew Patton, a forward-thinking individual who gave a block of land in the City of Albina to any group that would build a charitable organization for that purpose.

760 In 1965, when the Federal war on poverty program started, Oregon was chosen by Sargeant Shriver as **one of the first three states to start implementing the Federal poverty program**

761 On July 1, 1969, Governor Tom McCall created the nation's first independent Office of the Ombudsman. Marko Haggard was appointed the first Ombudsman for Oregon. The office is now called Citizen Representative.

762 **Community Gleaning Projects started in Hillsboro in 1972** with a cooperative canning project through the determination of housewife Monika Belcher. She saw crops remaining unpicked and approached Washington County Community Action Organization, Inc., with the idea of organizing people to pick otherwise wasted food. **WCCAO was the first agency in the U.S. to receive Office of Economic Opportunity monies for gleaning.** The Gleaning Project started as a direct service. Farmers donate windfall crops of fresh fruits, vegetables, and nuts which would otherwise rot in the fields to low-income pickers and preservers. In the first year, the number of families was 120, with over 670 low-income people total. Over 1,000 people participated. Produce valued at $39,165.50 was picked by gleaners in Washington County that year, with hundreds of tons more produce gleaned since. In 1980, 16 gleaning projects were operating in Oregon and over $597,000 worth of food was collected by and for the poor. In 1993, the community-based gleaning project served over 350 families in Washington County.

762• Another first nationally is Oregon's 10% tax-credit incentive for farmers who open fields and donate to the gleaners, low-income persons, and seniors the windfall crops of fruits, vegetables and nuts left after commercial harvests.

763 St. Mary's Home for Boys in Beaverton was, for a period up to 1990, one of the first residential homes for juvenile sex-offenders west of the Rocky Mountains.

764 Washington County's *Directory of Human Services (Medical and Social)* was initiated, designed, and produced for the Washington County Board of Commissioners by the author in 1975. Governor Robert Straub called the problem-oriented manual **the most comprehensive and sophisticated human resources directory ever compiled in the state**. The 320-page problem-oriented manual combined two Federal research and demonstration projects with local training for a decentralized information and referral system.   [*out-of-print*]

765 The **"Blue, Green, and Community Pages"** at the front of telephone books started in 1977 by the author for Community Action in Washington County and nationally. **It's now the single largest improvement in the information, referral, and outreach field for human services, government, schools, and community information** (maps, mass transit routes, statewide ZIP Codes, survival guides, civic information, energy conservation, recycling pages, etc.).

766 **In 1981 Oregon became the first state in the country to receive Medicaid waivers, which allowed development of a home- and community-based care system. Ten years later, Oregon was the only state to have an active approved Medicaid waiver.** Oregon makes a greater variety of long-term care services available to its citizens than most other states. Oregonians believe this alternative to institutionaliza-tion is less expensive and more humane. This Medicaid waiver allows Oregon's Senior and Disabled Services Division to place persons who are Medicaid-eligible and in need of health care in the community instead of in a nursing facility. This allows Medicaid recipients the right to live in their own homes as long as they like.

767 **Oregon serves more persons per capita in its community-based long-term care system than any of the other 49 states in the Union.** The state is second only to Nevada for the lowest expenditure for long-term care services of all the states. In 1983, the concept of "assisted living" did not exist. In 1993 there were 20 assisted-living facilities in Oregon.

768 Nursing homes have been suffering from increasing costs and extremely high inflation rates. **Because of its successful waiver program, Oregon became the first U.S. state to lower its nursing home population.** Through pre-admission screening and development of alternative care settings, more than 4,000 nursing home residents have been relocated to alternative care services. There were three times as many Medicaid clients living in adult foster homes in 1993 as in 1983, and more than twice as many Medicaid recipients received home care services in the same time period.

768• In 1992, the Confederated Tribes of the Warm Springs Reservation became the first Tribe in the Indian Country to initiate implementation of the Indian Tribal Governmental Tax Status Act when it secured funding from bonds for its Early Childhood Education Center.

769 In 1985, Portland Mayor J. E. "Bud" Clark's office was the first to acknowledge the extent of the problem and to develop the first 12-point Plan for the Homeless to break the cycle of homelessness. These planning efforts brought together all the relevant parties (government offices, Chamber of Commerce, churches, private groups, and others) to develop a continuum of services. Specific innovative efforts included renovating a hotel for a Single Room Occupancy Demonstration Project and an early use of Federal Low-Income Energy Assistance monies to buy sleeping bags and winter jackets. The doors of one of the first youth shelters in the northwest were opened by Burnside Projects in January, 1987.
The Mayor's 12-point **Plan for the Homeless** has been an exemplary effort replicated at least partially in several cities (including Reno, Phoenix, and San Francisco). In Vancouver, British Columbia, Canada, a hotel was renovated and renamed The Portland Hotel.

769• Ecumenical Ministries of Oregon (EMO) opened the **nation's first women's and children's alcohol and drug recovery house,** the Letty Owings House, in Portland, during April, 1987. Ecumenical Ministries of Oregon and its Center for Urban Education provided the first computer system to assist **refugees,** and the Information Technology Institute was the region's first **computer center for nonprofit organizations**.

769• Ecumenical Ministries of Oregon started the **first "free-standing" HIV Day Care Center in the U.S.** in March, 1989. ("Free-standing" means independent, not connected to a hospice or nursing home.)

769• The Old Town Reading Room started by the Multnomah County Library is the nation's **first and was the only library for the homeless** when it opened on June 13, 1988, at 219 NW Couch Street in Portland. The Old Town Reading Room may still be the only library for the homeless located in a storefront and not part of a traditional library building.

769• Hospice care had origins in Europe. Hospice provides a full-range of assistance, skills, and counseling for persons (and their families) with incurable diseases and a life expectancy expressed in months. In the U.S., beginning in New England states, hospice developed as a home care program.
Oregon became **the first and only state in the country to require accreditation standards for hospice care**. As one component of "death with dignity" legislation in 1987, State Senator Nancy Ryles (1938-1990), chairperson of that interim task force, sponsored Senate Bill 817 which created ORS 443.850-870, a law regulating hospice and recognizing Oregon Hospice Association as the hospice programs' accrediting body. Within Oregon, Providence Hospital in Portland started the first hospital-administered hospice in 1980. Visiting Nurse Association and Providence Hospital participated in the first federal Medicare benefit-eligible hospice pilot project, and operated the first home-based hospice. Mt. Hood Hospice in Sandy became the first accredited hospice and the first Medicare-certified free-standing hospice facility in 1983. The state's first community-based hospice dedicated to the memory and spirit of a person (Mary Ann Nimmo) in Forest Grove accepted its first patient in 1983.

Transportation, Trade, and Bridges

The Oregon Country's first means of interior transportation, communication, and trade was often via its rivers. Indians used large dugout canoes. Indian trails were the first roads. Fur trappers used pack horses. The low-tide beaches along Oregon's rugged coastline were the first coastal "highways." The military built some of the early roads. Other early overland roads were toll roads. There are no toll roads now.

770   **The Columbia River bar is one of the most dangerous in the world.** It is estimated that over 2,000 boats and vessels have been lost in or destroyed by the Columbia River bar.

771   Furs and farm products were sent from the **first shipping ports** at Astoria and Fort Vancouver to Europe, the Sandwich Islands, and China by the Hudson's Bay Company. The **first commercial use** of the Columbia River began when fur trading posts in the Oregon Country (Astoria, Fort Vancouver, Fort Walla Walla, Fort Okanogan, Fort Colville) were established.

772   John Jacob Astor's vessel, the *Beaver,* was the first sailing vessel to use this name in the Northwest.

773   The *Beaver,* the first steamboat to ply the waters of the Pacific Ocean, was built in 1835 in England on the Thames River. It sailed around the Horn to Oregon in five months, arriving at Fort George on April 4, 1836.

774   One of the first endeavors to send mail east from the Oregon Country across the continent was in 1838 and it took sixty days. Dr. John McLoughlin sent a courier from the Willamette Valley to Medpor, Missouri. The rider rested two full days at Lapwai and two days at Fort Hall.

775   In 1839-40, the landing of the ship *Maryland* and its cargo led to the establishment of the Oregon Country's first commercial business, a retail store.

776   The first shipment of women's wear and dry goods arrived in the Oregon Country in 1847 on the brig *Henry.*

Wagon trains that were coming overland brought news and mail. Postal service to Astoria and other Pacific points was via the ocean, not over land. Mail was shipped on water via rivers and by sea down the coast to Nicaragua and then taken by land to ships on the other ocean. Other ships sailed their journey around the Horn. When the first U.S. Post Office west of the Rocky Mountains opened at Astoria, Oregon Territory, May 9, 1847, letters cost 40¢ to or from places on the Pacific coastline within the U.S. territory, and packages cost more. Mail service to San Francisco was begun in 1850.

By the 1850s, Russian ships were in the Columbia and Willamette rivers trading for grain from the Tualatin and other valleys.

777   Japan was first shipped flour from the Oregon Territory in 1856.

778 Oregon is the only state for which a transcontinental highway is named. The Oregon Trail began in the 1840s at Independence, Missouri, and today travel along U.S. Highway 30 roughly approximates the route of the trail.

779 **The first locks in the Oregon Country and on the Pacific Coast was built in West Linn in 1872.** It was built by the Willamette Falls Canal and Lock Company with a 50 foot lift. The steamer *Maria Wilkins* became the first vessel to navigate up the west end of Willamette Falls when the locks first opened on New Year's Day, 1873. Tolls were charged at the Willamette Locks until purchased by the U.S. Government in 1915. Willamette Falls Locks was designated a National Historic site in 1974.

780 Twelve-year-old John Corbin Barnum was one of the youngest railway conductors in this nation's history. When he grew up he became both the Secretary and General Manager of the Rogue River Valley Railway, which had tracks from Medford to Jacksonville.

781 The *Columbia* was the first steamboat on the west coast to successfully utilize electric lights. It did so on a trip from Portland to San Francisco on May 2, 1880.

782 **The first transcontinental railroad connection from Portland to east coast points in 1883 was the Northern Pacific Railway,** which was controlled by Henry Villard. The first direct link to the rest of the country occurred September 4, 1883, with a gold spike about 60 miles east of Helena, Montana. The first train arrived in Portland on September 11, 1883.

783 The Old Yaquina Bay lighthouse became the **first beacon aid to navigation on mainland America's Pacific Coast.**

784 The 1891 Legislature created a state agency, the Port of Portland, and empowered it to dredge and maintain the Willamette River at a depth of 25 feet.

785 The first foghorn-equipped floating lighthouse, Lightship #50, began beaming a few miles west of the mouth of the Columbia River on April 9, 1892. Columbia River Lightship #50 was the **first U.S. Lightship** on the Pacific Coast. Lightships aided navigation until the 1950s, when widespread use of radar made them obsolete. Lightship #604, the **last U.S. Coast Guard lightship** in operation on the American Pacific Coast, went out of service on November 2, 1979.

786 Bicycling was a craze in Portland in the 1890s. Fred T. Merrill opened a bicycle store in Portland in a 100 foot by 200 foot building, making it the **largest bicycle store in the U.S.** In one year, 1898, Fred Merrill **sold more bicycles (8,850 total) than any other bicycle dealer in the western United States**.

Bridges

787 **When Portland's first bridge across the Willamette River, the first Morrison Bridge, opened on April 12, 1887, it was the longest vehicular bridge west of the Mississippi River.** On the first day, the bridge was toll-free, there was a parade, and a marching band played music. The wooden truss span bridge was constructed by a California company, and had tolls of 15¢ for horse-drawn rigs, 20¢ for a team of horses, and 5¢ for pedestrians. It was bought by the City of Portland in 1895 for $150,000 and operated toll-free. When the first Morrison Bridge was constructed, it soon put the Stark Street Ferry out of business.

789 The Wilson River Bridge was the first concrete-tied arch structure span in the U.S. It was built by state bridge builder Conde B. McCullough. The Coos Bay Bridge, the 3,200-foot-long Yaquina Bay Bridge, and the three other coast bridges were also built by Conde B. McCullough.

790 The Rogue River Bridge was the first bridge in the nation to be built using the Freyssinet technique, which is essentially a modern method of refabrication.

792 About 300 covered bridges had been built in Oregon by the 1920s. Oregon has one of the best collections of remaining covered bridges west of the Mississippi River. Oregon has the first state-wide comprehensive covered bridge preservation (rehabilitation and maintenance) program. Oregon had 49 covered bridges in 1989.

793 The bridge across the Columbia River to Longview was the highest cantilevered bridge when it opened for traffic on March 29, 1930. This was the first time people could cross over the lower Columbia River other than by a slow ferry. The bridge over the river between Longview, Washington and Rainier, Oregon has a cantilever span of 1,200 feet and a clearance of 196.5 feet above the river.

793• The second longest "continous truss" bridge in the world with a main arch (1,232 feet long) is the Astoria-Megler bridge across the Columbia River connecting Oregon and Washington.

A 1990 City of Portland Proclamation claimed that no other city in the world the size of Portland currently can boast so many unique bridges:

794 The Steel Bridge is the **world's only telescoping double deck vertical-lift bridge.** The bridge operator can raise the lower deck 45 feet in 10 seconds, and the upper deck in 90 seconds.

795 The Hawthorne Bridge, the **oldest vertical-lift bridge** in the world, is also Portland's oldest existing bridge (since December 19, 1910).

796 The Broadway Bridge, when it opened on April 22, 1913, was the **world's longest double-leaf bascule drawbridge.**

797 The St. John's Bridge, built in 1931, is a rope-strand suspension bridge considered one of the world's most beautiful. For many years, the St. John's Bridge **was the world's longest rope-strand bridge.**

798 Upon construction, **Oregon's first double-deck vehicular bridge**, the Marquam Bridge in Portland, was North America's third longest continuous-truss span.

799 The **tallest vertical lift ever made** was the 6,000-ton mid-span of the Fremont Bridge, which was hydraulically lifted 170 feet into proper position in 1973. This was roughly ten times heavier than any previous lift, and 32 jacks were used.

800 Built in Portland in 1905-06, the Burlington Northern railroad bridge was **the longest double-track swing span** (500+ feet) **in the world**, until its alteration in 1989.

800• The 658-foot Southern Pacific single-track swing-span at Coos Bay was one of the longest in the world when it was built.

801 **The nation's first interurban electric streetcar system** was built by East Side Railway Company in 1893 from Portland to Oregon City, 14 miles away. (The first car was named Helen and made the first actual trip on February 23, 1893, in one hour.)

802 Mabel Bretherton became **the first female lighthouse keeper** in 1903.

803 The Portland Lewis and Clark fairgrounds served as the destination and conclusion of the **first transcontinental auto race**. It took the winner forty-four days and five hours! On June 20, 1905, the Oldsmobile "Old Scout" driven by Dwight B. Huss became the **first automobile to cross the continent and the Willamette Valley and Cascade Mountain Wagon Road.** "Old Scout" raced its only competition, another Oldsmobile, "Old Steady" across the country and overtook it in Nebraska.

804 The *Peter Iredale* at Young's Bay is the **only presently visible sailing boat wreck on the entire coast of the Pacific U.S.** The 235-foot sailing vessel was driven aground on October 25, 1906.

805 **Silas Christoferson flew the first airplane to take off from a hotel roof** on June 11, 1912. The pilot took a 12-minute flight to Vancouver. The push-plane was lifted in pieces to the top of the Multnomah Hotel and assembled.

806 The **first flight of U.S. airmail** service was from Portland, Oregon, to Vancouver, Washington (August 10 and 11, 1912).

807 The Columbia River Highway was built in 1913 to 1915 from Portland to The Dalles and was one of the earliest paved highways in the Northwest. The 73.8-mile Columbia River Scenic Highway has been designated a **national historic civic engineering landmark,** in part because of four rock tunnels. The original highway engineer-designer was Samuel C. Lancaster, who was followed by engineers John Yeon and Amos Benson.

808 The Oregon State Board of Aeronautics was established on February 11, 1921, becoming **the first government aviation agency in the U.S.** Oregon was the first state to actively regulate fliers and flying—long before the Federal Government took over the regulation of flying. Over 20 states adopted state regulation of flying, modeled on the Oregon plan, as opposed to regulation by Federal authorities.

809 One of the country's **first inter-city buses** with hard rubber tires and air brakes was built at Gas Engine and Machine Company in Portland. The auto-stage made its first bumpy trip from Shaniko to Bend on April 13, 1905, in five hours, with 40 mph the top speed.

810 Two 45-horsepower Beaver Six cars were produced at Oregon's first automobile manufacturing plant, the **Beaver State Motor Company,** which was founded in 1912 in Gresham and went bankrupt in 1924. The company was successfully sued for patent infringement. Other than a special gear imported from England, all parts were made at the Gresham auto factory.

812 Tex Rankin operated the largest airplane stunt-flying school in the nation in Portland in 1929.

813 On May 15, 1931, at the Omaha, Nebraska Air Races, **20-year-old Milwaukie-born Dorothy Hester** set a **world record, performing 56 inverted snap rolls,** which remains unbroken. Two days later, Dorothy Hester set another **record for women pilots, executing 69 outside loops in an airplane.** These are maneuvers in which the pilot is on the outside of the turn at all times and flies upside down. She performed aerobatic exhibitions in 38 states in 1931. For 40 years, Dorothy Hester Stenzel lived west of Banks.

814 The first woman steamboat captain west of the Mississippi River was Minnie Hill, born in Albany, Oregon. She received her pilot license in 1886.

815 Early Coos Bay pilot Vern Gorst built a land-sea vehicle, the Amphibian, which he constructed from a Hupmobile with pontoons on either side. The Amphibian went 15 mph in the water and 70 mph on the beach.

816 **The first mall in the nation designed with one-way streets specifically for mass transit** opened in May, 1978, on 22 blocks of Portland's two busiest downtown streets. It was the largest transit mall. Philadelphia and Minneapolis had earlier, smaller transit malls which operated on two-way streets. The mall, which was planned and funded by Tri-Met and the City of Portland, has cut 15 minutes off the average trip through downtown during rush hour.

817 During 1934, the State's Port of Portland ranked first nationally in shipments of lumber, wheat, and wool.

818 The first vessel, *Charles L. Wheeler, Sr.*, went through the highest (66 feet) single-lift lock in the world as of July 9, 1938, at Bonneville Dam and steamed to The Dalles. McNary Dam's single lift lock, built in 1947, rises 92 feet and became the world's highest lift.

819 The **highest lift lock in the world** was built at John Day, 113 feet deep.

820 **The fastest ship-building in the U.S.** occurred when the first prefabricated ship to be completed in less than two weeks was the *Joseph N. Teal*, which had a trial run on September 27, 1942.

821 The last sailing vessel to take commercial cargo from the Columbia River was the big steel **360-foot six-masted schooner *Tango*,** which hauled lumber from St. Helens to South Africa in 1942. The *Tango* was the largest sailing ship of her kind still afloat. The *Tango* sailed 210 trips between Europe and South America's west coast.

822 The Port of Coos Bay has ranked as the largest shipping point for raw timber logs on the Pacific coast.

823 The Columbia River ports form the largest and longest export route for grain and forest products on the West Coast. The **Port of Portland is the largest deep fresh-water port on the Pacific Ocean. It exports a larger volume of dry goods than any other port on the American west coast.**

824 Since March, 1979, the Port of Portland has operated **the largest dry dock on the west coast (Dock #4)** and the **Pacific Rim's largest floating dry dock**. It's designed to serve the largest ships trading in the Pacific.

825 The Portland Ship Repair Yard (PSRY) ranks first in North America in very large cargo container (VLCC) repair, tank cooling repair, and propeller duct installation. PSRY is unique as **the only publicly owned-privately operated major shipyard in the U.S.**

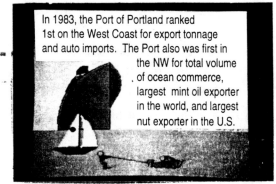

In 1983, the Port of Portland ranked 1st on the West Coast for export tonnage and auto imports. The Port also was first in the NW for total volume of ocean commerce, largest mint oil exporter in the world, and largest nut exporter in the U.S.

826 **The Port of Portland ranks or has ranked first among other ports in ocean commerce: mint oil, Japanese autos, nuts, and other goods.**

827 The fresh-water Port of Portland handles more than 12.5% of all automobiles imported into the U.S. from Asia and Europe. **More autos are distributed to more regions of the U.S. (30+ states) and to more Asian markets from Portland, Oregon, than any other U.S. port.** The Port of Portland has grown to become America's fifth largest auto port.

828 Built in 1947, the Sternwheeler *Portland* was the last working steam-powered stern-wheel ship-assist tug boat to operate in an American harbor when she was retired in 1981.

829 **The *Ticonderoga*,** a 72-foot vessel owned and skippered by Robert F. Johnson of the Portland Yacht Club, LaHaina Yacht Club, and New York Yacht Club, **set more elapsed-time sailing records than any other vessel ever built.** The *Ticonderoga* was built by the Quincy Adams shipyard in Marblehead, Massachusetts, and was launched in 1937. Perhaps the most notable records were made in the years 1964, 1965, and 1966, during which period she broke all previous records for these races:

830 the Miami to Jamaica Race

(approx. 844 miles in 4 days, 23 hours);

831 the Tahiti Race

(approx. 3,500 miles in 17 days, 6 hours);

832 the Honolulu Race

(approx. 2,350 miles in 9 days, 13 hours);

833 the Trans-Atlantic Race

(approx. 3,600 miles in 15 days, 23 hours).

834 When completed in 1926, the Pacific Highway (U.S. Highway 99) allowed people to travel from Canada to Mexico. It was the **world's longest paved highway**.

835 In 1946, Oregon became the first state to adopt a **"staggered expiration" for original and renewal driving licenses.**

836 In 1950, Oregon became the first state to adopt a **"staggered registration"** renewal cycle for vehicles.

837 The **nation's first prorated vehicle registration law** was enacted in 1951.

Traffic Safety Legislation

838 Oregon is the first state to have a law permitting **Victims Impact Panels** (with relatives of victims) to make presentations to persons convicted of driving under the influence of intoxicants (DUI). Only nine Oregon counties use Victims Impact Panels, a concept which started in Boston, Massachusetts. Utah has a stronger law than Oregon now.

839 Oregon is the first state to allow left turns (onto one-way streets) at red traffic lights. The State of California was the first to allow right turns on red traffic lights.

840 In 1967, Oregon became the first state to require motorcycles to have lights turned on while operating on public streets.

841 In 1967, both Oregon and Florida passed laws requiring helmets for motorcycle riders. Oregon repealed the law after ten years, but in 1988 Oregon voters approved a referendum (placed on the ballot by the legislature) requiring helmets.

842 Oregon is the first state to have allowed plea bargaining on DUI cases (1975 legislature). The law went into effect (1976), but was repealed (1981).

843 The state of Oregon **was first to set the strictest blood alcohol level (.08%)** in the U.S. for illegally driving a vehicle under the influence of liquor. Utah's law went into effect one month prior to Oregon's law. By 1992, six other states (including Maine, Florida, and California) had lowered tolerance levels to .08%.

844 In 1989, Oregon became the first state with 0% alcohol tolerance for anyone under the age of 18 years.

845 The 1991 Oregon Legislature enacted the nation's lowest (0%) tolerance level for drivers below 21 years of age, which matches the legal drinking age.

846 Oregon enacted a .04% tolerance level for commercial drivers as of April, 1990. This has become the national standard for commercial drivers.

847 To reduce recidivism, in 1987 Oregon passed the nation's first law to allow mandatory automatic ignition interlock in the vehicles of persons convicted of drunk driving who've lost their driving licenses. This law allows usage in only about a dozen counties. These people cannot drive any vehicle without this ignition interlock, which will work only if a sober driver blows into it. It rents for $40 per month.

848 Through a Federally-financed program, Oregon became the first state to use a court-mandated drug, Antabuse, which makes users ill when alcohol is swallowed.

849 Oregon was the **first state to implement the 55-mile-per-hour speed limit** (November 17, 1973; repealed September 27, 1988) which was intended to save fuel. More importantly, it saved lives. Governor Tom McCall went to Washington, D.C., and told President Nixon about it.

•

(For the strongest safety belt law in the nation, see **Citizen Initiatives** *#228, #229)*

850 In April, 1957, the **Don Rasmussen Company in Portland became the first franchised Mercedes dealership in the U.S.** It owns the 1968 diesel Mercedes 220 which is seen in television commercials and which placed second in an official Mercedes contest (1979) for the highest mileage on a Mercedes (1,020,000 miles).

From 1959 to 1963 the slogan on all Oregon automobile license plates was PACIFIC WONDERLAND. A current license plate is below.

851 In 1969, Oregon became the first state to use on-line computers to process and retrieve driver and vehicle records.

852 The 64-mile logging railroad through Ponderosa pine areas over Bly Mountain from Klamath Falls had the nation's last double-switchback track in use on its last train run on April 29, 1990.

853 In 1967, Oregon became the first state to allow triple-trailers on state highways, and by 1993 fifteen states allowed them. Triple-trailers are allowed on interstate highways and about half of the state's highway system. The Oregon Department of Transportation began tests in 1964.

854 The biggest private collection of Rolls-Royces in the world was the 93 cars collected by Bhagwan Shree Rajneesh, of Rajneeshpuram in central Oregon, during 1984. Indian guru Bhagwan Shree Rajneesh was arrested in 1985. The City of Antelope later re-formed.

855 Les Schwab started his tire business in rural Oregon towns, beginning with Prineville in 1952. The Les Schwab Tire Company is **one of the largest independent tire distributors in the U.S. and the largest tire dealer in the Northwest,** according to blue-book value (not ranked on the most number of chain stores). There are over 220 Les Schwab Company-owned and affiliated dealers.

856 The Les Schwab Tire Company operates the **largest tire retreading plant in the U.S. for passenger vehicle and light truck tires.** The Les Schwab Tire Company produces about 1,350 units/day and uses over 3.5 million pounds of rubber per year.

857 Ron Tonkin in 1959 became the first automobile dealer in the continental U.S. assigned a Honda automobile dealer franchise.

858 Emmert International, Inc., of Clackamas, Oregon, **moved the largest building ever moved on wheels, a three-story hotel (65' by 86') in San Antonio, Texas.** The 1,650-ton (3.3 million pounds) Fairmount Hotel was moved four blocks in April, 1985.

859 Emmert International, Inc., also hauled the **longest, heaviest, and most valuable load ever moved long distance on the highway.** A U.S. Department of Energy steam generator was pulled and pushed the longest distance by land highway from Pensacola, Florida to Long Beach, California in 1990.

860 The Mt. Hood Railroad is one of the few remaining train lines in the U.S. to have a switchback that is still in use. It runs 24 miles to Parkdale from Hood River through the Hood River Valley.

861 The Wallowa Lake tram is the **steepest tram in North America.** It whisks passengers 3,200 vertical feet to the summit of Mt. Howard in Wallowa County.

862 Instead of using lifts inside its rail vehicles, Tri-Met will implement the **first wayside lifts** to provide easy access for both wheelchair users and other people unable to use the train steps on the west side light rail. Tri-Met won a 1989-90 award as **"Best Transit Agency in the U.S."** from the American Public Transit Association (APTA) for efficient surface transportation, the same year Tri-Met General Manager James Cowens was the head of APTA. The Tri-County Metropolitan Transportation District of Oregon (Tri-Met) is a state agency.

862• On March 12, 1993, America's first two buses fueled completely by liquefied natural gas were operated by Tri-Met in Portland.

862• Another Tri-Met task will be the first "low step handicapped platform access" for the metropolitan Portland west side light rail. The west side light rail project to West 185th Avenue is the largest public works project in the state (costing about $600 million to $700 million).

862• **In 1971, Oregon became the first state to dedicate state monies for the construction of bicycle paths.** The law requires that a minimum of one percent (about $1.3 million/yr.) of state highway funds be expended annually for construction and maintenance of bicycle trails and footpaths during construction, reconstruction, or relocation of a highway, road, or street. **Over 530 miles of bike paths were constructed in the first twenty years.** The bike path bill passed April 2, 1971, and was signed by Governor Tom McCall on a bicycle seat in front of the capitol. A large group (about 200 people), including bill author Rep. Don Stathos of Jacksonville and the Bicycle Lobby of Oregon, cycled 3.5 hours from Oregon City to Salem on Highway 99 for the bill signing. Sen. George Wingard co-sponsored it. The Bicycle Lobby of Oregon provided strong citizen input for this bill. The bike path funding law has been copied in some form by many states and countries. The Oregon Recreation Trails Systems Act was passed by only a one-vote margin in each committee throughout the legislative process.

862• Oregon's Department of Transportation (ODoT) Bend Section was the first in the nation to use "cold-in-place-recycling" on a contractual basis. A "cold-in-place-recycling" machine chews and grinds up asphalt, mixes it, and sets it down again. ODoT began tests on Mt. Bachelor in 1984 with the first contract for 130 miles in central Oregon's high desert in 1985. Oregon State University's engineering department has documented **tremendous energy savings** from " **cold-in-place-recycling.**" ODoT received national energy awards for this road recycling process, and it's been a model used elsewhere.

862• The Oregon Department of Transportation is the first in the West to use cathodic protection to stop metal disintegration on the undersides of bridges. Cathodic protection switches electrical poles by using a zinc coating. It was first used on the Yaquina Bay Bridge in Lincoln County.

862• **The largest airplane in the world was built** from 1942 to 1947, mostly with birch and also with spruce from the Toledo-Yaquina area. The *Spruce Goose* plane has a 320-foot wingspan, eight 28-cylinder engines, and was built by Howard Hughes. On November 2, 1947, he piloted the plane on **its only flight, a flight of only about one mile** for 70 seconds. Peak elevation was 70 feet. The **largest wooden airplane** in the world, the Hercules HK-1 (the *Spruce Goose* or *Flying Boat*), was moved by Emmert International in 1992-93 from Long Beach, California, to its new home at the to-be-built Evergreen aviation museum at Dayton in Yamhill County.

862• The Washington Park Zoo Railway operates the only surviving railroad post office in the United States, and the post office has its own canceling stamp.

862• The oldest remaining depot of the Oregon & California Railroad is the one located at the Canby Depot Museum.

Unclassified Business Advances

Necessity is the mother of invention. Technology transforms society. There are too many inventions, patents, and marketing claims for this chapter to be complete. There were 640 patents (including 542 inventions, 90 designs, and three botanical plants) issued to Oregon corporations and inventors in 1990 alone. Most of the inventions described in this chapter are included in the Oregon Historical Society photo collection.

*According to the Oregon Corporation Division in Salem **well over 100 Oregon businesses currently use the word "FIRST" in their name.***
Advances that didn't fit the other chapters have been included in this chapter. It's tough to verify some historical business firsts, particularly those beyond Oregon's current borders.

863 **Meier & Frank is the oldest department store operating continuously under the same name in the Oregon Country** (now corner of 1st and Yamhill). Meier & Frank was established in 1857 by Aaron Meier, two years before Oregon became a state. Sigmund Frank became Meier's partner in 1873 and the store was known from then on as Meier and Frank's. In 1915, Meier and Frank built the **"largest department store west of Chicago."** Judi Hofer, the current Chief Executive Officer at Meier & Frank, is the first woman to hold that position and one of the nation's top female retailers.

864 Former Kentuckian Daniel Lownsdale located the **west's first tannery in 1846** where Portland's Civic Stadium now is. The Muir and McDonald leather tannery in Dallas is one of the state's oldest businesses (1863) and one of the nation's last tanneries still using a "vegetable process."

865 Some of the Pacific Northwest settlers' first pottery was the Smith and Company pottery made along the Willamette River in Polk County in 1865. Household pottery was made first. Later, stoneware, flowerpots, vases, and bricks were sold on the coast.

866 On August 24, 1867, **the first iron produced west of the Rocky Mountains** was near Lake Oswego with the first casting of pig iron at Oregon Iron Company.

Erickson's Cafe and Concert Hall

867 **Erickson's Saloon was the site of the world's longest bar** around 1893. Opened by a Russian Finn, August Erickson, as a simple bar in the early 1800s, it grew. The mahogany bar was horseshoe-shaped, 684 feet long, had fifty bartenders, covered one full block (Burnside at NW 2nd Avenue), and had five entrances.

868 Atiyeh Brothers, now the oldest Oriental rug dealer in the Northwest, started in 1900. Aziz and George Atiyeh came to Portland from South Bethlehem, Pennsylvania, and started a rug store on Washington Street between 10th and 11th. The store moved in 1906 and is the oldest continuously-operating rug store in Oregon.

869 Foster and Kleiser was founded in Portland in 1901. It moved, was sold a few times, and became MetroMedia, the largest outdoor advertising firm in America.

870 Oaks Park Amusement Park is the **oldest continuously-operating amusement park in the U.S. (since 1905).** Closed only two weeks in the past 85 years (during the Vanport and 1963 floods), the wooden park, built by the Oregon Water & Power Company, is now operated by a private, nonprofit organization. It's located at the east foot of the Sellwood Bridge. When built, Oaks Park was the largest and "finest" amusement resort west of New York and was called the "**Coney Island of the West.**"

871 The Electric Steel Foundry Company (ESCO), founded in 1913, imported an electric furnace, the first of its kind in the western U.S. The company says it was the largest distributor of steel and aluminum in the western U.S.

871• The Portland Livestock Association assembled the West Coast's largest livestock arena in 1922.

872 Doernbecher Manufacturing Company in Portland was the largest producer of furniture west of the Rockies.

FERRIS WHEEL
8½ Set

Erector Set
(courtesy of Gilbert House in Salem)

873 Salem-born Olympic sportsman Alfred C. Gilbert invented the Erector Set, chemistry kits, and the S-gauge model trains at his Mysto Manufacturing Company in New Haven, Connecticut. He filed over 150 patents. More than 10 million Erector Sets were sold.

874 The first automatic coal burner was conceived and produced in 1923 at the Portland Wire and Iron Works.

875 Iron Fireman in Portland had become the country's largest manufacturer of automated sawdust burners for home use.

876 In the 1940s, Johnny Trulliger's 3,000-unit frozen-food locker facility was the largest on the West Coast.

Inventors

881 Missouri native **Henry F. Phillips, Jr., in 1933 invented the Phillips recessed-head screw in Portland. Phillips' screw was the first major improvement in the single-slot screw industry in eight decades.** He tried to sell his invention to every major screw manufacturer in the U.S., including the American Screw Company, but originally was turned down. The American Screw Company got a new President, E.E. Clark, in 1932, who bought Phillips' idea.

Henry F. Phillips founded the Phillips Screw Company in Portland, serving as President and General Manager until his retirement in 1945. His company developed, engineered, and marketed the Phillips recessed-head screw, obtaining 90 licenses with domestic and foreign companies, including every automobile manufacturer. The Phillips Screw Company was backed financially by officers of the Jantzen Knitting Mills.

Billions of Phillips screws were made and are used today.

882 A patented hop dryer with a steam engine-driven fan used forced air to speed and improve the drying of hops. It was used in rural Linn County at the Templeton Hop Yard in 1878.

883 Ice cream cones were made by hand until F. Bruckman of Portland patented his ice cream cone rolling machine in 1902. It made leak-proof cones, saving parents the headache of ice cream drips. The ice cream cones created a sensation at the Lewis & Clark Exposition.

884 A device that automatically installs handle sticks in corndogs was patented by Carl Gerdlund of Warren.

885 The world's first quick-release ski-binding with the pivoting metal toe piece was invented in 1937 in Portland by Hjalmar Hvam who's now in the National Ski Hall of Fame. Hjalmar Hvam, a Norwegian immigrant, broke a leg while skiing, and conceived the idea in his hospital bed. He patented his invention in 1939 and founded a company in Portland with the slogan "Hvoom with Hvam."

886 Beaverton resident Roger Berg invented the Verti-Burger, which grills hamburgers vertically; a triple baby stroller; a bicycle wheel cover that reduces wind drag; a child's bed shaped like a racing car; carts designed for hauling extra gear while backpacking; and the infamous chug-a-lug machine, which allows six drinkers to race against a clock.

887 Hundreds of inventions, gadgets, and gimmicks were conceived by the late Carl Brandefels of Scappoose, including, in 1936, the hair-growing tonic which made him famous. He also developed photo patches designed to personalize luggage, a carpenter's hammer with a three-way level built into the handle, filbert huskers, fruit de-stemmers, clam diggers, tip-proof Christmas tree stands, and special fish bait. Brandefels Scalp and Hair Application generated $10 million in sales. He obtained 15 patents.

888 Former Portland mayor John Gates invented many things, including a flexible anchorage, an automatic oiler, a hydraulic steering gear, a sectional boiler, a spark arrester, an ash pan, a cut-off valve, a hydro-aeroplane, an early Wankel-style rotary engine, a combination pocket knife-fountain pen-automatic pencil, and a method for sluicing out river bars with a steamship propeller.

889 In 1950, the longest continuous escalator system ("up" and "down") in the world was installed to serve all twelve selling floors of the Meier & Frank store.

890 Bill Barton, who worked for the Mattel Corporation in 1958 and 1959 and who sculpted the Barbie Doll mold, now lives in Oakland, Oregon. The doll was named after the daughter of Ruth and Elliott Handler, founders of Mattel, which sold over 92 million Barbies.

891 On November 4, 1958, the first molybdenum centrifugal casting occurred in Albany.

892 Roscoe A. Fawcett proposed and demonstrated the concept of telephone news, a special entertainment service broadcasting 12 hours of news per day, for Home Telephone Company. The entertainment included music and phonograph records via telephone.

893 Earl Thompson, an auto mechanic at Covey's Garage on 21st and West Burnside in Portland, with his profitable invention of the synchro-mesh transmission "took the curse out of gear shifting."

894 The Nite-light, an additional light mounted on the left front of an automobile, was invented by J. A. Dawson of Portland.

895 An oil field draw works was invented by Frank L. Turney and manufactured by Portland Iron Works.

896 The Acroplane "Orientator," an electric-powered mechanism for cockpit simulation, was invented by Lee U. Eyerly of Salem.

897 A portable elevator and fire escape was invented in 1932 by M. E. Hayman of Portland.

898 An Astoria machinist, William Silvo, developed a frost eliminator that was tested at the Dellmoor Cranberry Bog (1932).

899 The "iron claw," a criminal torture device, was invented by Y. Smith-Strange in 1934.

900 C. L. Lantz of Portland invented a cheese slicing and packing machine in Portland in 1937.

901 Oregon's State Prison Warden J. C. Gardner patented a penal device, the Oregon boot, a heavy leg shackle for securing prisoners, in 1876. It was described as the cruelest, most torturous device in any prison system.

902 An improved Oregon boot, a device for transporting prisoners, was developed by Portland Police Detective Reginald Todd in 1937.

903 A soft ice cream server was invented by D. A. Fingerhooth, Portland (1932).

904 Sibberian Frozen Cream, a direct ancestor of soft ice cream, was invented by Portlander Si Berry. The frozen ice cream machine was the basis of a chain of restaurants in western states that began in Portland in 1931.

905 The Haulaway Home was invented by Allison Dean of Portland (May 21, 1941) and built by Drake, Wyman and Voss, Inc.

906 A motorbike with a washing machine engine was invented by C. O. Hanson of Oregon Shipbuilding Corporation.

907 The glass vacuum juice concentrator was developed by William Filz of Oregon State College, Corvallis, 1949.

908 The Sportster, a plastic blanket carrying case that inflates into a cushion, was invented by Mel H. Davis in 1949.

909 Mrs. Jean Coffey of Portland is credited with developing the pie wedgie in 1949.

910 A light meter for telephoto exposures was invented by Sam Muirhead (April 22, 1951).

911 A Hallicrafter, a model radio with printed circuit wiring, was invented by David Lindsey of Portland in 1952.

912 An improved drum pedal was invented by Bob Ramsey of Springfield in 1953.

913 A machine to harness power from the rise and fall of ocean tides was invented by Erik Johnson in 1953.

914 A plastic baby holder for bathing was invented by Louella Moore of Myrtle Creek. It was made by Beaman Plastic in 1956.

915 Batch processing for hard board was invented by R. Chapman in 1958 at an unknown Oregon location.

916 A moving strawberry-picking apparatus in which 14 pickers lay abreast as they picked strawberries was used near St. Paul in 1962.

917 A four-horse-power garden tractor, the Kutter King, was invented by James Gourly of Portland in 1936.

918 A 10.2-foot water wheel to generate electricity was invented by Frederick Hager of Milwaukie in 1950.

The Oregon Historical Society has over two million photographs and negatives, including photos of all the inventions on this page.

919 Tillamook's Frank Batter patented a portable foot and baby warmer in 1901. The contraption employs a heating system filled with spirit and brine connected with tubes to pads worn on the baby's hands or feet.

920 In 1918, an undertaker, H. J. Breeze, created a cheaper auto wheel made of a steel frame, resilient rubber, and a tough wood tread forced on the wheels with intense hydraulic pressure.

921 A translator used for satellites was invented by Harold Sterne in 1958 at Radio Specialty Mfg. Co. in Portland.

923 Miss Rosetta Washington of Portland invented a bedpan made of fiberglass which fit inside a special mattress.

924 Walter Brattain, born in southeast China and a 1914 University of Oregon graduate in physics, was co-inventor of the transistor and won a shared Nobel Prize in 1934.

925 In 1931, Oceanside inventor M.E. Howe built a 24-foot, 18- to 20-passenger amphibious vehicle that went 15 miles on land and 4 to 15 miles per hour in water. The patent was owned by Lotsafun Amusement Company.

926 The goal of the Hacky-sack game is to keep the footbag in the air the longest. The Hacky-sack game was created in 1972 by Mike Marshall and John Stalberger, Jr. By 1983, over a million footbags were sold. The Wham-O Company paid $1.5 million for rights to make the game. In 1985, Clackamas' Tricia Sullivan-George set a world record with 6,200 consecutive kicks.

927 The first and only known **self-cleaning house** was designed by a Newberg woman who uses a pseudonym, Frances Gabe. Frances Gabe's father built houses and her teenage dream was of a house that would make house cleaning unnecessary. The 36-by-32-foot house has been built since the 1950s with many labor-saving devices **in an attempt to revolutionize house cleaning**. Every room has a special cleaning unit in the ceiling, with nozzles to spray detergent and water. The furniture is made with a soft but sturdy, thick, leather-like covering for waterproofing. For drainage the floors are sloped slightly; drying is aided by forced air. Clothes can be cleaned on hangers in the closet. The dishwasher is the cupboard, and vice versa. The house includes 68 separate inventions, including a self-cleaning organic toilet. The only limitation of this livable work-in-progress is that there is no machine yet to pick up after people.
(telephone: (503) 538-4916)

(Photo of inventions courtesy of Frances Gabe)

Textiles and Apparel

929 The first woolen mill on the Pacific coast was organized and built at Salem in 1857 by early businessmen Joseph Watt and William H. Rector. Willamette Woolen Manufacturing Company produced its first finished product, white blankets, in 1858.

930 The restored Thomas Kay Woolen Mill, established in 1889 in Salem, is the only woolen mill museum west of Missouri. The mill burned in 1895 and was rebuilt in 1896. Manufacturing ended in 1958. It is the last of the intact water-powered woolen mills.

931 **Pendleton Woolen Mills is the oldest textile manufacturer still operating in the Oregon Country.** Pendleton Woolen Mills started in Pendleton in 1893 as a scouring plant.

932 Pendleton Woolen Mills was the first to convert the fine wool grown on the Columbia plateau into a lightweight flannel. Pendleton Woolen Mills uses the whole fleece of fine grade wools from Rambouillet sheep of the Columbia plateau. Pendleton blankets have the distinction that Native Americans have used them as wearing apparel.

933 A wool fringing machine that did the work of 45 people was invented by Portlander G. F. McDougall. The first machine was used by Pendleton Woolen Mills.

934 There were lots of sheep ranches east of the Cascade Range from about 1880 to 1911, making Shaniko one of the world's largest wool-shipping centers. The railroad from Shaniko to The Dalles was very financially productive for a short railroad line. Shaniko is now a ghost town.

935 The largest flax retting and scrutching plant in the U.S., with two linen mills, was located in Salem in 1926.

936 The first flax was grown in Oregon at Tualatin by Mrs. Charlotte Matheny Kirkwood in 1844. Western Oregon was one of the only places in the U.S. where fiber flax was grown. A 1939 survey showed that 95% of the flax was grown in Russia, Lithuania, Germany, and Poland. There was a demand for linen fiber during the wars.

937 Portland-based clothing manufacturer White Stag designed and produced the world's first pedal pushers in 1951.

938 Jantzen Knitting Mills was "the **world's largest manufacturer of swim suits**, and one of America's best known apparel names." The company started in 1910 as Portland Knitting Company producing sweaters, socks, and gloves. Its name was changed to Jantzen Knitting Mills in 1918. A red diving girl became its trademark in 1920. The word "swimming suit" was coined in 1921. The first American clothing business to distribute worldwide was Jantzen in 1928. Mergers in 1980 and 1986 now have Jantzen with VF Corporation (PA), the world's largest publicly-held apparel enterprise.

939 Oregon had the most woolen textile machines in the west in the 1940s.

940 Since the first half of 1990, **Beaverton-based Nike, Inc.** (est. 1968) has been the **largest sporting clothing and apparel company in the world.** The growth continued throughout 1992. Most Nike shoes are Indonesian-made.

941 Phil Knight and Bill Bowerman met at the University of Oregon in 1957. Bill Bowerman's handcrafted shoes helped University of Oregon runners and future Olympians break records in 1960. A common kitchen waffle iron gave University of Oregon track coach and Nike co-founder Bill Bowerman a model for the tread of Nike running shoes with the **first waffle soles.**

Phil Knight first started to use the name **Blue Ribbon Sports** in 1962. The first shipment of Tiger shoes from Japan arrived in December, 1963. The Swoosh ® design trademark was created and the company's new brand name, Nike, the Greek goddess of victory, came from a Jeff Johnson dream in 1971.
American multi-record-holder Steve Prefontaine of Coos Bay became the first major athlete to wear Nike® brand shoes in 1973.
In 1977, Blue Ribbon Sports started **Athletics West, the first U.S. track-and-field training club for Olympic contenders in 1977.**

942 Nike developed the **first air-pump shoes.** Nike's 1986 revenues went over $1 billion for the first time.
Nike's **"Just Do It"** ™ campaign experienced unprecedented success in 1989. The new Nike World campus was built in 1990.

Technology

Technological changes transform society and have been occurring at an increasing rate. Technological firsts are tough to nail down.

943 Started by inventor Howard Vollum and business manager Jack Murdockin in southeast Portland in 1945, Tektronix, Inc., invented, patented, and manufactured <u>dozens</u> of modifications and improvements in oscilloscopes. The now-Beaverton-based **Tektronix became the world's leading maker of oscilloscopes.**

944 **Tektronix made the first oscilloscope to have a calibrated amplifier and a calibrated timebase** (May, 1947). **Tektronix produced:**
- its first cathode ray tubes in 1951;
- first "transistor curve tracer" (1957);
- first oscilloscope camera (1961);
- first Tektronix digital readout oscilloscope (1962);
- first T4000 Series graphic computer terminals;
- first large-screen storage terminal;
- first hand-held storage oscilloscope (1974);
- first general-purpose, real-time gigahertz scope; and
- fastest writing scope in the world (1979).

The shipment of the one millionth Tektronix oscilloscope to a purchaser occurred in 1979. Liquid crystal technology is also being developed. For many years, **Tektronix was Oregon's largest employer.**

945 Electro-Scientific Industries, Inc. (ESI) secured zoning restrictions from the Washington County Board of Commissioners and started the **first science park in the northwest U.S.** in 1962. It was modeled after Stanford's Science Park.

946 Electro-Scientific Industries Inc. has developed innovations in lasers, laser trimming (1976), and laser processing, including **the first laser to be used as a machining tool in the micro-electronics industry.**

947 ESI worked with Bell Telephone Labs to develop **the first uses of lasers to repair large computer memories** in 1979 (dynamic random access memories). **ESI is by far the world's largest supplier of this equipment.**

948 **The nation's first appropriate technology (AT) periodical was *RAIN: Journal of Appropriate Technology*, begun in Portland, Oregon, in 1972.** Its founding members were Steve Johnson, Tom Bender, Lane DeMoll, and Lee Johnson. It served as a networking source and as the conscience of the U.S. AT movement, being based on the principles espoused by Fritz Schumacher in his book *Small Is Beautiful* and by Tom Bender in his book *Environmental Design Primer*. Before the original founders left, they also wrote and edited *RAINBOOK* and *Steppingstones: Next Steps in Appropriate Technology*, published by Schocken Books, N.Y.C.

949 **The Oregon Advanced Computer Institute's** (OACIS) mission is to speed the development of advanced computing technology through leading-edge research and the rapid transfer of such technology to industry. OACIS tracks development of software technology and relates it to parallel computing. The **OACIS** partnership includes the University of Oregon, Oregon Graduate Institute, Oregon State University, Portland State University, Willamette University, and the Oregon Center for Advanced Computer Technology, as well as Intel, NCUBE, Sequent, STRAND, Cogent, and FPS.

950 Washington County in northwest Oregon has **the highest concentration of parallel computer companies in the world.**

Founded in 1976 by Robert B. Hill, Eyedentify, Inc., in Beaverton was the first company to design and manufacture a device for using retinal patterns as a human characteristic identification means (for high-security applications, CIA, FBI, etc.). Eyedentify produced one of the first biometrics on the market.

951 Floating Point Systems (established 1970) announced in April, 1986, that it had constructed the **fastest computer in the world**. It is capable of 262 billion arithmetic operations per second.

952 Mentor Graphics in late 1985 (only four years after its inception) held the largest share of the computer-aided engineering equipment manufacturing field in the U.S.

California-based **Intel** is a large multi-national corporation and while it is difficult to give credit solely to Oregonians on major company breakthroughs, the following can be credited in part to **Oregon being home to several divisions of the #1 chip manufacturing corporation.**

953 Intel developed iSBC (R) 80/10, the **first single-board computer,** in 1976.

954 In 1989, Intel developed the i860 (TM) microprocessor, the **first one-million transistor processor,** which achieved the ability to bring supercomputing to the desktop. That same year, Intel

955 developed the i960 microprocessor used in embedded control applications; it implements superscalar techniques capable of executing two instructions in one tick of the its clock.

956 In May, 1993, Intel announced its fifth generation of personal computer chips, Pentium, made in Aloha, Ore. and Rio Rancho, New Mexico. The Pentium chip contains 3.1 million transistors on a thumbnail-sized chip five times faster and more powerful than its immediate predecessor, the 486 chip.

957 California-based nCUBE, Inc., of Beaverton displayed what it says was the **world's fastest computer** on June 18, 1989. The nCUBE 2 Scaler Super Computer can solve in minutes mathematical problems that no human could perform in a lifetime. The nCUBE 2 Scaler Super Computer will run at 27 billion "flops," or floating point operations, per second. **The nCUBE 2 supercomputer offers more main memory capacity than any other computer in the world.** nCUBE, Inc., supplied the Federal Government's Internal Revenue Service with a supercomputer that will enable it to track all U.S. citizens' tax returns for the past twenty years.

958 Oregon has 564 software companies, the most in the Northwest and near the top nationally. **Oregon has the most software companies per capita in the nation and perhaps the world** with a software company for approximately every 5,000 Oregonians.

959 Interactive Systems Corporation of Beaverton has developed VEIL, Video-Encoded Invisible Light, the **first interactive broadcast television in the world.** Their Universal Interactive unit was first used on a large scale in France, via TF1, the largest broadcaster in Europe. It has been used with *Wheel of Fortune,* where viewers play along with regularly-scheduled TV shows. Interactive applications include pay-per-play games, coupons, play-along contests, home shopping, information, and education. In 1991, Interactive Systems expanded usage of VEIL technology in Australia and the Netherlands, and by 1993 signed up 10,000 subscribers in Spain. One of the first small U.S. audience participation field trials began at KGW in Portland on December 13, 1993.

960 TriQuint Semiconductor, Inc., is the world's largest manufacturer of digital, linear, and microwave gallium arsenide integrated circuits (ICs). Gallium arsenide chips have advantages over using silicon for computer chips. TriQuint has built the world's fastest chips, used in the long-haul telecommunications industry. These chips transmit very high-speed digitally encoded voice signals down fiber optic lines.

Oregon Firsts $24.95

5 2 4 9 5

9 781882 635009

ISBN 1-882635-00-0

International Standard Book Number Bar Code

961 Spectra-Physics Scanning Systems, Inc., of Eugene is the **world's largest manufacturer of machine-readable laser optical scanners.** Supermarket cashiers almost everywhere worldwide pass items over electronic bar code readers (laser scanners) manufactured in Oregon. Spectra-Physics Scanning Systems has overseas offices and sells products bearing the names and logos of the leading merchants of point-of-sale scanners in America, Japan, and Europe (respectively, IBM, Tokyo Electric Company, and Siemens-Nixdorf).

962 California-headquartered Hewlett-Packard's Corvallis operation makes in 1987 (HP-28C) intelligent calculators, e.g.,the first calculator capable of doing symbolic mathematics.

962• In Corvallis, Hewlett-Packard made the first thermal ink jet printer cartridge (1980s) and the smallest DOS-based palm-top computers (11 ounces, April 23, 1991). The HP OmniBook 300 superportable PC in August,1993, is the smallest and lightest computer (2.9 pounds) with a full-size keyboard and VGA screen.

963 In the 1980s, Floating Point Systems in Beaverton built the fastest array processors.

965 Precision Castparts Corporation developed the technology for making large complex investment castings.

966 Wagner Mining Equipment Company in Portland is the largest manufacturer of non-rail (free-moving/trackless) underground mining equipment in the world, with more than 50% of the market.

967 "America's Largest Antique and Collectible Sale," which started in 1985, occurs three times each year at the Expo Center at 2060 North Marine Drive in Portland.

968 The "largest Christmas Bazaar in the country" has been held annually at the Expo Center in Portland since 1982. There are over 1,000 booths, with two-thirds for craftspersons, and 46,000 buyers.

970 Clackamas Town Center was the Northwest's largest enclosed shopping mall when it was constructed in 1978.

971 In February, 1960, ZOOMSI, one of the first large-scale non-profit charity auctions in the country, was held to raise funds for the Washington Park Zoo and the Oregon Museum of Science and Industry. Governor Mark Hatfield was one of the first auctioneers.

972 The largest and most complex theatrical pipe organ in a public place has been assembled since the 1950s with components from a couple of dozen pipe organs by Dennis Hedberg. It's located at the Organ Grinder in Portland.

973 According to statistics compiled for 1982-87, as a percentage of total revenues, Oregon was the state with the largest percentage (19.4%) of businesses that are female-owned (meaning at least 51% female-owned).

974 In 1990, Oregon had more small businesses per capita than any other state. Ninety-nine percent of all businesses in Oregon are small business, with only 100 big businesses statewide.

975 Soloflex became the first company to introduce a "home" weight-lifting machine. The exercise machine was invented by Jerry Wilson in Roswell, New Mexico, in 1978. In 1986, Soloflex of Hillsboro, Oregon, became the first company to jump heavily into cable television advertising via lengthy 30-minute videos ("info-mercials").

976 Leupold & Stevens of Cedar Mill ranked first in 1990 as manufacturer of rifle scopes in the U.S. market, with more than double the market share of any competitor.

977 Boeing of Portland has the largest metal heat treatment facility west of the Mississippi River.

978 Covering one full block in NW Portland, Powell's Books (43,000 square feet) is one of the largest bookstores in the U.S. in terms of the number of titles of new and used books (over one-half million titles). It was established in 1970 by Walter Powell, proprietor.

978• According to the American Booksellers Association in 1992, Portland had more bookstores per capita (1.7 per 10,000 people) than any large U.S. city except Washington, D.C., the nation's capital, which had 1.8 bookstores per capita.

979 **"Buy Oregon First,"** a promotional campaign that started in 1980 for consumption of products and services grown, processed, produced and manufactured in Oregon, was an idea of Irwin Starr of KGW-TV. The **"Buy Oregon First"** model has been used in other states.

979• Bend Research, Inc. is a research and development firm that developed new controlled-release membrane technologies utilized in biomedical and environmental applications.

979• Rodgers Organ Company, founded in Hillsboro by Fred Tinker and Rodgers Jenkins in 1958, produced the world's first all-transistor church organs. They were financially-backed by the founders of Tektronix (Howard Vollum and Jack Murdoch) where the stable transistorized oscillator, a main component of the Rodgers organ, was invented. The debut of the Rodgers house organ at Carnegie Hall in New York City was in 1974. The world's first commercial five-keyboard electronic organ was built by Rodgers that same year. The largest new pipe organ built since before the metal rush of World War II was installed in Houston by Rodgers Instruments at the Second Baptist Church (1985).

Oregon Zip Codes

City/Town	Zip Code
Adams	97810
Adel	97620
Adrian	97901
Agness	97406
Albany	97321
Allegany	97407
ALOHA	97007/6
Alsea	97324
Alvadore	97409
Amity	97101
Antelope	97001
Applegate	97530
Arago	97458
Arch Cape	97102
Arlington	97812
Arock	97902
Ashland	97502
Astoria	97103
Athena	97813
Aumsville	97325
Aurora	97002
Azalea	97410
Baker	97814
Bandon	97411
Banks	97106
Bates	97817
Bay City	97107
Beatty	97621
Beaver	97108
Beavercreek	97004
BEAVERTON	970++
BEND	977++
Birkenfeld	97016
Blachly	97412
BlackButteRanch	97959
Blodgett	97412
Blue River	97413
Bly	97622
Boardman	97818
Bonanza	97623
Bonneville	97014
Boring	97009
Bridal Veil	97010
Bridgeport	97819
Brightwood	97011
Broadbent	97414
Brogan	97903
Brookings	97415
Brooks	97305
Brothers	97712
Brownsville	97327
Burns	97712
Butte Falls	97522

City/Town	Zip Code
Buxton	97109
Camas Valley	97416
Camp Sherman	97730
Canby	97013
Cannon Beach	97110
Canyon City	97820
Canyonville	97417
Carlton	97111
Cascade Locks	97014
Cascade Summit	97425
Cascadia	97329
Cave Junction	97523
Cayuse	97821
Central Point	97502
Charleston	97420
Chemult	97731
Cheshire	97419
Chiloquin	97624
Christmas Valley	97641
Clackamas	97015
Clatskanie	97016
Cloverdale	97112
Coburg	97401
Colton	97017
Columbia City	97018
Condon	97823
Coos Bay	97420
Coquille	97423
Corbett	97019
Cornelius	97113
Corvallis	973++
Cottage Grove	97424
Cove	97824
Crabtree	97335
Crane	97732
Crater Lake	97604
Crawfordsville	97336
Crescent	97733
Crescent Lake	97425
Creswell	97426
Crooked River Ranch	97760
Culp Creek	97427
Culver	97734
Curtin	97428
Dairy	97625
Dale	97880
Dallas	97338
Days Creek	97429
Dayton	97114
Dayville	97825
Deadwood	97430
Deer Island	97054
Depoe Bay	97341
Detroit	97342
Dexter	97431
Diamond	97722

City/Town	Zip Code
Diamond Lake	97731
Dillard	97432
Donald	97020
Dorena	97434
Drain	97435
Drewsey	97904
Dufur	97021
Dundee	97115
Durkee	97905
Eagle Creek	97022
Eagle Point	97524
Eastside	97420
Echo	97826
Eddyville	97343
Elgin	97827
Elkton	97436
Elmira	97437
Empire	97420
Enterprise	97828
Estacada	97023
Eugene	974++
Fairview	97024
Fall Creek	97438
Falls City	97344
Fields	97710
Finn Rock	97488
Florence	97439
Forest Grove	97116
Fort Klamath	97626
Fort Rock	97735
Fossil	97830
Foster	97345
Four Corners	97301
Fox	97831
Frenchglen	97736
Friend	97021
Gales Creek	97117
Garden Home	97223
Gardiner	97441
Garibaldi	97118
Gaston	97119
Gates	97346
Gaylord	97458
Gearheart	97138
Gervais	97026
Gilchrist	97737
Gladstone	97027
Glendale	97442
Gleneden Beach	97388
Glide	97443
Gold Beach	97444
Gold Hill	97525
Goshen	97401
Gov't. Camp	97028
Grand Ronde	97347
GRANTS PASS	975++
Grass Valley	97029

City/Town	Zip Code
GRESHAM	970++
Haines	97833
Halfway	97834
Halsey	97348
Hammond	97121
Harbor	97415
Harper	97606
Harrisburg	97446
Hebo	97122
Helix	97835
Heppner	97836
Hereford	97837
Hermiston	97838
HILLSBORO	97123/4
Hines	97738
Hood River	97031
Hubbard	97032
Huntington	97907
Idanha	97350
Idleyld Park	97447
Imbler	97841
Independence	97361
Ione	97843
Ironside	97908
Irrigon	97844
Jacksonville	97530
Jamieson	97909
Jasper	97438
Jefferson	97352
John Day	97845
Jordan Valley	97910
Joseph	97846
Junction Valley	97448
Juntura	97911
KEIZER	973++
Keno	97627
Kent	97033
Kerby	97531
Kimberly	97848
King City	97224
Kinzua	97830
KLAMATH FALLS	976++
Lafayette	97127
La Grande	97850
LAKE GROVE	970++
Lakeside	97449
Lakeview	97630
Langlois	97450
La Pine	97739
Lawen	97740
Leaburg	97489
Lebanon	97355
Lexington	97839
Lincoln City	97367
Logsden	97357
Long Creek	97856

Oregon Zip Codes

City/Town	Zip Code
Lorane	97451
Lostine	97857
Lowell	97452
Lyons	97358
Madras	97741
Malin	97632
Manning	97125
Manzanita	97130
Mapleton	97453
Marcola	97454
Marion	97359
Marquam	97362
Marylhurst	97036
Maupin	97037
Mayville	97830
McMinnville	97128
McNary	97882
Meacham	97859
MEDFORD	975++
Medical Springs	97814
Mehama	97384
Merlin	97532
Merrill	97633
Metolius	97741
Midland	97634
Mikkalo	97861
Mill City	97360
Milton-Freewater	97862
MILWAUKIE	972++
Mitchell	97750
Mollalla	97038
Monmouth	97361
Monroe	97456
Monument	97864
Moro	97039
Mosier	97040
Mount Angel	97362
Mount Hood-Parkdale	97041
Mount Vernon	97865
Mulino	97042
Murphy	97533
Myrtle Creek	97457
Myrtle Point	97458
Nehalem	97131
Neotsu	97364
Neskowin	97149
Netarts	97143
Newberg	97132
New Pine Creek	97635
Newport	97365
North Bend	97459

City/Town	Zip Code
North Plains	97133
North Powder	97867
Norway	97460
Noti	97461
Nyssa	97913
Oakland	97462
Oakridge	97463
O'Brien	97534
Oceanside	97134
Odell	97044
Ontario	97914
Ophir	97464
OREGON CITY	97045
Orenco	97124
Oretech	97601
Otis	97368
Otter Rock	97369
Oxbow	97840
Pacific City	97135
Paisley	97636
Paulina	97751
Pendleton	97801
Philomath	97370
Pheonix	97535
Pilot Rock	97868
Pistol River	97444
Pleasant Hill	97455
Plush	97637
Pony Village	97459
PORTLAND	972++
Port Orford	97465
Post	97752
Powell Butte	97753
Powers	97466
Prairie City	97817
Princeton	97721
Prineville	97754
Prospect	97536
Rainier	97048
Redmond	97756
Reedsport	97467
Remote	97468
Rhododendron	97049
Richland	97870
Rickreall	97371
Riddle	97469
Riley	97758
Ritter	97872
Riverside	97917
Rockaway	97136
Rogue River	97537
Roseburg	97470
Rufus	97050
Saginaw	97472
Saint Benedict	97373
Saint Helens	97051
Saint Paul	97137

City/Town	Zip Code
SALEM	973++
Sandy	97055
Scappoose	97056
Scio	97374
Scottsburg	97473
Scotts Mills	97375
Seal Rock	97376
Seaside	97138
Selma	97538
Seneca	97873
Shady Grove	97539
Shaniko	97057
Shedd	97377
Sheridan	97378
Sherwood	97140
Siletz	97380
Silver Lake	97638
Silverton	97381
Sisters	97759
Sixes	97476
South Beach	97366
Sprague River	97639
Spray	97874
SPRINGFIELD	974++
Stanfield	97875
Stayton	97383
Sublimity	97385
Summer Lake	97640
Summerville	97876
Sumpter	97877
Sunriver	97707
Sutherlin	97479
Sweet Home	97386
Swisshome	97480
Taft	97367
Talent	97540
Tangent	97389
Tenmile	97481
Terrebonne	97760
The Dalles	97058
Thurston	97482
Tidewater	97390
TIGARD	972++
Tillamook	97141
Tiller	97484
Timber	97144
Toledo	97391
Tolovana Park	97145
Trail	97541
Troutdale	97060
Tualatin	97062
Turner	97392
Tygh Valley	97063
Ukiah	97880
Umatilla	97882
Umpqua	97486

City/Town	Zip Code
Union	97883
Unity	97884
Vale	97918
Veneta	97487
Vernonia	97064
Vida	97488
Waldport	97394
Wallowa	97885
Walterville	97489
Walton	97490
Wamic	97063
Warm Springs	97761
Warren	97053
Warrenton	97146
Wasco	97065
Wedderburn	97491
Welches	97067
Westfall	97920
Westfir	97492
Westlake	97493
West Linn	97068
Weston	97886
Westport	97016
West Stayton	97325
Wheeler	97147
White City	97503
Wilbur	97494
Wilderville	97543
Willamina	97396
Williams	97544
Wilsonville	97070
Winchester	97495
Winchester Bay	97467
Winston	97496
Wolf Creek	97497
Woodburn	97071
Wren	97397
Yachats	97498
Yamhill	97148
Yoncalla	97499
Zig Zag	97073

*CAPS for multi-Zip cities

The **USPS** abbreviation is **OR**, the alternative state.

A single-sheet All-Oregon Zip Code list was first presented by the author to the phone companies and USPS headquarters as one part of the original "Blue/Green Pages" concept in 1977. Statewide Zip Code lists are now published widely in phone books in many states.

CITIES

MUSEUMS

City	Museums
Albany	•Albany Fire Museum, 120 34th St. SE, 967-4389
	•Albany Regional Museum, 302 Ferry St. SW, 967-6540
	•Monteith House, 518 2nd Ave. SW, 928-0911
Ashland	•Schneider Museum of Art, Southern Oregon State College, 552-6245
Astoria	•Columbia River Maritime Museum, 1792 Marine Drive, 325-2323
	•Fort Clatsop Nationall Memorial, east of Rt. 101, south of Astoria, 861-2471
	•Flavel House Museum, 8th and Duane Street
	•Heritage Museum, 16th and Exchange Street
	•Uppertown Firefighters Museum, 30th and Marine Drive
Aurora	•Old Aurora Colony Museum, 2nd and Liberty, 678-5754
Baker City	•Oregon Trail Regional Museum, Campbell and Grove Streets, 523-9308
Bandon	•Historical Society Museum, Historic Coast Guard Station, Old Town, 347-2164
Bend	•DesChutes Historical Center, Wall and Idaho Streets, 389-1813
	•High Desert Museum, 59800 S. Highway 97, 382-4754
Brownsville	•Linn County Museum, 101 Park Avenue, 466-3390
Canby	•Canby Depot Museum, 888 NE 4th Avenue, 266-9421
Cascade Locks	•Cascade Locks Historical Museum, Marine Park, 374-8535
Clackamas	•Oregon Military Museum, Camp Withycombe, 657-6806
Columbia City	•Caples House Museum, 1915 First Street, 397-5390
Condon	•Gilliam County Historical Society, Highway 19, 384-4233
Coos Bay	•Coos Art Museum, 235 Anderson Street, 267-3901
Corvallis	•Corvallis Arts Center, 700 SW Madison, 754-1551
Cottage Grove	•Cottage Grove Museum, Birch and H, 942-3963
Crater Lake	•National Park Visitor Center, 594-2211
	•Steel Center, located at park headquarters
Creswell	•Creswell Area Historical Society, PO Box 157, 97426
Dallas	•Polk County Museum, 187 SW Court Street, 623-6251
Eaglepoint	•Butte Creek Mill and Museum, 402 Royal Ave. N., 826-3531
Echo	•Echo Historical Society, Bonanza and Main Streets, 376-8137
Eugene	•Lane County Historical Museum, 740 W. 13th, 687-4239
	•Lane Education Service District Planetarium, 2300 Leo Harris Parkway, 689-6500
	•Aviation & Space Museum, Eugene Airport, 461-1101
	•University of Oregon Museum of Art, 1430 Johnson Lane, 346-3027
	•University of Oregon Museum of Natural History, 1680 E. 15th Avenue, 346-3024
	•Willamette Science and Technology Center, 2300 Leo Harris Parkway, 484-9027
Florence	•Siuslaw Pioneer Museum, 85294 Highway 101 South, 997-7884
Forest Grove	•Pacific University Museum, 2043 College Way, 357-6151
Gold Beach	•Curry County Historical Society Museum, 920 S. Ellensburg, 247-6113
Grants Pass	•Grants Pass Museum of Art, 304 SE Park Street, 479-3290
	•Schmidt House Museum, 508 SW 5th, 479-7827
	•Wiseman Gallery, 3345 Redwood Highway, 471-3500
Gresham	•Gresham Pioneer Museum, 410 N. Main Avenue, 661-0347
	•Gresham Pioneer Church, Main Street Park, 661-0347
Haines	•Eastern Oregon Museum, 3rd and School, 856-3233
Halfway	•Pine Valley Community Museum, 742-2983
Hammond	•Fort Stevens State Park Museum, 861-2000
Heppner	•Morrow County Museum, North Main Street, 676-5524
Hood River	•Hood River County Historical Museum, Exit 64 off I-84, 386-6772
Independence	•The Heritage Museum, 112 S. 3rd Street, 838-4989
Jacksonville	•Catholic Rectory, 210 N. 4th, 773-6536
	•Children's Museum, 206 N. 5th, 773-6536
	•Beekman Bank, 101 W. California, 773-6536
	•Beekman House, 470 E. California, 773-6536
	•Jacksonville Museum of Southern Oregon History, 206 N. 5th, 773-6536
John Day	•John Day Fossil Beds, Highway 19 two miles north of U.S. Hwy 26, 987-2333
	•Kam Wah Chung Co. Museum, NW Canton/City Park, 575-0028
Joseph	•Wallowa County Museum, Main Street, 426-3811/432-9482
Junction City	•Lee House-Junction City Historical Society, 655 Holly Street, 998-3657
Klamath Falls	•Baldwin Hotel Museum, 31 Main Street
	•Fort Klamath Museum, Hwy 62 (42 miles north of Klamath Falls)
	•Klamath County Museum, 1451 Main Street
Lafayette	•Yamhill County Historical Museum and Barn, 6th & Market Streets, 864-2589
Lakeview	•Schminck Memorial Museum, 128 South E Street, 947-3134

CITIES	MUSEUMS

Lincoln City	•North Lincoln County Historical Museum, 1512 SE Hwy 10, 996-6614
Medford	•Southern Oregon History Center, 106 N. Central Avenue, 773-6536
Milton-Freewater	•Frazier Farmstead Museum, 1403 Chestnut Street, 938-4636/938-3480
Milwaukie	•Milwaukie Museum, 3737 SE Adams Street, 659-5780/659-2998
Molalla	•Historic Dibble House, 616 S. Molalla Avenue 266-5571
	•Vonderahe House, 625 Metzler Street (Open Mother's Day, 4th of July, Apple Festival)
Monmouth	•Paul Jensen Arctic Museum, 590 Church Street, 838-8468
Moro	•Sherman County Historical Museum, 565-3232
Myrtle Point	•Coos County Logging Museum, 7th and Maple Streets, 572-3153 or 572-2186
Newberg	•Hoover-Minthorn House, 115 S. River Street, 538-6629
Newport	•Hatfield Marine Science Center Aquarium, OSU, S. side of Yaquina Bay, 867-0226
	•Lincoln County Historical Society Museums, 545 SW 9th, 265-7509
North Bend	•Coos County Historical Society Museum, 1220 Sherman, 756-6320
Oakland	•Oakland Museum, 130 Locust Street (1-4:30pm)
Oakridge	•Oakridge-Westfir Pioneer Museum, 76433 Pine St., 782-2703/782-2666
Oregon City	•End of the Oregon Trail Interpretive Center, 500 Washington Street, 657-9336
	•McLoughlin House National Historic Site, 713 Center Street, 656-5146
	•Barclay House, adjacent to McLoughlin House
	•Rose Farm, William Holmes House, Holmes Lane
	•Clackamas County History Museum, 211 Tumwater Drive, 655-5574
	•Stevens Crawford Museum, 603 6th Street, 655-2866
Pendleton	•Umatilla County Historical Society Museum, 108 SW Frazer, 276-0012
Philomath	•Benton County Historical Museum, 1101 Main Street, 929-6230
Portland	•American Advertising Museum, 9 NW 2nd Avenue, 226-0000
	•Bybee House & Howell Territorial Park, Sauvie Island
	•Children's Museum, 3037 SW 2nd Avenue, 823-2227
	•The Old Church Society, 1422 SW 11th Avenue, 222-2031
	•Oregon History Center, 1200 SW Park Avenue, 222-1741
	•Oregon Maritime Center & Museum, 113 SW Front Avenue, 224-7724
	•Oregon Museum of Science and Industry (OMSI), 1945 SE Water Avenue, 797-4000
	•The State of Oregon Sports Hall of Fame, 900 SW 4th Avenue, 227-7466
	•Pittock Mansion, 3229 NW Pittock Drive, 823-3624
	•Portland Art Museum, 1219 SW Park Avenue (at Jefferson), 226-2811
	•Portland Police Museum, 1111 SW 2nd Avenue, 796-3019
	•Washington County Museum, 17677 NW Springville Rd. (N. of Hwy.26, E. off 185th), 645-5353
	•Washington Park Zoo/Lilah Callen Holden Elephant Museum, 4001 SW Canyon Road, 226-1561
	•World Forestry Center, 4033 SW Canyon Road, 228-1367
Prineville	•Bowman Museum, 246 N. Main Street, 447-3715
Roseburg	•Douglas Co. Museum of History and Natural History, I-5 exit 123, 440-4507
	•Lane House, 544 SE Douglas, 459-1393
Rogue River	•Woodville Museum, First and Oaks Streets, 582-3088
St. Helen	•St. Helens Museum, Old County Courthouse, 397-3868
St. Paul	•Robert Newell House Museum, 8089 Champoeg Rd. NE, 678-5537
	•Pioneer Mothers Memorial Cabin Museum in Champoeg Park, 633-2237
Salem	•Gilbert House Children's Museum, 116 Marion Street NE, 371-3631
	•Historic Deepwood Estate, 1116 Mission Street SE, 363-1825
	•Marion County Historical Society Museum, 260 12th Street SE, 364-2128
	•Bush House, 600 Mission Street SE, 363-4714
	•Historic Mission Mill Village, 1313 Mill Street SE, 585-7012
Seaside	•Seaside Museum, 570 Necanicum, 738-7065
Silverton	•Silverton County Museum, 428 Water Street, 873-4766
Springfield	•Springfield Museum, 590 Main Street, 726-2300
Sweet Home	•East Linn Museum, 746 Long Street, 367-4580
Tillamook	•Blimp Hangar Museum, 4000 Blimp Boulevard, 842-1130 or 842-2413
	•Tillamook County Pioneer Museum, 2106 2nd Street, 842-4553
Troutdale	•Harlow House, 726 E. Historic Columbia River Highway
	•Troutdale Rail Depot, 473 E. Historic Columbia River Highway, 665-0423
Union	•Union County Museum, 311 S. Main Street, 562-6003
Vernonia	•Columbia County Historical Society Museum, 511 E. Bridge Street, 429-3713
Warm Springs	•The Museum at Warm Springs, 2189 U. S. Highway 26, 553-3331
Woodburn	•Settlemier House, 355 N. Settlemier Avenue, 982-1897

Cities and Towns

Incorporated cities, towns, post offices, and ghost towns have unique histories and in-city firsts.

980 **Astoria was the first permanent Euro-American settlement west of the Missouri River.** Astoria, Oregon Country, was founded by John Jacob Astor's Pacific Fur Company in April, 1811. Fort Astoria was the headquarters, and it was later named Fort George after British fur traders bought it and dominated the area until American farmers settled there in the 1840s.

981 **Perhaps the oldest gravemarker in the Pacific Northwest** is behind Fort George, for Donald McTavish. Donald McTavish brought Jane Barnes, the **first white woman to land on the Pacific coast,** to Astoria from Great Britain in 1814. Jane Barnes Day is celebrated annually in Astoria. Jane Barnes had blonde hair, blue eyes, and a wardrobe of new clothes.

982 The first customs house west of St. Louis was established in Astoria on April 3, 1849. *(See photo page 162)*

983 John Adair, the first customs agent, recorded that the brig *Veladora* was **the first vessel officially entered at the port of Astoria.**

984 The first Federal building west of the Rockies was built in Astoria for the U.S. Customs House. It was completed in April, 1852.

985 The first salmon cannery was established at Astoria in 1864. **Astoria was also the home of the oldest continuously operated salmon cannery in the U. S.** The Samuel Elmore Cannery was built along the Columbia River in 1881, and was later operated by Bumble Bee Seafoods, Inc., until 1980. It was **the largest salmon cannery in the contiguous U.S.**

986 **The first distribution of television signals via cable** (Community Antenna TV) **started on the roof of the Astor Hotel in Astoria in 1947** with signals from KING-TV in Seattle, Washington. Millions of people spent time watching cable television today. *(See #511)*

987 In 1862, Auburn, Oregon, was the largest town in the greater **northwest. Auburn** materialized after the October 25, 1861, discovery of gold started a roaring **gold** strike and settlers filed over 1,700 mining claims. Some of the emigrants traveling west on the Oregon Trail heard about the gold, were caught up in the gold rush, and stayed. Within six months it had about 5,000 residents. By 1864, **Auburn** was declining in population. (The population of Portland was about 3,500 at that time.) Baker County was created because the nearest county seat was over 200 miles west at The Dalles. The ghost town of Auburn, a few miles southwest of Baker City, has had no buildings since 1945.

988 **Aurora** was the site of a Christian communal utopian society that was founded in 1856 and thrived for more than two decades. Aurora was the

only communal settlement in the pioneer Northwest, and it was in some ways similar to utopian communes in the eastern U.S., such as the Harmony, Amana, and Shaker colonies. Aurora was widely famous for its musicians, who made excellent clarinet reeds. One of four towns in the American west founded by Dr. Wilhelm Keil, the communal enterprise dissolved after his death in 1877. **In 1990, Aurora may have had the most antique stores per capita in the Northwest and beyond.**

989 In **Baker City,** the Cavin Rock Collection at the Oregon Trail Regional Museum includes the **largest** known **collection** of Tempskysa, which is the pertrified form of a **rare prehistoric fern** which grew between 200 and 300 feet tall and has been found only at Greenhorn, southwest of Baker. The **largest** known specimens of fluorite crystals are found there as well.
The **Oregon Trail Association** organized in Baker City in 1922. The National Oregon Trail Interpretive Center is in Baker City.

990 The **only northwest city to fall into the ocean** is the City of Bayocean Park. T. B. Potter began selling Bayocean spit real estate in 1907, and 59 houses were built. By 1952, all the houses and other buildings had eroded into a very wet ghost town's history.

990• **Cannon Beach** was named for the cannon from the 1846 wreck of the U.S. schooner *Shark.* The *Shark's* flag was the first U.S. flag to wave over undisputed Oregon Country in 1821.

Champoeg

991 This was originally a Calapooyan Indian village called **Champooick.** Champoeg, the first clearing along the tree-lined Willamette River, was first visited by fur-traders and hunters from Astor's fur company in 1811. **Champoeg is where the Hudson's Bay Company set up the first grain market in the Oregon Country.** A granary was built there as early as 1829 or 1830 and a warehouse was built on the Willamette River. With the great fluctuation in river depths through the seasons, Champoeg was considered the "year-round head of navigation."

Federal Government representatives negotiated treaties with Willamette Valley Indian tribes in April, 1851, at Champoeg. Though these treaties were never ratified by the U.S. Senate, they were significant because the treaties signed at Champoeg were the **first official procurement agreements for land titles of Indians in the Oregon Country by the U.S. government.**

Champoeg is regarded as the "birthplace of Oregon" because it was the site of the first provisional government meetings in 1843. A thriving community was built on the Donation Land Claims of Andre Longtain and Robert Newell surveyed at that site. The 1860 census showed approximately 180 persons living at Champoeg until water from Willamette River floods inundated and buried the entire frontier community on December 2, 1861. *(See #119, #122)*

992 **Cornelius is the only incorporated city in the U.S.** that Pacific Telecom's 3,270-mile trans-Pacific fiber optic cable between Alaska, Seattle, and Japan goes through on its way to Pacific Telecom in Vancouver, Washington. The PTI cable started carrying messages on May 13, 1991, with three optical pairs, each capable of carrying at least 280 megabits of information.

Corvallis (Marysville) was the site of the Oregon territorial capitol building, 1855-56. Corvallis is home of the state land grant agricultural college.

Old College Hall on the campus of Pacific University in **Forest Grove** is the oldest educational building still in use west of the Rocky Mountains.

Eugene is known as the "track capital of the world."

Jacksonville was formed after gold was discovered by prospectors James Cluggage and J. R. Poole in Jackson Creek in 1851. Jacksonville is the oldest town in southern Oregon, and it was registered as a National Historic Landmark in 1966 by the U.S. National Park Service.

Joseph, in the Wallowa Mountains, has a population of 1,500 and is world-renowned for metal sculptures.

Newberg was the boyhood home of Herbert Hoover, the 31st President of the United States of America.

Orenco is a turn-of-the-century community that "unincorporated" in 1938 after 25 years. The nursery industry (Oregon Nursery Company) moved from Salem in 1907 and flourished there. The 1908 the Oregon Nursery Company catalog advertised and shipped nursery stock around the world.

994 A park at John Day is the location of the unique Chinese Kam Wah Chung Museum, **which was one of the first Chinese apothecaries to be established in the Pacific Northwest.** The museum has a large collection of Chinese herbs. Doctor Ing Hay and Lung On started the Kam Wah Chung and Company about 1887. They had definite success healing the ill. The U.S. Postal system took medicine to distant patients in Portland, Boise, and Walla Walla. The building was given to the City of John Day to use for a museum to signify the contributions of the Chinese community of John Day to the development of eastern Oregon.

996 The City of Lebanon made the **"world's largest strawberry shortcake"** at the 1986 World's Fair, Vancouver, British Columbia, Canada.

997 **Ontario** is one of the nation's largest shippers of onions (Ore-Ida Foods, Inc.).

998 The **only town in the northwest where only some consumers pay a sales tax is New Pine Creek.** The Lake County town is split by the California-Oregon border, with only the south half of the town paying the California sales tax.

Oregon City

999 Willamette Falls, a 42-foot waterfall, was the site of an **Indian salmon fishing village**. Dr. John McLoughlin, chief factor of the Hudson's Bay Company, located a land claim near Willamette Falls as a trading post in 1829. Dr. John McLoughlin paid Etienne Lucier in 1829 to build three cabins and a log storehouse at Willamette Falls, **that site's first construction**. John McLoughlin renamed Willamette Falls Oregon City in 1842. John McLoughlin built the first house in Oregon City in 1845, and it's a National Historic Site.

Oregon City was the capital of the first Provisional Government (from 1843-48) and Territorial Government (from 1848-52). The most firsts and historic sites of any place in the Oregon Country are in Oregon City.

1000 **Oregon City is the western end of the Oregon Trail. The Oregon Trail starts** 2,200 miles east in Independence, Missouri. The Barlow Road stretches the final 110 miles from The Dalles over the Cascade Mountains to Oregon City. The Oregon Trail's first overland immigrants arrived in Oregon City in 1842.

1001 The Clackamas District was established July 5, 1843, and stretched from Alaska to the Rocky Mountains. **Oregon City was the first incorporated city west of the Rocky Mountains, an act by the Provisional Government in 1844.** Oregon City was the only town to hold a charter under the Oregon Provisional Government.

Oregon City Is Site of the Oregon Country's:

1004 first court of record
1005 first public library
1006 first Catholic archdiocese
1007 first mint
(**Gold coins with a beaver imprint** were privately minted and circulated: $58,500 worth of $5 and $10 coins made of California gold; coins from the U.S. Mint in San Francisco came into use later.)
1008 first water-powered industry
first newspaper *(see #165)*
1010 first Protestant church west of the Rockies was built by Methodists in 1844 *(see #1102)*
1011 first temperance society, 1838
1012 Oregon's first furniture factory, 1844
1013 first debating society (Falls Debating Society), 1843
1014 first jail, 1844
1015 first paper mill, 1867
1016 first fish ladder, built at Willamette Falls

1017 Oregon City in 1848 was the site of the **first Oregon legislative session.**

1018 The original and first plat for the **City of San Francisco** was officially filed in Oregon City on February 1, 1850. **Oregon City had the only district and Federal court west of the Rocky Mountains.**

1019 The first vote to fund a public elevator to replace wooden steps was defeated in 1912. **Oregon City built the only municipal elevator in the U.S. in 1914.** The elevator was originally water-powered and consumed 200,000 gallons per day until 1924, when it was connected to electricity. A new elevator (90 feet) was built in 1954, and it's operated by a person. There were once four municipal elevators in the world; three remain (in Oregon City, Switzerland and Germany). The Oregon City elevator can be considered a "vertical street." It's a quick, free ride with a good view of a history-filled town. The longest-ever operator of a municipal elevator was Patricia Wheeler from 1973 to 1991.

Pendleton

1021 The Eastern Oregon District Fair was **the first and hence largest rodeo in the Northwest,** with 4,500 attending the first show in 1912. The Pendleton Round-Up is the largest rodeo in the state. Women rode in the Pendleton Round-Up for the first dozen years. Except for an interruption during the Second World War (1942-1943), the Pendleton Round-Up has been held in September every year. All-time record attendance figures at the rodeo occurred Saturday night at the 1985 Pendleton Round-Up with 17,800 spectators.

An extensive network of underground rooms and tunnels with a variety of businesses operating in them was built by Chinese laborers at Pendleton. The Chinese population was approximately 800 in the late 1870s. Today, visitors can enter the tunnels at First Avenue and Emigrant Street for tours.

Portland

A copper coin was flipped at an Oregon City dinner party in 1845 to give the settlement ***"Stumptown"*** *a new name, either Portland or Boston. The plat for the City of Portland was and still is filed at the Tuality (now Washington) County Courthouse in Hillsboro, 1852. Portland's first city charter went into effect on April 6, 1851.*

1022 Consolidation of the City of Portland with the the cities of Albina and East Portland in 1891 made the City of Portland the largest in the Northwest. Portland had the second largest Chinese population on the west coast at that time.

1023 Portland was the westernmost large city in the U.S. until 1959, when Hawaii became a state. It then became the westernmost large city in the continental U.S., with Forest Park being the city's westernmost part.

1025 Portland has the best "raw" unfiltered municipal water in the U.S. Portland's forefathers were smart enough to have chosen the Bull Run Watershed (25 miles east of the city), which receives an average 80" to 120" of rain, compared to the 40" to 46" of rain in downtown Portland. The Bull Run watershed is one of the most protected watersheds in the U.S., because it was set aside for exclusive use. When parts of the Bull Run watershed were logged, it was done by horses wearing diapers! In comparison to most other cities, Portland's water is so pure it can be used to fill car batteries and irons.

1026 Portland's tap water is very soft and some of the purest in the country. The City of Portland is believed to be the first city to bottle and sell its water (from 1985 to 1989).

1027 **Forest Park** (with about 4,900 acres) **stretching along the Tualatin Mountains' northeast face is the largest municipal wilderness park in the U.S.** Fairmount Park in the City of Philadelphia, Pennsylvania, is very close to the same size as **Forest Park,** which was established in 1947. Over 160 parks exist in Portland, with approximately one acre for every 45 people. Portland parks have **one of the largest-acreage-per-capita ratios.**

1028 **Mill Ends Park in downtown Portland is in the *Guinness Book of World Records* as the smallest park in the world.** The park came into existence when Dick Fagan, a reporter for the *Oregon Journal,* saw that a utility pole was being removed from a SW Front Street traffic island. Patrick O'Toole is the resident leprechaun of Mill Ends Park, which is roughly 452.16 square inches.

1029 **Pioneer Courthouse Square** (April 6, 1984) was built with over 65,000 personalized bricks, which were sold to pay for construction of the square. This is believed to be a first in construction funding. In 1858, this was the site of Portland's first public school.

1030 **The Portland Rose Festival** is the **largest all-floral parade in the northern U.S.,** and the second largest in the country (since 1907). The Rose Society held an informal floral parade in 1904 down Third Street.

1031 The Portland Police Bureau was the **first in the world to have 100% of its officers attend a training academy,** as reported in 1927 by Portland Chief of Police Leon V. Jenkins to the International Chiefs of Police Association.

1032 The **first police agency in the U.S. to use radio** to communicate with detectives and staff was the Portland Police Bureau (1934). Though the initial transmitter was one-way, use of two-way radio revolutionized law enforcement as it did other phases of life.

1033 Portland became **the first city with a civil rights law** when the Portland City Council approved one in 1950 while Dorothy McCullough Lee was mayor. Later, voters rejected it.

1034 Portland was the first jurisdiction in the U.S. to take away the cars of repeat drunk drivers and customers of curbside prostitutes. Confiscated cars are sold. Earl Blumenauer and Bob Koch sponsored these statutes.

Weather Machine
(foreground)
Pioneer
Courthouse
(background)

1035 **The weather machine at Pioneer Courthouse Square is the only one in existence** (August 23, 1988). On top of a 25-foot column, the three-foot-high creatures are **Helia, a stylized sun** for clear sunny days, **a dragon** for those darker, gloomy days, and **a heron** for days with drizzle, mist, and transitional weather. The machine, which took five years to plan and build, moves, plays trumpet, sprays water, blinks its lights, and signals the weather. **Each day at noon**, a musical fanfare initiates a two-minute sequence involving the appearance of one of the weather creatures/symbols through clouds of mist. Additional features of the machine include a new-fangled thermometer and a pollution index. Credits for the weather machine go to historian Terrence O'Donnell (idea) and Dick Ponzi (design).

1037 In the early 1970s, Portland became the first, if not **the only, city to remove a freeway through its downtown.** Harbor Drive along the Willamette River was removed and symbolically given back to the people when it was replaced with a park (now Tom McCall Waterfront Park).

1038 Based on the July, 1987, Consumer Price Index (CPI), Portland had the lowest cost of living of any major West Coast city. The Consumer Price Index of 321.6 was clearly below the U.S. city average of 340.8.

1039 The City of Portland was one of the nation's first, and the first city in the Northwest, to ban polystyrene foam fast-food packaging for restaurant take-out businesses.

1040 Portland is one of the few large cities in the U.S. with neighborhood associations, and has the largest city-supported neighborhood program in the Northwest. Citizen participation includes 90 active neighborhood associations in the City of Portland determining needs, issues, problems, and solutions. Portland was the first U.S. city to permanently fund neighborhood crime prevention programs.

1041 The City of Portland was the only Northwest city with a horse-mounted patrol as a working unit for law enforcement (1991-92).

1041• After President Dwight Eisenhower established the sister city program, Portland adopted a sister city relationship with Sapporo, Japan, in 1959. This was one of the first and hence longest sister city relationships in the nation.

1042 The first city in central Oregon, the City of Prineville, operates the nation's first and only municipally-owned railroad.

1043 Port Orford is the westernmost incorporated city in the contiguous U.S.A.

1044   **St. Paul,** the central area of **French Prairie,** is second only to Astoria in order of white settlement in Oregon. French Prairie, the **earliest permanent agricultural region,** was settled in 1828 by French Canadians who completed contracts with the Hudson's Bay Company. Two of the original Lewis and Clark Expedition members are buried in St. Paul.

Salem

1045   Salem was confirmed by Congress as the Territorial Capital in 1852, incorporated in 1857, and became the state capital by popular vote in 1864.

1046   **The Jason Lee House (1841) in Salem is the oldest known remaining frame house in the Pacific Northwest.**

Willamette University in Salem is one of the **oldest educational institutions** west of the Rocky Mountains (1842; chartered 1853).

1047   Salem became the **state capital** by a popular vote in 1864. **"Salem" means peace.** Oregon City and Corvallis were previous capitals of the Territorial and Provisional governments.

1048   The restored Thomas Kay Woolen Mill (since 1889) is **the only woolen mill museum west of Missouri.** The mill burned in an 1895 fire and was rebuilt in 1896. Manufacturing ended in 1958, and the wool-dying plant closed in 1965. **It is the last of the intact water-powered mills.**

1049   Salem is the **largest food processing center in the Northwest** and one of the largest in the U.S.

1050   **Seaside is the end of the Lewis and Clark Trail.** On January 2, 1806, three Lewis and Clark explorers found Clatsop Indians on the beach boiling seawater to render salt and they built the **first American salt works on the Pacific coast.** Approximately 1,400 gallons of seawater were boiled in a 45-day period to produce 20 gallons of salt.

1052   **Seaside, the oldest beach resort city in the Pacific Northwest,** was founded by Ben Holladay, a pioneer railroad builder who constructed the Seaside House as a "destination resort." Seaside has an 8,000-foot seawall, the **only seawall of its kind on the west coast.**

1053   The Dalles is the **only northwest site of a branch building of the U.S. Mint,** which was constructed following the gold rushes of the 1860s. No money was coined there.

1053•   Early French Canadian voyageurs knew the falls of the Columbia River as the trough. In French, "dalles" means a rapid river flowing swiftly through a narrow channel over flat rocks. The Columbia River rapids drop 50 feet in elevation over a three-mile stretch.

1054   **The Dalles is the only place where two national trails meet** (the Lewis and Clark Trail and the Oregon Trail).

Courtesy of Keith Townsend

1055 **The Tillamook County Fairgrounds has the world's only PIG 'N FORD Races.** It was conceived by J. A. Bell and Doug Pine in 1925, after two pigs jumped out of the bushes and raced along in front of Pine's Model T Ford. The Pig 'N Ford (and human) races have since been an annual event at the Tillamook County Fair each August. The cars lost their metal tops for the WWII effort. The Pig 'N Ford races delight the spectators! The humans sprint across the track, grab a pig from the portable pigpen, race with it back to the Model T Ford, crank up the engine, hop on, put it in gear and race a lap. Each racer grabs another piggy, cranks up the Model T for another lap, then stops, picks up another piggy and gives it a third and final ride. During the race, the pigs squeal with excitement, and after the race, spectators' sides ache. Tillamookians say the race is even more fun after a rain. Bob Wassman is the 1992-93 world champion driver.

1056 Voters in the City of Warrenton elected the **first woman mayor west of the Rocky Mountains in 1912**, the same year women won the right to vote. Miss Callie Cynthia Munson began her term on January 6, 1913.

1057 Warrenton also had the **first woman city manager in the nation in 1923**, Callie Cynthia Munson.

City of Vanport (1942-48)

1058 By May, 1948, the **largest housing project in the nation** (and perhaps the world) was the City of Vanport, located south of Jantzen Beach. Originally called Kaiserville, **Vanport was conceived, designed, and constructed within one year. The largest local housing authority in the nation,** it had 5,295 families containing 18,700 "actual registered tenants."

1059 **Vanport had the nation's first public library designed exclusively for a housing development, and it was the only public library in a war housing project.**

1060 **Vanport had the largest public school system for a housing development in the U.S.** Vanport had the second largest school system in the entire state of Oregon.

1061 Vanport was Oregon's second largest city until a Columbia River flood swept over the dikes and wiped out the entire city. The flood started at 4:17 pm on May 30, 1948, and almost 19,000 residents lost their homes. Though 200 people were originally reported as "missing," the death count was 15-18 Oregonians. The flood at Vanport was the **worst flood in the U.S. since the Johnstown flood 49 years earlier.**

The flood focused the most national attention on the Portland area since the Lewis & Clark Exposition in 1905.

People

The following tribes and bands of people lived freely in hundreds of villages throughout the area that became the State of Oregon. The following is not a precise list of total tribes and bands in that pre-reservation era government records and anthropological names are incomplete and spellings vary. The arrival of the pioneers and their diseases, fevers, customs, and concepts led to the disappearance, consolidation, or freedom limitations of these Indian tribes and bands:

Agai-tika
Alsea/Yaquina
Bannock
Calapooya (Kalapooia)
Callico
Cascade
Cayuse
Chafan
Chaftan
Chetco (Nultunnatunne, Chetati)
Chetlesentun
Chinook (Clatsop, Kathlamet)
Clackamas (1860)
Clatskanie
Clatsop
Clowerwalla
Cow Creek
Dakubetede (Applegate Athabascan)
Euchre Creek
Galice Creek Athabascan (1856)
Gidi-tika
Grave
Gwi-nidin-ba
Hokan
Hood River
Hunipwi-tika
John Day
Joshua (Chemetunne)
Kalawatset
Kalapuya (Calapooya, Kalapooia)
Karok
Kathlamet
Khwaishtunnetunne
Klictitat
Kusan

Oregon Firsts

Kusotny
Lakimuit (1855)
Lohim
Long Tom Creek
Lower Coquille
Lowland Takelma
Luckiamute (Lakmiut)
Maddy
Macanotin
Mary's River (1855)
Mikonotunn
Mishikhwutmetunne
Modoc
Mohawk
Mollala (Southern and Northern)
Moses - Columbia
Muddy Creek
Multnomah
Munsel Creek
Nahankhuotana
Netunnetunn
Nez Perce (Idaho Reservation)
Northern Paiutes
Patikichi-tika
Pistol River
Nekutameux
Port Orford
Pudding River
Rogue River
Salishan
Santiam (1855)
Scoton
Shasta
Shasta Costa/Chasta Costa
Shoshonean
Siuslaw/Lower Umpqua
Sixes River (Quatoma)
Skilloot
Sloton
Snake (Yahooskin)
Tagu-tika
Takelma (Rogue Band)
Tenino
Tillamook (Nehalem, Nestucca, Siletz Bay, Salmon River Bands)
Tolowa (Smith River, Earl Lake)
Tsankupi
Tualatin/Atfalati
Tututni/Tututunne
Tututui
Tygh (Upper Deschutes)
Umpqua (Upper, Main)
Upper Coquille (mid 19th cent.)

Upper Santiam
Wada-tika
Wa-dihtchi-tika
Walla Walla
Wasco
    (Dalles, Ki-gal-twal-la, Dog River)
Wyam (Lower Deschutes)
Yakonen
Yamhill (Yamel) (1855)
Yapa-tika
Yoncalla (Yonkalla) (1855)
Yuki (Euchee/Euchree)

The above list was compiled from the following sources:
Native Americans at the Oregon Trail Finale, Oregon City, 1993
Tribal Distribution in Oregon, Joel Van Meter Berreman, 1937, American Anthropological Assoc.
Oregon Indians, J. Zucker, et al BIA, Confederated Tribes of Siletz Grande Ronde, and Warm Springs.

Indian Tribes in Oregon

The nine Federally recognized Indian tribes are:
• **The Burns Paiute Tribe**
• **The Confederated Tribes of Coos, Lower Umpqua, and Siuslaw**
• **The Confederated Tribes of the Grande Ronde**
• **The Confederated Tribes of the Siletz**
• **The Confederated Tribes of the Warm Springs**
• **The Confederated Tribes of the Umatilla Indian Reservation**
• **The Cow Creek Band of Umpqua Indians**
• **The Coquille Tribe**
• **The Klamath Tribe**
The Fort McDermitt Paiute-Shoshone (Nevada Headqtrs.)

Not Federally recognized:
• Celilo-Wyam Community
• Chetco Tribal Council
• Tchinouk Tribe

People

The First Oregonians

People have been native to Oregon for thousands of years. Natives, immigrants, and emigrants have created Oregon firsts. Somebody had to be first.

Evidence uncovered indicates very early inhabitants of this continent lived in a cave near Fort Rock about 10,000 years ago. The Fort Rock sandals were discovered by Oregon's first professional archaeologist, Dr. Luther Cressman, during excavations in Lake County in the 1930s. These sandals made of sagebrush are, according to carbon dating, about 10,000 years old.
(See photo page 6)

White people have been in Oregon for less than 190 years, a short time compared to native Indians. Successive cultures are evident throughout Oregon. (See #30)

Originally there were about one hundred tribes and bands of Indians living in the area which became the state of Oregon, but there are only nine tribes now. Indian words were adopted as names of many Oregon towns, rivers, and geographic features. Over fifty Indian languages were spoken in North America, with a dozen distinct languages spoken in the Oregon Country.

1063 On April 19, 1851, the Atfalati (Tualatin Indians) gave up lands for a small settlement at Wapato Lake (near the current Gaston). Other early reservations for Oregon Indians were established at the Table Rock Agency and the Umpqua Sub agency in 1853.

1064 Over 1,900 Calapooyas Indians from all parts of western Oregon were placed in the Grand Ronde Valley to reside. The Grand Ronde Valley near the coastal range in what is now Yamhill County was the site of the first permanent Indian reservation.

1065 Native Americans were made full U.S. citizens in 1924. Three dozen tribes in Oregon were terminated by the Western Oregon Termination Act of 1954. All of these tribes except the Coquille tribe (527 members) were returned to tribal status as the U.S. Government realized that the benefits Indians lost were protections they needed to survive.

1065• **Celilo Falls was the first large center of commerce in the Oregon Country.** Tribal members would travel from California, Idaho, Montana, and British Columbia, Canada, to trade at Celilo Falls. On the morning of March 10, 1957, when the gates of The Dalles Dam flooded the 80-foot plunge at Celilo Falls, an age-old (~8,000 years) salmon fishery was lost forever. As many as 50,000 native people lived and fished along the Columbia River.

Millions of acres of CEDED LANDS OF THE YAKIMA, UMATILLA,
WARM SPRINGS AND NEZ PERCE TRIBES

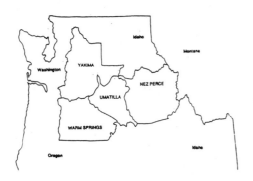

*Ceded Lands of the Yakima, Umatilla,
Warm Springs and Nez Perce Tribes*

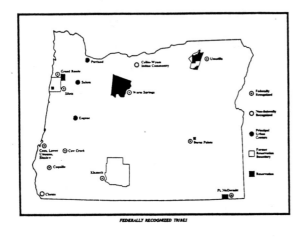

FEDERALLY RECOGNIZED TRIBES

Federally recognized Indian Tribes in Oregon

1066   In 1788, a young black man named **Marcus Lopius was the first person killed while serving under an American flag in the Oregon Country.** He worked for Captain Robert Gray. He died at a place Gray called Murderer's Bay that is now called Tillamook Bay.

1067   **New Yorker John Jacob Astor** was by far the largest fur trader in the region of the Great Lakes and upper Mississippi River. John Jacob Astor, perhaps the first American millionaire, established a fur trade base at Astoria. He never set foot in Oregon. Though it was Astor's only major unsuccessful business venture, this marked the beginning of continuous development of the Pacific Northwest and it established the white man's presence in the region.

1068   In 1846, Sheriff Joe Meek as the first Provisional Government tax collector found Dr. John McLoughlin to be the **richest man in the territory.**

1069   **John McLoughlin** (born Riviere Du Loup, Canada, October 19, 1784) came to the Oregon Country **as chief factor of the Columbia Department of the Hudson's Bay Company in 1824. In 1829, he staked his claim to the present site of Oregon City.** In 1845, he resigned his position with Hudson's Bay Company and moved to Oregon City. **He built his house in Oregon City, which is now a National Historic Site. He laid out Oregon City, he became an American citizen, and he served as mayor, establishing Oregon City as capital and trading center of the Oregon Territory** The 6'4"- tall McLoughlin died September 3, 1857, and was buried with his wife Margeurite at St. John's church in Oregon City. McLoughlin was called the "White-headed Eagle," and he's regarded as the **Father of Oregon.**

1071 **Nathaniel J. Wyeth**, a Bostonian, went back east to the Rocky Mountains and **built Fort Hall**, known as the midpoint of the Oregon Trail. He also opened a route over the Blue Mountains.

1072 The law forbidding slavery in Oregon was tested by **Robin and Polly Holmes**, married black slaves who lived in Polk County and brought a lawsuit against their owner for custody of their still-enslaved children. The Holmeses won their case in 1853.

1073 **Ewing Young** led a first cattle drive from California to Oregon, delivering over 600 Mexican longhorns to the settlers in the Willamette Valley and aiding their independence from the British.

1074 **Ewing Young was the initial settler of the Oregon Country to die and leave possessions.** When Ewing Young died he left a large herd of cattle. Following his funeral (February 17, 1841), **American settlers took initial steps toward forming Oregon's provisional government by electing a supreme judge, Ira Babcock, with probate powers over Young's estate.**

1074• Judge Ira Babcock also presided as chairman of the May 2, 1843, Champoeg meeting which began formal organization of the Provisional Government.

1075 Joe Meek was a trapper and trader before settling north of Hillsboro in 1840. He was an influential founder of the Provisional Government in Oregon. Joseph Lafayette Meek

served as the Provisional Government's first sheriff (1843), first tax collector, and census taker (1845). In 1847, Joe Meek and party rode horses to Washington, D.C. and carried word of the Whitman Massacre with a petition asking President James K. Polk for protection as a U.S. territory. President Polk, whose wife was Meek's cousin, received him and named him the first U.S. marshall of the Oregon territory.

1076 **Ranald McDonald** was born February 3, 1824, at Fort George in Astoria and attended school at Fort Vancouver. In 1848, at the age of 24, he set adrift alone in a small boat and entered Japan on Rishira Island. He deliberately and successfully defied a 200-year-old imperial edict which barred foreigners from Japanese soil and threatened reprisals. Later, in Nagasaki, Ranald McDonald tutored 14 Japanese in the English language to serve as interpreters, and hence, he became the **first English instructor on Japanese soil.**

1077 William Simon U'Ren (1859-1948) **led a revolutionary movement in American government for direct legislation.** William U'Ren led a revolution in American democracy with the Oregon initiative and referendum powers, which **remade constitutional law.** Initiative and referendum powers gave more control to citizens. William U'Ren was a member of the American Civil Liberties Union when it was formed in 1920. U'Ren believed that reform could only be achieved by citizens taking a direct role in legislation.

1078 **Anna Maria Pittman Lee** (1803-1838) accomplished many Oregon Country firsts. She was the first white woman to stand at Oregon's first mission.

1079 The first poetess was Anna Pittman.

1080 Miss Anna Maria Pittman became Oregon's first white bride on July 16, 1837.

1081 Finally, at age 34, Anna Maria Pittman Lee was the first white woman to be buried under the Oregon Country's soil.

Mary Ramsey Wood
(courtesy of Washington County Museum)

1082 **Mary Ramsey Wood of Hillsboro, an Oregon pioneer, was claimed to be the oldest woman in the world at her death in 1908. Mary Ramsey Wood lived in three centuries to the age of 120 years** . She was born in Knoxville, Tennessee, on May 20, 1787, as authenticated by her family Bible.

1083 **Illinois native and early Oregon school teacher Abigail Scott Duniway** organized the Oregon State Equal Suffrage Association in 1871. She moved to Idaho in 1887 and helped women there get a constitutional amendment for suffrage. Returning to Oregon, which still had unequal voting privileges, she maintained her advocacy. Oregon had unsuccessful votes on a woman's right to vote in 1900, 1906, 1908, and 1910. Victory came in 1912. **Abigail Duniway was the first voter in the first election open to women. It took six campaigns to gain women the right to vote. No other state voted as many times.** Abigail S. Duniway and Susan B. Anthony went together on a three-month Northwest speaking tour. *(See #224)*

1084 **Lola Baldwin was the first woman police officer hired by a city (under civil service) in the U.S.** In 1908 her official title was City Superintendent of Detective Work for Women. Lola Baldwin came to Portland in 1905 and was employed by the Traveler's Aid Society. She was so helpful to young women that women's groups convinced the City of Portland to hire her. **Later, Lola Baldwin headed all women's services in the military for the Federal Government.** She came back to Portland to consult and live.

1085 Beatrice Cannady was an early civil rights worker for black Americans. An educator, she became one of the region's first black lawyers in 1922.

1086 **Dorothy McCullogh Lee, who was Portland's first female mayor, was the first woman to chair the Federal Parole and Probation Board.** The Women's National Press gave her an achievement award, presented to her by President Truman in 1949.

1087 **Portland-born revolutionary jour-
nalist John Silas Reed (1887-1920)
is the first American citizen buried in the Kremlin at Red Square,
Moscow.** John Reed was educated
at Portland Academy and Harvard
University (1910). He became a
correspondent in Mexico, Europe,
and Russia. He wrote seven books
and many poems, and he's one of
Oregon's foremost literary figures.
His book, *Ten Days That Shook
The World*, is a lively, detailed, 351-
page eyewitness account of the
events surrounding the 1917 Russian Revolution.

1088 **Fred G. Meyer** (1886-1978)(born
Fred Grubmeyer in Brooklyn, N.Y.)
**started one of the first self-service
pharmacies in Portland in 1930.
Fred G. Meyer** also started one of
the earliest self-service grocery stores
(1922) in Portland. (Piggly-Wiggly
stores preceded with self-service.)
The rooftop parking at the Hollywood store in NE Portland was also
one of the earliest. Fred Meyer was
one of the first users of fluorescent
lightbulbs in Portland stores. By 1993
there were over 120 stores in seven
western states, with over 20,000 Fred
Meyer Corporation employees.

1089 **The original Bozo the Clown,** Vance
DeBar **"Pinto" Colvig** (1892-1967),
was born in Jacksonville and graduated from Oregon State University
in 1914. He performed at the Lewis
& Clark Exposition (1905) and
worked for Walt Disney Studios as
the first voice of Pluto (1930) and
Goofy (1932).

*Black and white version of six-color
InfoVision electronic graphic displayed at
the 1986 World's Fair.*

1090 Penny Harrington served 17 months
in 1985-86 as Portland's police chief.

1092 Before artificial fertility procedures,
the **oldest woman on record to give
birth** was Mrs. Ruth Ann Kistler,
(1899-1982), who raised Karakul
sheep in Myrtle Creek, Ore. On October 18, 1956, when she was 57
years 129 days old, she gave birth to
a daughter, Suzan, in Glendale, California.

1093 Linus Carl Pauling is the **only person to receive two unshared Nobel
Prizes. Linus Pauling** was born in
Portland on February 26, 1901, and
is a 1923 graduate of Oregon State
University. **His first Nobel prize
was in the field of structural chemistry in 1954. Pauling won the
second Nobel Prize in 1962 for his
work to attain a nuclear test ban.**

1094 **Nancy Ryles** was the first and only
woman PUC Commissioner in the
U.S. appointed by a governor of the
opposite political party. As a school
board member, Nancy Ryles advo-
cated use of athletic budgets for both
boys and girls. As a State Representative, she initiated legislation for
mandating kindergarten attendance
and for medical ethics related to death
with dignity.

Fishermen at Celilo Falls of the Columbia River, the first large commerce center. During warm months for thousands of years (May to October), Celilo Falls was the major gathering and trading place for northwest tribes. *(OHS Negative 373-A)*

Missionaries and Churches

Early missionaries started trails west looking for native souls to convert to Christianity. The missionaries sent back east encouraging words of the rich soil, good farming and many trees.

1095 On July 3, 1834, the first petition was sent by French Canadian Catholics in the Willamette Valley to the Catholic Bishop of Red River asking for priests to live with them.

1096 Jason Lee preached the first Protestant sermon west of the Rocky Mountains to Captain McKay's men at the site of Fort Hall, July 27, 1834. At Mission Bottom, 31-year-old Methodist Reverend Jason Lee was first to start a mission for Indians in the Oregon Country.

1097 Dr. Marcus Whitman and Narcissa Whitman established the Waiilatpu Mission along the lower Walla Walla River in 1836. Waiilatpu has an Indian meaning of "place of rye grass." Dr. Whitman guided the first immigrant group with a wheeled cart over the Oregon Trail as far west as Fort Boise in 1842.

1098 The first Catholic mass said in the Oregon Country was by Fr. Modeste Demers on the banks of the Columbia River at Big Bend, 250 miles north of the international border.

1099 The first Catholic missionaries in the Oregon Country arrived at Fort Vancouver on November 24, 1838.

The next day, Francois Norbert Blanchet, the first archbishop in the Oregon Country, celebrated the first Catholic mass in the Fort Vancouver schoolhouse with an estimated 26 Catholics.

First printing press in the Sandwich Islands and the Oregon Country (OHS Neg. 26237)

1100 The press shown above was acquired by the Presbyterian mission at Lapwai as a gift from missionaries on Oahu in the Sandwich Islands. Over four dozen native Hawaiian women raised $450 to send the printer, paper, and ink. It was shipped with printer E. O. Hall and transported up the Columbia, Snake, and Clearwater rivers, then carried by horseback to Lapwai. Rev. Henry Spalding printed the first book in the Oregon Country, *Nez Perces First Book*, (8pp.) in the tribal language at Lapwai in 1839 on the first printing press at Clear Water Mission. Lapwai is one of the earliest permanent settlements in the present State of Idaho. The printing press was transported to The Dalles for use there in 1846. The following year it was moved to Hillsboro to print issues of the *Oregon American and Evangelical Unionist*. This press is preserved at the Oregon Historical Society, 1200 SW Park Ave. Portland, OR 97205-2441. *(See also #1419)*

1102 The first Protestant church west of the Rocky Mountains was the Methodist Church in Oregon City established by Alvan Waller in 1840. The first Methodist parsonage west of the Rockies was built in 1843. The first Protestant church west of the Rockies was built by the Methodists in 1844 in Oregon City by the Rev. Gustavus Hines.

1103 The first Congregational church west of the Rockies was organized at Oregon City in 1843 by Vermont native Harvey Clarke.

1104 The first Baptist congregation in the Oregon Territory was formed on May 25, 1844, by David Thomas Lenox. The West Union community is the site of the first Baptist church built west of the Rocky Mountains (1853). The church, which is now owned by the American Baptist Church of Oregon, is the oldest Protestant structure still in use statewide.

1105 Harvey Clark was an independent pioneer missionary who organized congregational churches in Forest Grove and Oregon City. An early educator, he helped Tabitha Brown in the founding of the first orphanage in the territory (1846), which was known as Tualatin Academy (and was eventually chartered as Pacific University). Harvey Clark also helped in the formation of the Oregon Institute (later called Willamette University). He was chaplain of the first Oregon Provisional Government.

1106 Joseph Kellogg brought the first Masonic Charter over the Oregon Trail to Oregon City and first convened the first meeting on September 11, 1848. The Multnomah Lodge No. 1 A.F. & A.M. was the first Masonic Lodge west of the Missouri River.

1107 Thomas F. Scott in 1853 became the first Episcopal bishop of the Oregon and Washington territories. He dedicated the first Episcopal church building on the Pacific Coast in Portland in 1854.

1108 St. James Lutheran Church (1890) in SW Portland is the first English-speaking Lutheran church in the Northwest. The first Lutheran seminary in the Northwest started at St. James in 1910, and it had the nation's first female faculty member (theologian), Miss Jennie Summer from Iowa.

1110 A survey reported in *The Oregonian* newspaper cited Oregon residents as ranking lowest nationally in membership or affiliation in an organized religion (church, synagogue, mosque, temple, etc.).

1111 The Ecumenical Ministries of Oregon (EMO) is 75 years old, and from 1982 to 1992 it grew from being the smallest ecumenical ministry in the U.S. to being the largest, with 17 denominations and over 200 congregations. EMO ministers to the poor, the powerless, the sick, and the addicted.

Sportswomen and Sportsmen

Twenty-eight of over 730 U.S.-earned gold medals reside with athletes who grew up in Oregon, attended Oregon schools, trained in Oregon, or once had connections with the state. The first Oregonian to win an Olympic gold medal was A. C. Gilbert (pole vault). The only Oregonian to win five gold medals is Don Schollander (swimming).

Baseball

1112 Ken Williams (a left-hander from Grants Pass) and the St. Louis Browns led the American Baseball League with 39 home runs and 155 RBIs in 1922.

1113 Bobby Doerr set **a major league record with 73 consecutive error-less games in 1948.** He was the American League's Most Valuable Player in 1944, and seven-time All-Star second baseman for Boston's Red Sox (1937-51).

1114 **Mickey Lolich is the only major league pitcher to win three games in one World Series (1968).** Mickey Lolich graduated from Lincoln High School in Portland, where he pitched the Cardinals to the Oregon State High School title by striking out 18 batters in the championship game. **Mickey Lolich was the American League's all-time lefty strike-out artist, with 2,670 strikeouts, a record that stood for over a decade.** He won 217 games for the Detroit Tigers.

1115 The first ball thrown in Colorado Rockies' franchise history was caught before the Bend Rockies beat the Boise Angels (6 to 4) during 1992 in Bend.

1115• Wilson High School graduate Dale Murphy, who played for Atlanta's Braves, is the only Oregonian to win major league baseball's Most Valuable Player award twice (1982, 1983).

Basketball   *"The Tall Firs"*

1116 **In 1939, at the first-ever National Collegiate Athletic Association basketball championship, the winning team was the University of Oregon Ducks team.** The team was nicknamed **"The Tall Firs."** The Ducks basketball team defeated Ohio State 46 to 33 in a small gymnasium in Evanston, Illinois. The founder of the game of basketball, Dr. James Naismith, attended the first tournament game. Naismith started basketball in 1891, using a soccer ball and peach baskets hung on a gymnasium wall, in Springfield, Massachusetts.

1117 The **Tall Firs** won every one of the NCAA playoff games by at least 13 points. This **record** stood throughout the history of the eight-team playoff series. Sixty-four teams compete in the NCAA play-offs now. **Everyone on the Tall Firs starting team was an Oregon native.**
   • Bob Anet was captain and guard
   • John Dick was forward
   • Lauren "Laddie" Gale, **top scorer**, is in the National Basketball Hall of Fame
   • Urgel "Slim" Wintermute was the tallest member of the **Tall Firs** at 6' 8"
   • Wally Johansen

Tall Firs coach Howard "Hobby" Hobson was one of the earliest coaches to suggest more points for baskets made from a greater distance and use of a time clock to speed up the game.

Basketball is a team game, and numerous Oregon athletes have been members of gold medal-winning U.S. Olympic basketball teams, including:

1118 **Lew Beck,** Pendleton, OSU, was on the basketball team at London's Olympics in 1948. Two transplanted Oregonians, **Terry Dischinger** and **Darrell Imhoff**, were members of the Olympic basketball team in 1960.

1119 **Mel Counts** (originally from Coos Bay) was a gold medal winner on the 1964 U.S. Olympic basketball team. This Gervais resident played on two Boston Celtics championship teams.

1120 **Carol Menken-Schaudt** won gold on the 1984 women's basketball team in Los Angeles.

1121 **Cynthia Brown** was on the women's 1988 Olympic basketball team.

1121• **Clyde Drexler** was on the 1992 Olympic basketball team (Barcelona).
(See front cover photo)

1122 **Freeman Williams of Portland State University (1975-78) was NCAA Basketball Scoring Champion in 1977 and 1978. Freeman Williams was NCAA all-time scoring leader with 3,249 points** in 1978. He scored the second most points (81) in one game in NCAA history.

1123 Former OSU guard **Gary Payton** was the first Oregon college basketball player to be named to the Associated Press All-American Team. He won the 1990 *Sports Illustrated* Basketball Player-of-the-Year Award, was an All-American, and was a **first-round** NBA draft pick by the Seattle Supersonics.

1123• On February 6, 1970, Portland was granted a National Basketball Association franchise. Harry Glickman deserves credit for bringing professional basketball to Oregon. The first owner was Larry Weinberg and the second owner, Paul Allen, is the richest owner in professional sports. The **Portland Trail Blazers, Inc.,** is the only professional major league team in Oregon, and it holds the following NBA records:

1124 Geoff Petrie was the first-ever draft choice of the Portland Trail Blazers. The first Blazer shared Rookie-of-the-Year honors with Dave Cowens of the Boston Celtics (1970-71). He is now Senior Vice-President of Team Operations.

Portland Trail Blazers fans hold the all-time professional sports record with over 650 consecutive sell-outs at Memorial Coliseum (since April, 1977).

1125 **The Trail Blazers continue to hold the longest consecutive sell-out record in both professional sports and the NBA.** The record total after the 1992-93 regular season was 651 consecutive games sold out at Memorial Coliseum since April 5, 1977. At the last game not sold out, only 12,539 of us fans saw the Trail Blazers beat the Detroit Pistons 110 to 105. The typical sell-out attendance was 12,666.

1126 The Portland Trail Blazers *(above)* became the **National Basketball Association Champions** (1976-77) on June 5, 1977, when they beat the Philadelphia 76'ers 109 to 107. The championship team members coached by Dr. Jack Ramsay were Bob Gross, Maurice Lucas, Bill Walton, Lionel Hollins, Dave Twardzik, Johnny Davis, Corky Calhoun, Lloyd Neal, Larry Steele, Wally Walker, Herm Gilliam, and Robin Jones. Bill Walton holds the record for the most blocked shots in an NBA finals game (eight).

1126• Bill Walton, the Blazers' first pick in the 1974 draft, was the NBA's Most Valuable Player in 1978.

1127 The Portland Trail Blazers won the 1989-90 NBA Western Conference Championship.

1128 The Portland Trail Blazers are the **NBA's 1990-1991 Pacific Division Champions with the best record in the league.**

The Trail Blazers were one of the first three NBA teams traveling to games in a chartered jet **(Blazer 1, Blazer One, Blazer Won)**.

1129 **Memorial Coliseum,** where the Trail Blazers play home games, **is the smallest arena in the NBA.** A new arena seating over 19,000 is scheduled to be ready in September, 1995.

1129• **Portland is the NBA's smallest city.**

1130 The **largest margin of victory in an overtime game**, 17 points, was Portland at Houston, January 22, 1983.

1131 The Trail Blazers set the NBA record for **fewest turnovers** per game (three) on February 22, 1991, against the Phoenix Suns.

1132 **The Portland Trail Blazers were the first NBA team to produce television coverage of basketball games in-house. The baseline camera and microphone in the backboard were concepts originated in Portland. For** years, the television ratings for the Portland Trail Blazers have been the highest among all 27 NBA teams, with a 50% share of the local viewers. In its local market (1990-91), Blazer games beat the top-rated prime-time program nationally.

1133 **The most three-point baskets made in one NBA game is 21** combined goals on December 30, 1990, at Milwaukee, Wisconsin. The Bucks had 12 and the Blazers made nine three-point field goals. Portland won the game 117 to 112.

1134 **The 1991-92 NBA Pacific Division and Western Conference champions were the Portland Trail Blazers.** The Blazers lost to the Chicago Bulls four games to two in the 1991-92 NBA championship series.

1135 On May 11, 1992, the Phoenix Suns and Portland Trail Blazers set an NBA playoff game scoring record with 304 points. The Blazers won in double overtime by a score of 153 to 151.

1136 Terry Porter set an NBA playoff series record by scoring 18 three-point goals against the Utah Jazz, May, 1992.

1137 On November 14, 1992, against Golden State, Terry Porter hit all seven of his three-point attempts, an NBA regular-season record for a year.

1137• Portland Trail Blazer coach Rick Adelman won 200 games faster than any other coach in NBA history. By November, 1992, his teams had won 200 games and lost 88 games for a .694 winning percentage.

1137• Short-term 1982 Blazer 7'0" Carl Bailey took only one shot and he made it, hence achieving 100% accuracy.

1138 **Individual Blazers holding NBA season titles:**

Larry Steele, '73-'74	217 steals
Bill Walton, '76-'77	934 rebounds
Bill Walton, '76-'77	211 blocked shots
K. Vandeweghe, '80-'81	.481 3-pt. FG %
Buck Williams, '90-'91	.602 FG %
Buck Williams, '91-'92	.604 FG %

1139 On June 12, 1991, **Portland was chosen over 26 other cities as the site for the first-ever U.S. Olympic basketball trial games with both amateur and professional athletes.** The bid was initiated by Brian Parrott of America's Best, Inc.

1139• The **Tournament of the Americas** was played at Memorial Coliseum from June 27 to July 5, 1992, with teams from ten countries: **Argentina, Brazil, Canada, Cuba, Mexico, Paraguay, Puerto Rico, United States, Uruguay, and Venezuela.** It was the **first time some NBA professional athletes played together, with and against amateurs.** The U.S. team was undefeated and won gold, winning each game by an average of 52 points. Larry Bird made the first and last U.S. points in the tourney, and his last points on U.S. soil. Television coverage was transmitted from Portland throughout the hemisphere and world. The U.S.A. basketball team *(see front cover photo)* with Oregonian Clyde Drexler beat the basketball team from Croatia (which starred the late Drazen Petrovic) for the Olympic gold medal at Barcelona, Spain.

1140 **The first NBA draft of college players ever held outside New York City was held in Portland** at Memorial Coliseum on June 24, 1992. **The first collegian chosen was Shaquille O'Neal** (by the Orlando Magic).

Boxing

1141 Denny Moyer of Portland won the World Boxing Association world junior middleweight title in 1962.

Football

1142 In 1962, Terry Baker (OSU) became the first Heisman Trophy winner from the Pacific Northwest.

1142• The first Canadian Football League game held in the U.S. since 1958 was played at Civic Stadium on June 25, 1992. This exhibition game, a 1991 Canadian Grey Cup rematch, was won by the Calgary Stampeders 20 to 1 against the Toronto Argonauts.

1142• The football rivalry since 1894 between Oregon State and University of Oregon is the oldest on the west coast (94 years). No game was played in 1900, 1901, 1911, 1943, or 1944.

Golf

1143 The Oregon Golf Course was site of the NFL quarterbacks tourney and the Fred Meyer Challenge. The Fred Meyer Challenge is unique in that it is a Monday-Tuesday tournament, and it's a **best-ball** format competition shown on national cable television.

1143• Pumpkin Ridge Golf was ranked in the January 1993 *Golf Digest* as the #1 best public and second-best private new course in the nation. Pumpkin Ridge Golf will be the site of the 1996 U.S. Amateur Golf tournament, the oldest major golf tourney in the U.S. Pumpkin Ridge uses bent grass on the tees, greens, and fairways.
Some of the U.S.A. Olympic Basketball "Dream Team" members and coaches used Pumpkin Ridge Golf as their unofficial headquarters.

Hockey

1144 The first professsional hockey championship in North America was won with members of a team originally formed in Portland as the Rosebuds.

1144• The Portland Buckaroos dominated the Western Hockey League by finishing in first place eight times, 1960-71.

1144• In 1976, the Portland Winter Hawks became the first U.S. junior hockey team. In 1983, the Portland Winter Hawks hosted the first Memorial Cup tournament held outside of Canada, and they won it. The team had a league record seven 100-point scorers.

Mountain Climbing

1145 Lige Coalman climbed Mount Hood a record 586 times from 1896 to 1927. Coalman Glacier is named for him.

1145• On September 29, 1988, Portlander **Stacey Allison became seventh woman and the first American woman to climb the world's highest peak, the 29,028-foot Mt. Everest.** Stacey Allison was part of a 13-person climbing team based in Seattle. She stayed on the summit for 45 minutes. She graduated from Woodburn High School in 1976. Stacey Allison had already ascended Alaska's Mt. McKinley (20,320 feet) and the former Soviet Union's Pik Communism in the Pamir Range (24,590 feet).

Rodeo

1146 **Salem-born cowboy Larry Mahan from Brooks is a six-time all-around rodeo championship title winner.** Larry Mahan won five consecutive world all-around rodeo championships from 1966-70, and he won his sixth all-around championship in 1973.

1146• The first rodeo of the year, the Tygh Valley Rodeo, is the only all-Indian rodeo in the Northwest.

Skating

1147 Tonya Harding of Beavercreek became the first American woman to successfully complete the physically challenging triple-axel jump in national competition on February 16, 1991, in Minneapolis where she won the U. S. Senior Ladies figure skating championship. In Detroit on January 8, 1994, she beat her competition and won that skating championship again.

Skiing

1148 Tacoman **Gretchen Fraser is the first U.S. woman skier to win a gold medal**. She won at the racing special slalom in 1948 Olympics at St. Moritz, Switzerland. Gretchen lived in Vancouver, Washington, but trained in Oregon on Mt. Hood and at the Multnomah Athletic Club (MAC Club).

1148• Bill Koch is the first American to win an Olympic Nordic cross-country skiing medal (silver in 1976 at Innsbruck).

1148• Bill Johnson of Sandy won a gold medal in alpine downhill racing at the 1984 Olympics (Sarajevo, Yugoslavia)

Soccer

1149 The Portland Pride on August 1, 1993, won the first shoot-out in Continental Indoor Soccer League history.

Swimming

1150 Norman Ross won **two gold medals in 400-meter and 1500-meter freestyle swimming** at the 1920 Antwerp, Belgium, Olympics.

1150• MAC Club coach **Louis "Happy" Kuehn became the first American to win a diving gold medal when he won in the springboard competition** for the U.S. team in 1920.

1151 **Brenda Helser** of Lake Oswego was a gold medalist on the U.S. 400-meter freestyle relay team at the Olympic games in London in 1948.

1152 **Suzanne Zimmerman** of Hillsboro won the backstroke silver medal at the 1948 London Olympics and tied the world's record at a California meet.

1153 **Carolyn Wood,** a 14-year-old Beaverton High School freshman and the youngest member of the 1960 U.S. Olympic team, swam a leg on the winning **4x100-meter freestyle relay team that set a world record** in Rome.

1154 Florida-born **Don Schollander** (a graduate of Lake Oswego High School and Yale University) became the **first American swimmer to win four gold medals at the Olympic games** at Tokyo in 1964. **Don Schollander was the world's first swimmer to break the two-minute barrier in the 200-meter freestyle. And he won one gold and one silver at the 1968 Mexico City Olympics. At age 19, he was World Athlete of the Year.**

1154• **Kim Peyton** won an Olympic swimming 400m relay gold medal in 1976.

1154• **Carrie Steinseifer won a 100-meter freestyle swimming gold** and was a member of the 4x100-meter relay team at the 1984 summer Olympics.

1155 Brent Lang was a member of the 400-meter relay gold medal-winning team.

Tennis

1155• At the first national collegiate tennis championship (Austin, TX, 1929), the co-champions were Texas and Oregon.

1155• The largest crowd ever to watch a Davis Cup match in the U.S. was in 1981 at the Memorial Colisum. This record was broken in Atlanta (1984).

1155• Two personal firsts: Tracy Austin (age 14) and Boris Becker (age 17) broke into professional tennis in Portland.

Track

1156 Dan Kelly (Baker City) was **the first world record holder from Oregon**, running the 100-yard dash in 9.5 seconds and 220 yards in 21.1 seconds in 1906. He was also a silver medalist at the 1908 Olympics.

1157 Forrest Smithson won a **gold medal in the 110-meter high hurdles at the 1908 London Olympics.**

1158 In 1901, **A. C. Gilbert** (born in Salem in 1884) simultaneously held world records of 40 chin-ups on a horizontal bar, in the running long dive (15' 9"), and in rope climbing while at Tualatin Academy in Forest Grove.

1159 **A. C. Gilbert set the world's record in the pole vault at 12 feet 7 and 3/4 inches** in the Olympic trials in 1908. **He was co-Olympic gold medal winner in the pole vault** at 12' 2".

1160 **In 1929, Ed Moeller set a new world record with a discus throw of 160' 7.7".** He graduated from the University of Oregon.

1161 George Varoff from the University of Oregon **set a world pole vault record of 14' 6.5" using a bamboo pole in 1936.**

1162 Les Steers, Oregon, was **world record high jump holder at 6' 11" in 1941.**

1163 Australian Jim Bailey, a University of Oregon student in 1956, was the NCAA mile champion.

1164 **Otis Davis,** University of Oregon, ran for two gold medals in the 1960 Olympics: the 400 meters (setting Olympic and world records) and the 1600-meter relay team.

1165 **Dick Fosbury, 1968, won a gold medal in high-jump (7'4.5") at the Mexico City Olympics.** The "Fosbury Flop" is named for his head-and-back-first over-the-bar technique, which **every recordholder in the high jump since has utilized and worked to refine.** Dick Fosbury grew up in Medford and graduated from O.S.U.

1166 Sheridan High School student Joni Huntley (age 17) **set the American high jump record** in Portland in 1973. She became the **first American woman to high jump six feet in 1974** at Oakland, CA when she leapt 6' 3/4".

1167 **Steve Prefontaine** (born January 25, 1951 in Coos Bay) in his first year at the University of Oregon became the **first freshman ever to win an NCAA title (the three-mile race).**

1168 **Steve Prefontaine was the first collegian to win four straight NCAA track championships. He also won three National Collegiate Athletic Association cross-country titles.**

1169 **At the time of his death in a one-car accident on May 30, 1975, Steve Prefontaine held American running records over many race distances: 2,000 meters, 3,000 meters, 2 miles** (indoor and outdoor), **3 miles, 5,000 meters, 6 miles, and 10,000 meters.**

1170 **Bill Bowerman was coach of the University of Oregon track team (1948-73) which won four NCAA titles.** He coached the University of Oregon cross-country team that won the 1971 NCAA title. He was U.S. Olympic Track Coach in 1972, and coached 28 Olympians.

1170• Bill Bowerman is also a **co-founder of Blue Ribbon Sports** (BRS), **which in 1977 started Athletics West, the first U.S. track and field training club for Olympic contenders.** BRS became Nike, Inc., the world's largest sporting-apparel manufacturer in 1990, 1991, and 1992.

1171 NCAA national discus champion Mac Wilkins, from Beaverton and the University of Oregon, set an **Olympic record discus throw** at the 1976 Montreal Olympics.

1172 **Bill Dellinger** was on three U.S. Olympic teams as a 5,000-meter distance runner, winning the bronze in 1964. Bill Dellinger was **coach of the 1984 National Track Champion University of Oregon Ducks.**

1173 **Mary Decker Slaney,** a graduate of Long Beach State and resident of Eugene, **has held many American running records for women, including the best indoor 1500-meter race in February, 1980. In 1982, she ran to over eight world records and 11 American distances ranging from one mile to 10,000 meters. She ran the fastest mile ever run by a woman** (4:16:71) in Zurich, Switzerland, on August 21, 1985.

1174 **Alberto Salazar,** a graduate of the University of Oregon, was the winner of the New York City Marathon in 1981 and 1982, during which he **set a new world marathon record (1981)** of two hours, eight minutes, and 13 seconds.

1174• Dan O'Brien of Klamath Falls set the world decathlon record with 8,812 points in 1991.

Volleyball
1175 Aldis Berzins was a member of the **U.S. Volleyball gold medal team** in 1984.

Wrestling
1176 **In the Paris Olympics of 1924, wrestlers Robin Reed and Chester Newton,** both wearing Multnomah Athletic Club colors, dominated the 124-pound freestyle wrestling, winning gold and silver medals respectively.

1177 **Rick Sanders** (born in Bly, Oregon) **was America's first freestyle wrestling champion in 1969. Rick Sanders won five national titles** at Portland State University from 1965 to 1968. He was a silver medalist in the 1968 Mexico City and 1972 Munich Olympics. Sanders was considered one of the most accomplished amateur wrestlers in the country. He was responsible for some of the sport's innovations.

1177• Olympic wrestling gold medals were won by **William (Bill) Smith,** freestyle, 1952, and **Mark Schultz,** 82-kilo wrestling, 1984.

Recreation

Beyond the Oregon Trail, there are more than 10,000 miles of trails from the high desert, up and down the Cascade Mountains, and westward to the Pacific shoreline. Outdoor recreational opportunities abound with 1,829 miles of wild and scenic rivers, 35 wilderness areas, and 429 miles of sometimes rugged ocean coastline.

1178 The first recorded people to reach the summit of Mt. Hood, the highest place in Oregon, did it on July 11, 1857. Mt. Hood is the second most climbed glacier-covered peak in the world.

1179 The U.S. Government's program aimed at accommodation of visitors at publicly-owned recreation areas began with construction of Mt. Hood's Timberline Lodge as its first building. The Works Progress Administration (WPA) used a broader variety of labor than on any project in Oregon at this year-round resort. It's 3.6 miles from Timberline Lodge to Mt. Hood's summit by trail.

1180 The first Magic Mile chair lift was dedicated at Timberline by the Prince (and later King) of Norway as the **first ski lift in the West,** and the nation's second ski lift, in 1939.

1181 Timberline Lodge is the **first ski resort ever on a U.S. postage stamp** (1987). The City of Lake Placid, New York, also had a postage stamp.

1182 **The only year-round snow skiing in the United States today** is at the Palmer Snowfield Lift, Timberline Lodge, on Mt. Hood.

1183 The Columbia River Gorge has some of the best winds in the world for the sport of windsurfing or sailboarding. Hood River is known as the **sailboarding capital of the world.**

1183• The Eagle Creek Campground in the Columbia River Gorge (Mt. Hood National Forest) is the **first U. S. Forest Service auto campground.**

1183• The first audience card stunt at an event occurred in 1927 at a University of Oregon football game.

1184 Oregon's Tourism Department started **the nation's first state-sponsored annual bicycle tour, Cycle Oregon**. In 1993, 2,000 cyclists rode 450 miles.

1185 The **"biggest fireworks in the West"** each Fourth of July are visible from Oregon over the Columbia River. The Fort Vancouver fireworks originate in Washington and use large shells. These biggest fireworks have a Portland sponsor. The state's largest fireworks display explodes on the first night of Rose Festival in June.

1186 The Multnomah Athletic Club (MAC Club) is one of the largest (areawise) private athletic clubs under one roof in the U.S., with 18,000 members. The MAC Club is the **oldest continuously-operating athletic club in the Northwest** (third oldest in U.S.). Thirty-eight U.S. Olympic athletes were products of the Multnomah Athletic Club and its coaches, or, as members, they chose to compete in MAC Club colors.

1187 The Multnomah Exposition and Recreation Commission, which operates Memorial Coliseum, etc., is **one of the** few city-operated sports complexes in the U.S. which operates in the black financially.

1188 **The oldest children's parade in the U.S.** started in Portland's Hollywood district in 1918. During the first World War, there was no Rose Festival Parade for adults, but only one for children. In the nation's largest children's parade, about 13,000 kids march, dance, ride, twirl, roll, and tumble along the two-mile route of the Children's Parade.

1189 The Multnomah Kennel Club attracts **the biggest crowds to see dogs race in the Northwest, and has the second largest attendance in the nation.** Multnomah Kennel Club's large purses attract some of the nation's best greyhounds. At the first MKC Derby, at Portland's Civic Stadium on August 11, 1933, the unbeatable Fawn Warrior won in front of **the largest crowd ever (33,000) to see dogs race.**

1190 The Hood-to-Coast Relay is the **nation's longest road-running relay (160-190 miles) and the largest, with 750 teams and about 9,000 runners.**

1191 **The Cascade Run-Off used a precise 15-kilometer course over which eight of the fastest ten times in world history were recorded,** including four world records and seven U.S. records for both men and women. From 1980 to 1993, up to 7,500 runners per year from most states and twenty countries ran the Cascade Run-Off, bringing $2.5 million into the local economy.

1192 Fiddler's Green in Eugene was the "largest on-course golf shop" in the U.S. in terms of both sales dollars and size (over 17,000 square feet) in 1990.

1193 The Mazamas Trails Club of Oregon, founded on top of Mt. Hood in 1894, is the oldest mountaineering club in the Northwest, and the third oldest in the U.S. behind the Appalachian and Sierra Clubs.

1194 The **world's largest marching band is the One More Time Around Again Marching Band,** which in 1992 had 536 members. An idea of Clayton Hannon of the Portland Rose Festival Association, the **One More Time Around Again Marching Band** started in 1985 with 80 musicians. Qualifying criteria are former high school, military, or college band experience and being able to march and play music, preferably at the same time. The **OMTAAMB** practices one week (in May) and performs half a dozen times per year. Its first appearance at the Tournament of Roses Parade in Pasadena, California was on January 1, 1989.

1195 The Cascade Run-Off, organized by an Oregon nonprofit corporation, never paid runners for appearances, but in 1981 became **the first major road race to pay prize money to the top men and women finishers based on the order of the top ten finishers.** Before this, major races paid "appearance money" to compensate for expenses. The significance of the Cascade Run-Off payment system is that every major running race has changed and now pays prize money to winners.

IN-STATE FIRSTS

This chapter describes firsts within Oregon's borders. The Oregon Historical Society is the historical center of Oregon and is an excellent source for information concerning early events within Oregon. **In-State Firsts categories** *are similar to those in the preceding Oregon Firsts and Beyond chapters.*

AGRICULTURE

1197   The first potatoes in Oregon were planted at Astoria by members of New York merchant John Jacob Astor's Pacific Fur Company in 1811. The first crop yielded 119 potatoes.

1198   French Canadian Etienne Lucier was the first farmer in the Willamette River Valley. He began cultivating the soil in 1829.

1199   The West Coast's first grafted fruit (apples, peaches, pears) were a result of Henderson Luelling and son Alfred hauling 700 fruit tree seedlings from Iowa by ox team to Oregon. The Luellings planted the trees in Milwaukie in 1847 and 1856.

Seedlings of cherries were brought over the Oregon Trail in 1847 by Seth Lewelling and his brother, Henderson Luelling. Royal Ann, Kentish, Black Hart, Black Tartarians, May Duke, and other varieties were planted near Milwaukie. From these varieties were grafted the Black Republican and Bing cherries.

1200   In 1840, the first white clover seeds were brought by Reverend J. L. Parrish.

1201   Flax grew wild before it was cultivated.

1202   On the mission farm a few miles north of Salem, the first grain cut with a cradle was cut by Reverend Jason Lee during the 1837 harvest.

1203   A thresher was built in Oregon City in 1848. A thresher and separator of grain was brought around Cape Horn in 1850. It was first used on the farm of Thomas Otchin north of Hillsboro.

1204   The first honey bees to arrive in Oregon were from California in 1849. Honey bees were brought overland by Dr. Davenport in 1854.

1205   Wild cranberries were noted in Lewis and Clark Expedition diaries, and they previously existed in Coos County. Charles Dexter McFarlin, from a Massachusetts family of cranberry growers, started cultivating cranberries in Coos County in 1885 and has been called the father of the Pacific coast cranberry.

1206   Prunes and plum seedlings were brought out the Oregon Trail and introduced in Oregon by Seth Lewelling in 1858. In 1871, the first commercial prune orchard started growing in Portland.

1207   When pioneers arrived, strawberries grew wild. Oregon's 1988 cultivated strawberry crop totaled a record 101.4 million pounds.

1208   Agriculture has been Oregon's top income-producing industry since 1990.

ANIMAL HUSBANDRY

1209   Simeon G. Reed imported one of the first herds of purebred cattle into the state.
1210   The first man to pioneer the improvement of sheep for wool growing was Joseph Watt. Watt also originated the first woolen factory on the Pacific coast.
1211   The first sheep brought across the plains were from Missouri by Joshua Shaw in 1844.
1212   Five trappers, all men from the Astor expedition, came to the Willamette Valley and introduced the art of animal husbandry.

ARCHAEOLOGY

1212•   The state's largest prehistoric site is the Stockoff Basalt Quarry in Union County which covers about 3,000 acres.

ATTENDANCE

1213 The Washington Park Zoo has the highest attendance of any attraction requiring an entrance fee in Oregon.

1214 Multnomah Falls is the most visited place in Oregon, with 1.6 to 1.8 million visitors yearly.

1215 The entire Oregon coast draws an estimated 28 million visitors annually for sightseeing, ocean fishing, hiking, etc.

1216 Greyhound racing at Multnomah Kennel Club is Oregon's most popular spectator sport, outdrawing the Portland Trail Blazers in numbers of paying fans.

BANKS

1217 Oregon's first bank, the Ladd and Tilton Bank, was founded in 1859.

1218 Glencoe High School in Hillsboro is the location of the first student branch bank in a high school west of the Mississippi River. Credit goes to the principal, Joel Rodriguez, who approached First Interstate Bank.

1218• Students at Poynter Jr. High School in Hillsboro on April 29, 1993, made the largest negotiable check in the world (30 feet by 65 feet). U. S. Bank cashed the check.

EARLY BIRTHS

Native Indians have legends about the first people.

1221 The first surviving quintuplets in Oregon were born on April 26, 1973, at Bess Kaiser Hospital in north Portland. The mother of two adoptees, Karen Anderson gave birth to five children weighing from 2 lbs. 8 oz. to 2 lbs. 15 oz. between 2:48 pm and 2:59 pm.

1223 Andrew Best of Eugene was born December 22, 1986, at Oregon Health Sciences University, becoming the first Oregon baby conceived through in vitro fertilization. In the first five years after his birth, 61 "test tube" babies were born to Oregon parents.

1224 The first triplets conceived through artificial insemination were born November 2, 1987.

BILLIONAIRE

1225 Philip Knight of Nike, Inc., is Oregon's first billionaire and was named by *Sporting News* "the most powerful person in sports in 1992."

BOOKS

1226 The first book in English printed in the Oregon Country was by W. P. Hudson, printer for the *Oregon Spectator*, in Oregon City, February 1, 1849. It was an abridgment of Webster's *Elementary Speller*.

1227 The first fictional book written in Oregon, *The Prairie Flower* was authored in 1842 by Sidney W. Moss, a pioneer from Kentucky. It was published in Cinncinnati, Ohio, in 1849.

1228 The first City Directory was printed of businesses and residences in Portland in 1863. It was updated and printed annually by J. J. McCormack, the publisher for thirty years.

1229 The 800-page "Flora of the Northwest" was the most complete list of plant species in the region. It was compiled and written by Thomas Jefferson Howell and published in 1903.

1230 Binford & Mort was the largest publisher of books about the Northwest in the 1930s.

1230• The Northwest Association of Book Publishers in 1993 was the west coast's largest group of book publishers.

BRIDGES

1231 Oregon's first bridge was built of logs across Dairy Creek, a western Tualatin River tributary. Its first tree was felled by Alvin T. Smith, a missionary, on February 14, 1843.

1232 The first bridge over the Willamette River was at Albany in 1871.

1233 The first toll-free suspension bridge over the lower Willamette River was in Oregon City.

1234 The oldest remaining covered bridge is the Drift Creek Bridge, in Lincoln County (1914).

1235 Lane County has the most covered bridges (19) in the state.

BUILDINGS

1236 The West's first brick house was built by George Gay near Hopewell in 1841-42. That house is on the boundary line between Yamhill and Polk counties.

1237 In 1844, George Abernethy constructed the first brick store at Oregon City.

1239 The Granada Theatre in The Dalles is the first theatre built in Oregon for talking motion pictures. Built in 1929, it had 800 seats.

1240 The first brick church in Oregon is the St. Paul Roman Catholic Church erected in 1846.

1241 The first frame house was constructed by Methodist missionaries at Wascopam (The Dalles) on October 1 and 2, 1839.

1242 Brickyard owner Charles H. Piggott built the first castle in Oregon in 1892 (now along Buckingham Avenue in SW Portland).

1244 The ten-story Baker Hotel in Baker City was the tallest building in eastern Oregon.

1245 Cottage Grove and Aurora have two of the only octagonal buildings in Oregon.

1246 The First Interstate Bank Tower in Portland, with 44 levels and 554 feet from its basement, has been the tallest building since 1972.

BUSINESS

1247 On January 10, 1964, Tektronix became the first company incorporated in Oregon to appear on the "Big Board" of the New York Stock Exchange.

1248 For many years, Tektronix was Oregon's largest employer. The State of Oregon was the largest employer in the state subsequently.

1249 Bipolar Integrated Technology was the first Oregon-based semiconductor manufacturer.

1250 The longest continuously operating microbrewery in Oregon is the Bridgeport Brewing Company (since 1984).

CAPITAL

1251 The Territorial Capital was in Oregon City until February 7, 1851, when it was moved to Salem. In April, 1855, it was moved to Corvallis. and then in December, 1855, it was returned to Salem. John L. Morrison built the building known as the first capitol in 1850.

CENSUS

1252 An early unofficial census was taken by Thomas H. Smith in 1844. Sheriff Joseph L. Meek enumerated the first official Census in the five districts in the spring of 1845. The first Federal census of the Oregon Territory in 1850 counted 110 persons of color.

District	Male	Female	Total
Champoeg	400	305	705
Clackamas	232	129	361
Tuality	309	229	538
Yamhill	257	158	415
Clatsop	61	30	91
Totals	1,259	851	2,110

(See Population for totals)

CHURCHES

1253 The first Catholic church was a log structure built at St. Paul in 1836 by Catholic settlers. The first Catholic mass was celebrated there at the French Prairie area on January 6, 1839.

1254 The first Catholic services were celebrated by Fr. Blanchet from January 5 to February 4, 1839, with 74 baptisms and 24 marriages. The first Catholic cemetery in the Pacific Northwest is at St. Paul.

1254• The first Catholic sisters arrived in Astoria on August 1, 1844, and were greeted by Mr. James Birnie of the Hudson's Bay Company.

1255 The first clergyman of the Episcopal faith, Reverend Herbert Beaver, arrived in Vancouver at the Hudson's Bay Company in 1836.

1256 The first Protestant house of worship was the Methodist Episcopal church built in Oregon City from October, 1842 to 1844.

1257 The first Presbyterian church to be formed in Oregon was by Reverend Lewis Thompson, Mr. and Mrs. William H. Gray, and Mr. and Mrs. Alva Condit on September 19, 1846, at Clatsop Plains.

1258 The initial Episcopal bishop of the Oregon and Washington territories was Thomas F. Scott in 1853. The next year in Portland, he dedicated the first Episcopal church building on the West Coast.

1259 The Grotto, Sanctuary of Our Sorrowful Mother, in northeast Portland is presently the only important, internationally-known Catholic shrine (1993).
(See also Churches #1095-#1111)

CITIES

1260 Pendleton is the only place in Oregon with underground tunnel tours. Chinese laborers dug the tunnels in the late 1800s.

1261 The Reed Opera House in Salem was the site of the first suffrage meeting.

COMMERCE

1262 The first cargo of wheat was dispatched to Liverpool, England, via Cape Horn by Joseph Watt in 1868.

DAMS

1263 John Day Dam is the largest in the state and the third largest in the nation.

DIVORCES

1265 Mary Ann Smith became one of the first three Oregon women to obtain a divorce when the Oregon Provisional Court granted her a decree on November 2, 1846. To Mary Ann Smith were restored "all the rights and immunities of a state of celibacy."

1265• Attorney Robert Nordyke opened the first drive-up divorce service by utilizing the drive-up window of a former bank in Salem (1987).

DEATHS

1266 The oldest cemetery, a resting place for pioneers, is near the community of West Union in the Tualatin Valley.

1267 Charity Lamb, contrary to her name, was Oregon's first murderess when she killed her husband with two gashes of an axe in 1854. Convicted of second-degree murder, she was sentenced to a life of hard labor.

1268 Governor Earl Snell, Secretary of State Robert S. Farrell, Jr., and President of the Senate Marshall E. Cornett were killed in a private plane crash on October 29, 1947.

1269 The 461 suicides in Oregon in 1988 were an all-time state record. In 1989, 459 Oregonians committed suicide. This rate is 30% above the national rate.

1270 An August, 1988, car accident on Interstate 5 caused by smoke from field burning took the lives of seven motorists.

1271 Tobacco smoking is the leading preventable cause of death in Oregon; it is a contributing factor in 23% of all deaths.

EARTHQUAKE

1271• Mother Nature awoke most Oregonians on Thursday, March 25, 1993, at 5:35 am with Oregon's most costly earthquake. Centered about 3 miles east of Scotts Mill, it caused about $30 million damage (magnitude 5.6). On September 21, 1993, the epicenter of a stronger earthquake (magnitude 5.7) occurred 15 miles northwest of Klamath Falls.

EDUCATION

1272 In 1876, the University of Oregon was established in Eugene as Oregon's first liberal arts university. Deady Hall was the first educational building on campus.

1273 Willamette University became Oregon's first medical institution.

1274 In 1883, Oregon's first law school was established at Willamette University in Salem.

1275 Starting in 1948 at Baker High School, grades 13 and 14 were beginnings of Baker Community College, the first community college.

1276 Hopkins Elementary School in Sherwood became the first school in Oregon and one of 28 nationally to speak with an astronaut, Ron Parise, aboard the space shuttle *Columbia*. About 500 people gathered in the gym on Dec 9, 1991, for communication with and from outer space from 7:07 pm to 7:15 pm.

ELECTIONS

1277 The first general election was May 14, 1844.

1278 The first mail ballot was used to gather the results of a Port of Newport levy vote.

ELECTRICITY

1279 The first electrical energy usage was on May 25, 1879, on the steamship *The State of California*. It provided the first showing of electrical light with arc lights on board its anchor at Ainsworth Dock in Portland. A public display of brilliant light brighter than any previous sight at night in Portland was seen by more than 500 Portlanders.

1279• The first Public Utility District was formed in western Lane County (the Blanchly Lane Cooperative Association, 1932).

1280 The Trojan nuclear power plant along the Columbia River in Rainier was the only operating commercial atomic plant (1975-1992). The most deadly wastes in Oregon are the spent radioactive nuclear fuel rods, temporarily stored at the Trojan Nuclear plant by Portland General Electric since 1975. There are at least 60 hydroelectric plants and eight thermal (steam) plants. *(See #1387)*

ENERGY

1281 The first discovery of commercial quantities of natural gas was by Northwest Natural Gas in 1979 near Mist in Columbia County.

FAIRS

1282 The first county fair was held at Forest Grove in Washington County in 1855-56.

1283 The first Oregon State Fair was held in what is now Gladstone October 1st to 4th in 1861; it was moved to Salem in 1862. *(For the Lewis & Clark Exposition, see #190-#193)*

FERRIES

1284　The first ferry across the Willamette River was built by Jesse Applegate across from Wheatland near the Jason Lee mission in 1843-44. The first ferry across the Willamette River in Portland was a canoe.

FILMS

1285　The first moving picture shown in Portland was on August 8, 1897. By 1915, Portland had 20 movie "places."

1286　The first motion picture film made in Oregon and successfully distributed nationally was a 1914 documentary about the Pendleton Round-Up titled "Where Cowboy Is King."

FISH

1287　Salmon is the state's most valuable fishery. In the 19th century, river salmon fishing was the subject of U.S. treaties with Indian tribes. Treaties guarantee the fishing as an Indian resource.

FLEAS

1288　The first fleas recorded to be on white people were those experienced by Narcissa Whitman in 1836 near The Dalles. "She was covered from head to foot."

FLOODS

1289　Big floods of the Willamette River occurred in 1861 and 1894, and lesser floods occurred in 1890, 1923, 1945, 1955, and 1964. A 25" steelhead was caught inside Union Station during the flood of 1894.

1290　The *St. Clair,* a steamwheeler, was the first and only steamboat to ride over Willamette Falls was during the flood of 1861. Captain George Taylor started off above the falls and three minutes later blew a loud safety signal below the falls.

1291　The Heppner flood, which resulted from a downpour up Willow Creek and a dam failure, killed 225 people on June 14, 1903.

FLOUR MILL

1292　The first flour mill in the Oregon Country was built in 1828 on Mill Plain, near Vancouver, by William Cannon.

FOOD

1293　The first foods recorded to have been eaten in Oregon included antelope, elk, and buffalo meat, which were popular either fresh or dried. Venison was eaten when available. Meat was baked on the hearth. Salmon was served with fried cakes. Some buffalo tongue was pickled. "When desperate, we ate wild horses," Narcissa Whitman wrote.

Camas resembles an onion and grows near rivers. Indians were fond of it. Camas is a genus of the lily family and when cooked it tastes sweet, like a fig. It was the chief food of many tribes in the winter. Tarweed and wapato were other favorite foods. Berries were gathered.

One fried cakes recipe called for "a little flour, little water, make a dough, roll thin, cut in squares, fry in buffalo fat."

1293•　Portland's first pizza restaurant was Caro Amico ("dear friend"), started by Fred K. Baker and Kenneth Baker in October, 1949.

GEOGRAPHY

1294　Mt. Hood is the tallest point in Oregon, 11,240 feet above sea level. (Its summit is the border between Hood River and Clackamas counties.)

1295　About 25% of Oregon is desert, including the Alvord Desert, the High Desert, and coastal dunes. Oregon's desert is mostly in Deschutes, Lake, Harney, and Malheur counties.

1296　Lakeview is the highest city in Oregon (elevation 4,800 feet above sea level).

1297　Old Perpetual, the geyser just north of Lakeview, erupted 60 feet into the air every 90 seconds since 1923, before the drought slowed it to 15-20 minutes to build up steam.

1298　The Lilliputian Geyser in the Alvord Desert (six to eight feet) is a hot spring, the state's only mud pot has 200 degree water.

1299　Upper Klamath Lake is the state's largest freshwater lake (58,922 acres), with over 100 miles of shoreline. Malheur Lake was the largest body of water before recent drought.

1300　Oregon's longest lake is Owyhee Lake in Malheur County.

1301　The oldest known rocks are in the Siskiyou Mountains along the California state line.

1302　Harney County, largest of Oregon's 36 counties, with 10,228 square miles, is larger than the states of Connecticut, Delaware, and Rhode Island combined.

GOVERNMENT

1304 The first Provisional Government organized in an open field at Champoeg on May 2, 1843.

1305 The first incorporated city west of the Rocky Mountains was Oregon City, December 24, 1844.

1306 Harney County government has jurisdiction over Oregon's largest county. With 10,228 sq. miles, the county is larger than Connecticut, Delaware, and Rhode Island combined.

GOVERNMENT SERVICE

1307 The first mail service between Oregon City and the "stump town" settlement at Portland was begun in May, 1851.

1310 William Knighton is Oregon's first and last, to date, State Architect.

Cecil Edwards, Legislative Historian

1311 The oldest and longest-term employee of the state was Cecil Edwards, the only Legislative Historian. He started working for the State of Oregon in 1933, and he has held various positions, mostly with the legislature. Cecil Edwards turned 86 years old in 1992; he contributed to this book at times from 1990 until he retired on June 30, 1993.

GOLD

1314 Apparently, the first gold found and lost in Oregon was just off the Oregon Trail by the Stephen Meek-led group of pioneers. This was the legendary Blue Bucket mine.

1315 The first gold discovered and claimed in the Pacific Northwest was near Gold Hill (January 19, 1848).

1316 The largest gold nugget (80.4 oz.) in Oregon was found June 19, 1913, by George Armstrong on Pine Creek in Baker County. The nuggest is on display at the U. S. Bank in Baker City.

GRINDSTONE

1317 The first grindstone was made in 1848 by Peter Scholls at Scholls Ferry from a block of sandstone transported from Astoria.

HISTORIANS

1319 Frances Fuller Victor was Oregon's first historian (*River of the West, The Adventures of Joe Meek*, published 1870).

1320 Pennsylvania native George Himes was secretary of the Oregon Pioneers Association (est. 1873) for over four dozen years. He was a founder of the Oregon Historical Society, which incorporated on December 17, 1898.

1321 The first state archivist, David C. Duniway, was appointed on January 5, 1946, for keeping and verifying state records.

1322 With 35 years of service Thomas Vaughan was director of the Oregon Historical Society (1954 to 1989) for the longest time.

1322• The OHS Library first started charging nonmembers for admission on September 1, 1992.

HOTELS

1323 About 1854, the first hotel in Hillsboro was managed by Mrs. Mary Ramsey L. Wood. *(See #1082 for photo)*

HORTICULTURE

1324 The first rosebush was planted at the mission near Chemawa. John Minto bought the property, and he divided the roots and cuttings and sent them to various parts of the Northwest.

HOLIDAYS

1325 The first Thanksgiving Day in Oregon was approved by Governor John Whiteaker on December 29, 1859, in response to a petition by over six dozen ladies of Oregon City to appoint a day of thanksgiving. Oregon celebrated two Thanksgivings in 1893.

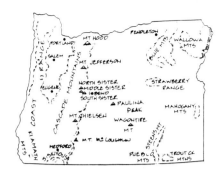

IMMIGRATION

1326   The first immigrants to cross the plains were led by Marcus Whitman. Some 80 wagons from Fort Hall traveled 600 miles. They helped break the first wagon road.

1327   In 1843, the first large immigration to Oregon had about 1,000 men, women, and children, bringing 126 wagons and 1,300 horses and cattle. These pioneers were educated, refined, sturdy, able, and willing to work. They raised Oregon from camp sites of hunters, trappers, and missionaries to the status of a territory ready for civil government.

1329   Thomas Fitzpatrick was the guide on the 1842 immigration west.

1330   The first naturalization in the Oregon Country was when Hugh Byrne of Great Britain became a U.S. citizen, recorded in Clatsop County Courthouse, 1856.

LABOR

1331   The first craft union, the Typographical Society, organized in Portland June 11, 1853. Resolutions adopted by the society called for a minimum wage, an attempt to control the labor market, and discouragement of machinery in the trade. In 1862, the National Typographical Union granted the journeymen in and around Portland a charter as the Typographical Society of Portland.

1332   The first general labor organization, Portland's Workingman's Protective Association, organized in September, 1869. The PWPA was against Chinese labor and resolved to boycott those who employed Orientals.

1334   The first labor newspaper, *Labor Gazette*, began publishing in Portland during the campaign of 1878.

1335   The first successful strike was a three-day strike in 1880, after which harness makers in Portland received raises of $1 from $2.50 to $3.50 a day and piece workers were granted a 20% increase.

1336   Though Oregon was second only to the State of Wisconsin in adopting regulations pertaining to apprenticeships, Oregon was a leader in apprenticeship protections in some occupations (e.g., forestry).

LAND USE

1337   The first city to have its land use plan reviewed and acknowledged by the Oregon Land Conservation and Development Commission (LCDC) was the City of Central Point on October 8, 1976.

1338   The first county to have its land use plan reviewed and acknowledged by the Oregon Land Conservation and Development Commission was Gilliam County on July 8, 1977.

1339   Gilliam County has the highest percentage (93%) of privately-owned land.

1340   Deschutes County has the lowest percentage (only 21.1%) of private ownership statewide.

1341   The first and only exception to Oregon's land-use planning and public beach laws is the 1988 Oregon Supreme Court case McDonald vs. Halvorson, regarding private use of Little Whale Cove in Lincoln County.

LEGISLATION

Many legislative acts passed by the Assembly are in-state firsts. Just a few of the significant laws not noted elsewhere, are noted below.

1343   The state's first legislative session, a special session, was held in May, 1859.

1344   In 1971, the Legislature enacted a comprehensive revision of the state's criminal laws, the first such revision in over 100 years.

1345   The Billboard Control Act was enacted in 1971. Though Oregon was the 30th to do so, Governor Tom McCall called it "**landmark legislation**" in anticipation of the removal of over 3,700 "landmarks" from interstate highways, primary highways, and other roads.

1346   Other significant laws include: Willamette Greenway Act, HB 2497, 1973; Field Burning, SB311, 1975; Rules of Civil Procedure HB 3131, 1979; Workers Compensation, SB 1197, 1990 Special session, The first smoking control law, allowing no smoking in meetings at state buildings passed (1975).

1347 In March, 1992, Hillsboro businessman Jerry Wilson started the first successful direct mail campaign to obtain signatures for an initiative. The measure called for "closure of Portland General Electric's Trojan Nuclear Power plant if a permanent waste storage site isn't opened within 30 days after the measure is approved, or if the Energy Facility Siting Council determines the plant can't withstand an earthquake of a magnitude of 9.5 on the Richter scale." The direct-mail campaign to all Oregonians cost at least $400,000 and, with personal canvassing, garnered enough signatures to place it on the November 2, 1992, election ballots. Two independent ballot measures were heavily outspent by the utilities and lost at the ballot box.

One week after defeating the initiatives, PGE closed Trojan anyway because of safety problems. In the **first week** of January, 1993, PGE announced it would keep Trojan closed permanently.

LIGHTHOUSES

1348 The first lighthouse was built inside the mouth of the Umpqua River in 1857. In part due to advancements in radar, only five of Oregon's nine lighthouses are still in operation (Tillamook Rock, Yaquina Bay, Cape Meares, Coquille River, and Cape Blanco). Only the Tillamook Lighthouse stands offshore.

LOTTERY

1349 Joyce Givens of Eugene won the northwest's largest jackpot, ($30,460,327.33) in the 14-state Powerball via a computer quick-pick in 1992. The largest lottery within the state ($23 million) was won by Oregonians Jan and Mike Maginnis on July 28, 1991.

MARRIAGES

1349• Beyond common law marriages, the first two weddings were performed on July 16, 1837, between Rev. Jason Lee and Miss Ann Maria Pittman and for Cyrus Shepard and Miss Susan Downing. Joseph Gervais later served as the first tour guide when he led Jason Lee and his bride to the coast for a honeymoon.

MEDICAL

1350 The first dentist was Dr. Griffin (1851).

1350• In 1865, the Medical Department at Willamette University was founded.

1350• St. Vincent in Portland was the first hospital, founded by the Sisters of Providence in 1875.

1351 The Oregon Health Sciences University (OHSU) pioneered the first open-heart surgery (1957), coronary bypass, and heart transplant (1985).

1352 OHSU is the only center in Oregon performing heart (1985), liver (1988), kidney (1959), pancreas (1987), and bone marrow (1990) transplants.

1353 The first lung transplanted in Oregon was on April 14, 1992, at OHSU into Lynda Chandler, a 50-year-old Hermiston resident, with Dr. Adnon Cobanoglu the chief surgeon.

1355 The first heart-lung transplant was a 13-hour operation on 21-year-old Jack Jones on April 2, 1993, at OHSU.

MILITARY

1356 The first Oregon Cavalry was organized in 1861 and had 19 commissioned officers.

MILLINERY AND DRESSES

1357 The first millinery and dress shop was in Olympia, Oregon Territory, and was owned by Mrs. Elizabeth Frazier. She received orders from all parts of the Northwest.

MISSIONS

1358 The first mission was established by Rev. Jason Lee ten miles north of the present Salem at Mission Bottom in October, 1834.

1359 Marcus and Narcissa Whitman established Waiilatpu Mission after guiding the first major immigrant train over the Oregon Trail.

MUSIC

1360 The first musical instrument, a piano, was bought to Oregon City by M.M. McCarver. General John Adair gave a piano to his wife, Mary Ann, in 1849 in Astoria.

1361 The musicians and instrument makers of Aurora were the best in Oregon and, some claimed, the "best in the West."

NEWSPAPERS

1362　The first weekly news sheet published on this side of the continent was the *Free Press* in Oregon City, March, 1848.

1363　The first newspaper in Oregon south of Portland was the *Umpqua Valley Gazette,* issued at Scottsburg, Umpqua County, Oregon Territory, April 28, 1854. Politically, it was a Democratic paper.

1364　The oldest continuously operating newspaper is *The Oregonian*, which was founded by two Portland businessmen, Stephen Coffin and William W. Chapman, on December 4, 1851. Portland had three other newspapers at the time, the *Oregon Journal, Evening Telegram*, and *Portland News*. The first *Sunday Oregonian* was published December 4, 1881.

1365　The first illustrated paper was the *West Shore*, established by L. Samuel in Portland, 1895.

NEWSPAPER EDITORS

1366　The earliest editor of the *Oregon Spectator* at Oregon City was William G. T'Vault, in February, 1845. John Fleming printed the paper.

1367　One of the first Black editors of a major newspaper in the U.S. is William Hilliard of *The Oregonian*. In 1993, Bill Hilliard became the first black man to serve as head of the American Society of Newspaper Editors.

ORGANIZATIONS

1369　The Citizens' Utility Board of Oregon (CUB) is the only non-governmental organization in Oregon to be approved and established by voters (637,698 voters) in November, 1984.

PHOTOGRAPHY

1370　Prior to photographers, there were a few daguerreotypists who didn't last long. The first four photographers were L. H. Wakefield, Peter Britt, D. H. Hendee, and Joseph Buchtel.

1371　Jacksonville's Peter Britt (Swiss-born) took the first photgraphic images of Crater Lake in 1874. These photos were used in the successful legislative proposal that led to making that scenic lake a national park.

POLICE

1372　F. X. Matthieu was one among the first four constables in the state.

POLITICS

Governors of Oregon

Oregon Provisional Governor
George Abernethy - 1845-1848

Oregon Territorial Governors
Joseph Lane - 1848-1850
Kintzing Prichette - 1850
John P. Gaines - 1851-1853
Joseph Lane - 1853
George L. Curry - 1853
John W. Davis - 1853-54
George L. Curry - 1854-59

Oregon State Governors
John Whiteaker - 1859-1861
Addison C. Gibbs - 1861-1865
George Lemuel Woods - 1866-1870
Lafayette Grover - 1870-1877
Stephen F. Chadwick - 1877-1879
William Wallace Thayer - 1879-1883
Zenas Ferry Moody - 1883-1887
Sylvester Pennoyer - 1887-1895
William Paine Lord - 1895-1899
Theodore T. Geer - 1899-1903
　　(first native Oregonian elected governor)
George Earle Chamberlain - 1903-1909
Frank W. Benson - 1909-1910
Jay Bowerman - 1910-1911
Oswald West - 1911-1915
James Withycombe - 1915-1919
Ben W. Olcott - 1919-1922
Walter M. Pierce - 1923-1927
Isaac Lee Patterson - 1927-1929
Albin W. Norblad - 1929-1930
Julius L. Meier - 1931-1935
Charles H. Martin - 1935-39
Charles Arthur Sprague - 1939-43
Earl W. Snell - 1943-1947
John Hubert Hall - 1947-1949
Douglas McKay - 1949-1953
Paul L. Patterson - 1953-1956
Elmo E. Smith - 1956-1957
Robert D. Holmes - 1957-1959
Mark O. Hatfield - 1959-1967
Tom McCall - 1967-1975
Robert Straub - 1975-1979
Victor Atiyeh - 1979-1987
Neil Goldschmidt - 1987-1991
Barbara Roberts - 1991-

POLITICS (continued)

1373 The first Republican convention in the Oregon Territory was held in 1847.

1374 The State of Oregon's first elected governor was John Whiteaker in 1859. He was the only person in Oregon history to serve as speaker of the state House of Representatives, president of the state Senate, governor, and as a member of Congress (1879-81).

1375 Although his term lasted only 17 days, Lafayette Grover was the first U.S. representative from Oregon. Grover, a Salem businessman, was elected to Congress in 1858 believing the assumption Oregon would soon become a state, but his term only lasted from statehood to expiration of Congress on March 3, 1859. While governor, Lafayette Grover worked to preserve salmon resources.

1376 Similarly, one of the first two U.S. Senators from Oregon, Delazon Smith, also served the briefest term: from statehood, February 14, to March 3, 1859.

1377 Luther Elkins was the first President of the Senate and B.F. Harding was the first Speaker of the House in 1860.

1378 G. Lemeux Woods was Oregon's youngest elected governor at 34 years.

1379 When U.S. President Benjamin Harrison visited Oregon in 1891, Oregon Governor Sylvester Pennoyer refused to see him.

1380 Charles Wickliff McBride was the first native Oregonian in the U.S. Senate (1895-1901).

1381 Jay Bowerman became Oregon's youngest governor at 33 years and 10 months. He was president of the Senate and took office when Governor Benson became incapacitated.

1382 Governor Oswald West had the most vetoes of legislation. Ranking close behind, Victor Atiyeh vetoed the second most legislative bills to reach the governor's desk.

1383 Miss Kathryn Clarke from Douglas County became Oregon's first woman State Senator from 1915-16, when she was elected to fill a vacancy for one term.

1384 Portland native Nan Wood Honeyman was the first woman to serve as a U.S. Congressional Representative from Oregon when she won a term in office 1937-39.

1385 Julius Meier was the first Independent (and first Jew) elected governor.

1385• Grace O. Peck from Multnomah County was elected and served the most terms by any woman in Oregon's House of Representatives: 11 terms (22 years) beginning in 1949.

1386 The first male Black judge, Aaron Brown, Jr., was appointed a full-time municipal judge for the City of Portland on November 20, 1969.

1387 Mercedes Diez became the first Black woman judge in 1970. Though competent, this 75-year-old judge was constitutionally required to retire because of her age in December, 1992, while still the only Black woman judge.

1387 Norma P. Paulus was the first woman to win a statewide office in Oregon in a statewide race, the Secretary of State position in 1978.

1388 Betty Roberts was the first woman judge on the Oregon State Court of Appeals (1977-82).

1389 Mary Wendy Roberts became the youngest woman legislator when she was elected a State Representative from Dist. 20 at age 27.

1390 Mary Wendy Roberts and her father Frank Roberts were the first father-daughter combination in the Oregon Senate simultaneously.

1391 Mary Wendy Roberts became the first woman to serve as state Labor Commissioner (1979).

1392 Mary Wendy Roberts was the first elected official in Oregon and perhaps the U.S. to bear a child while in office (a girl, Alexsandra), in 1980.

1393 Betty Roberts became the first woman State Supreme Court Justice (1982-86).

1394 Barbara Roberts became the first woman House Majority Leader (1983).

1395 Miss Marion B. Towne from Jackson County was the first woman elected to the Oregon House of Representatives (1919).

1396 Vera Katz, the first woman elected Speaker of the Oregon House of Representatives, became the first legislator to serve three terms in the Speaker position.

1397 Belle W. Cook was the first woman clerk in the Oregon Legislature.

1398 Hedy Rijken was elected the legislature's first woman Sergeant-at-Arms in 1981.

1399 Edith Bynon (Lowe) was the first woman in Oregon to serve as Chief Clerk.

1400 Charles Hanlon (1918-1990) of Mountaindale from Senate District #1 (Route 1, Cornelius) was the only State Senator elected as an Independent this century.

1401 Lt. Colonel Adria Hernandez was appointed Oregon National Guard's first female Battalion Commander on January 5, 1991. She had responsibility for approximately 450 soldiers.

1402 Raul Soto-Selig (1941-87), a Cuban immigrant, was appointed to the Oregon Senate (District 10, Portland) on September 26, 1977.

1402• Rocky Barilla became the first Hispanic elected to Oregon's House of Representatives in 1988.

1403 William (Bill) McCoy became the first African-American to serve as a State Representative in 1972.

1404 William McCoy was the first African-American in the Oregon Senate when appointed to replace Bill Stevenson in December, 1974. Bill McCoy was elected to the Oregon Senate in 1976 and has been re-elected four times.

1404• Pat Whiting was the first minority woman elected to the Oregon House (serving 1973-79). She is Filipino, Icelandic, and Indian.

1405 Gladys McCoy became the first African-American to serve as chairperson of a county commission in Oregon in 1987, after being the first African-American elected to the Portland School Board.

1406 Margaret Carter is the first African-American woman elected to Oregon's Legislature.

1407 Senator Paul Phillips of Tigard received the highest fine ever ($17,000) from the State Ethics Commission for violations of laws.

1408 Norma P. Paulus was the first woman elected as State Superintendent of Schools in 1990.

1409 Barbara Roberts in 1991 became the first elected woman governor.

1411 Judith Ramaley is the first woman to serve as president of a state university in Oregon (Portland State University).

1412 In 1990, Representative Jackie Taylor became the first Native American woman elected to the Oregon Legislature. An Astoria resident, Jackie is a member of the Potawatomi Tribe in Oklahoma.

1413 Gail Shibley is the first representative in the Oregon Legislature to openly declare herself a lesbian. She was appointed for the 1991-92 legislative term, ran for office, and won.

1414 Oregonians for the first time elected a person of color to a statewide position on November 3, 1992. The State Treasurer race offered the choice of Stan Chen or Jim Hill. The voters chose Jim Hill, a Black man, for treasurer.

1414• Elizabeth Furse may be the first professional peace activist elected to Congress (November 3, 1992, U.S. Congressional District #1).

1414• The voters approved a charter for Metro in the November, 1992, election. The charter is a first for a regional government in the U.S.

1414• On October 18, 1992, *The Oregonian*, the only statewide newspaper, endorsed a Democratic presidential candidate for the **first time ever** (since pre-Civil War) when it endorsed Governor Bill Clinton of Arkansas.

POPULATION

1415 Estimates indicate that over 100,000 Indians/ Native Americans lived within Oregon's borders. In 1843, the non-tribal population was about 350. From 1829-1843 there were at least 91 French Canadian families living at French Prairie. Many of the Americans who later came to Oregon were Confederates (Southern Democrats). The U.S. Census counted these totals of people living in Oregon:

1860	12,093
1870	54,465
1880	90,923
1890	174,768
1900	317,704
1910	413,536
1920	672,765
1930	783,389
1940	953,786
1950	1,089,684
1960	1,521,341
1970	1,768,687
1980	2,633,156
1990	2,842,321
estimate mid-1993	3,038,000

1990 Census and Race (as of April 1, 1990):

White	2,636,787
Black	46,178
Native American Indian	38,496
Asian-Pacific Islander	69,269
Other	51,591

Hispanics are Oregon's largest minority population. According to the U.S. Census Bureau, "Hispanic" is not a race. Hispanics are counted in the above total figures, and categorized by the U.S. Census into the following racial categories:

White	57,055
Black	1,196
Native American Indian	2,747
Asian-Pacific Islander	1,847
Other	49,862

Hispanic/Latino total population was 112,707.

1415• Washington County has been the fastest-growing county in the state since 1973.

POTTERY

1416 The first pottery in Oregon was made in Yamhill County near Newberg. J. C. Nelson worked there in 1844.

PRINTING

1417 Rev. Henry Spalding obtained the first press in the Oregon Country from a mission on the Sandwich Islands. The first printing press arrived in Oregon in 1839 and was immediately transported to Lapwai, accompanied by Edwin O. Hall, a Yankee printer.

(See photo #1100)

1419 Roselle Applegate Putnam was the west coast's first woman typesetter with her husband, who was printer for the *Oregon American and Evangelical Unionist* at Tualatin Plains in 1848.

1420 Asahel Bush, who founded the *Statesman Journal* in Salem in 1851, became the first and only "territorial printer" in 1859.

PUBLIC WORKS

1421 The largest public works project is the Westside Light Rail Project (about $688 million dollars) through the Tualatin Mountains to West 185th Avenue in Washington County.

1422 The first planetarium in Portland was dedicated on June 5, 1950.

RECREATION

1423 Cloud Cap Inn, built in 1889 at the 6,000-foot level of Mt. Hood, is the oldest mountain resort in Oregon.

1424 Crater Lake became the first National Park in Oregon in 1902.

1425 The seven-mile Larch Mountain Trail, the first hiking trail, was completed in 1915.

1425• The State Highway Commission received its first donation of lands for park purposes on February 15, 1922; it became the Sara Helmick State Park.

REFORESTATION

1426 An island in the Willamette River near Harrisburg was the site of the first reforestation effort in 1893. A crew of men from Oregon City's Willamette Pulp and Paper Company planted thousands of seedlings.

ROADS

1427 The first paths/trails were made by Indians. Later, some roads were built by settlers, and tolls were charged and sometimes paid.

1428 The West's first plank road was built up and over the Portland West Hills (Tualatin Mountains) in 1851.

1428• The City of Portland raised the speed limit from 8 mph to 10 mph in 1906.

1429 One of the first highways in Oregon, the Columbia River Highway, was completed in 1916 from Portland to Hood River.

1430 The first statewide bond issue was in 1917 for road construction "to pull Oregon out of the mud."

1431 The first official statewide road map was published in 1919.

1432 The first person with an Oregon driver's license was Arthur F. Allen, a druggist (1920).

1433 The low-tide "Hug Point Highway" was the first northern Oregon beach highway for pioneers around the point.

1434 The Steens Mountain Road is the highest road in Oregon at 9000+ feet above sea level.

SAWMILLS

1435 The first sawmill on the Pacific Coast was built at the mouth of a small creek six miles east of Vancouver about 1827. This sawmill was built by William H. Crate, who came from Canada for that purpose.

1437 The first sawmill in the state was built and operated near Champoeg in 1836.

1438 In 1850, the first steam sawmill was built in Portland at the bottom of Jefferson Street by Stephen Coffin and Cyrus Reed.

SCHOOLS

1439 In the summer of 1834, Solomon H. Smith established the first school at the farm of Joseph Gervais (pronounced jer-vay). The students were French Canadian and Indian.

1440 One of the few schools in Oregon from 1838-1842 was a log cabin on Cornelius Plains.

1441 Rev. Harvey Clark, an independent missionary, settled on the west Tualatin Plains in 1840. His gift of 200 acres helped establish Tualatin Academy (now Pacific University at Forest Grove).

1442 The first night school was started by A.D. Danburn in Oregon City in 1851.

1443 In 1869, the first public high school was established in Oregon City.

1444 Chemawa Indian School, the only Indian boarding school in Oregon, started in Forest Grove in 1880 and moved to Salem in 1885. Henry Minthorn was one of the first school superintendents in Forest Grove.

1445 Massachusetts native George Atkinson, who arrived by ship in 1848, brought the first school books sold in Oregon. He wrote the education portion of Territorial Governor Joseph Lane's inaugural address, which resulted in passage of the first school law, including a tax to fund schools.

1446 Fifty years ago there were lots of little schools. Most of these schools have been consolidated into centralized schools and districts.

SERMONS
1447 The first sermon was preached by Rev. Jason Lee at Fort Vancouver, September 28, 1834.

1448 The first sermon preached in the Willamette Valley was by Rev. Jason Lee in the home of Joseph Gervais, a Roman Catholic.

SETTLEMENTS
1449 The first European settlement west of the Rockies was established by the English at Fraser Lake in 1805.

1450 French Prairie was settled by French Canadians who had completed contracts with the Hudson's Bay Company. These British subjects built comfortable homes. Some of the houses were even painted. The French Canadians were kind and hospitable to newcomers. Recent excavations by the University of Oregon Anthropology Department have identified 53 sites and 93 families that lived at French Prairie from 1829 to 1843.

1451 The first white settlement on Sauvie Island (Wapato) was made in the fall of 1834 by Captain Nathanial J. Wyeth.

SETTLERS
1452 The first white settlers in the Willamette Valley included French Canadians Etienne Lucier and Joseph Gervais in 1829, and American William Cannon.

1453 Jason Lee and two companions representing the Methodist Mission settled just below the townsite of Salem in October, 1834.

1454 Miyo Iwakoshi, who came to Oregon in 1880 and settled near the current Gresham, was the first permanent Japanese settler.

SHIPWRECKS
1455 A Spanish galleon, *San Augustin,* homeward bound for the Phillipines which drifted off its course and was lost off Nehalem Beach, was the first shipwreck of record (1595). Beeswax from the cargo was found in 1813 and 150 years later was carbon-dated to being about 300 years old.

STOVE
1457 The first iron stove ever to be cast in Oregon was received by the Ladd and Tilton Bank from the Oswego Smelting Works on March 3, 1868.

TAXES (See #134)

TELECOMMUNICATIONS
1459 The first telegraph station was opened between Portland and Oregon City (November 16, 1855); Corvallis (1856); Salem (1863); San Francisco, transcontinental points (1864).

1460 The first transcontinental telephone message over Pacific Telephone Company wires from Portland to New York City was on December 27, 1916. Robert Gumbert Smith, aged 3.5 years, was the youngest person to talk by telephone across country.

1461 The first radio broadcasting in Oregon took place when Charles Austin broadcast phonograph records from his home at Mt. Tabor in Portland in 1921 under an experimental license and the call letters 7XG.

1462 The first regular radio license in Oregon was issued to Clifford Watson and Joe Hallock on January 7, 1922. Their radio station, KGG, was the first of several stations licensed early in 1922 (including KGW).

1463 KGW Radio was Oregon's first local commercial radio station. It went on the airwaves March 25,1922, for two to three hours daily.

1464 Oregon Public Broadcasting (OPB) is the only statewide radio and television network. It started in 1922. By 1993 OPB had five TV and four radio stations.

1465 KGW became Oregon's first station to connect to a major radio network (NBC) on February 22, 1927.

1466 KPTV-TV Channel 27 became Oregon's first television station in 1952, and the first UHF television station in the world.

1466• KGW-TV broadcast the first network progam in color in 1954.

TRADE and TRANSPORTATION
Trade

1467   Celilo Falls was the first large trading place for many tribes drawing people from as far away as Montana, California, the Great Plains, British Columbia, Canada, for thousands of years. They traded foods (especially salmon), clothes, blankets, baskets, horses, shells, beads, seeds, and more. *(See photo page 162)*

1467•   The first trading post in the Willamette Valley, the Willamette Post, was established on French Prairie in 1811 to trade for fur by the Astor Company. Game was cured and sent downriver to Fort Astoria. A granary and grain market were set up in 1829 or 1830. It was the first warehouse of the Hudson's Bay Company on the Willamette River.

1468   Seid Back, once the Northwest's largest importer of Oriental goods, was a nationally-known Chinese immigrant in Portland. He owned a 400-acre hop farm in Independence. His son was the nation's first Chinese lawyer.

1469   The Legislature created the Port of Portland in 1891, and empowered it to dredge and maintain the river channel at a 25-foot depth.

Automobiles and Trucks

1470   In 1899, the first automobile arrived in Oregon. It was an 1898 Locomobile purchased by Henry Wemme for $600 from the Stanley Brothers plant in Newtown, Massachusetts, and shipped by rail to Oregon.

1470•   Oregon Governor Oswald West declared the ocean beaches as state highways in 1913.

1471   Emmert International, Inc., of Clackamas moved the largest building ever moved in Oregon, a 300-ton building that was the Finnish Hall.

Aviation

In 1905 dirigible flights above the Lewis & Clark Exposition introduced the aviation era in Oregon.

1472   Charles Lindbergh of New Jersey flew the *Spirit of St. Louis* into Portland to help formally dedicate the first municipal airport on Swan Island on September 14, 1927. (Lindbergh flew the *Spirit of St. Louis* across the Atlantic Ocean on May 20-21, 1927, the first trans-Atlantic and longest non-stop solo flight in history.)

1473   The Long Brothers were one of the state's first kit plane manufacturers. Operating from Long Airfield one mile north of Cornelius in the 1920s, the Long Brothers were among the best-known kit makers in the country.

1474   Faye "Tiny" Carter was the first woman to sign up for flying lessons in the Northwest and the first woman pilot to solo.

1475   Ann Bohrer, Faye Carter, and Dorothy Hester (in that order) were the first women to parachute from a plane in the Northwest.

1477   Direct Air Mail service was established between Portland and points east on September 15, 1929, when Varney Air Plane, piloted by Joe Taft, left Swan Island airport.

1478   Bernard Airport in Beaverton (1914) was the oldest airport in the 1960s.

1479   The Port of Portland-Hillsboro Airport is the busiest airport in the state.

Boats and Vessels

1481   The first ocean-going boat built in Oregon was the *Star of Oregon* in 1840-41, by eight men led by Joseph Gale.

1482   The first state portage law passed in 1846, and S. C. Reeves became the first licensed pilot for the Columbia River Bar in 1847.

1483   The steamboat *Canemah* was the first waterborne Oregon post office. It served all riverside communities (1852-53).

1484   The state's first steamboat, the *Columbia*, was a little sidewheeler built at upper Astoria. Its first trip was July 3, 1850, to Portland and Oregon City.

1485   The Oregon Steam Navigation Company had a monopoly on the Columbia River in 1862.

1486   Cape Arago had the first U.S. life-saving station (1876).

1487   The ocean-going ship *Glenesslin*, constructed in Glasgow, Scotland, in 1865, held the speed record of 74 days, sailing between Portland, Oregon and New Jersey. The *Glenesslin* shipwrecked at the foot of Neah-Kah-Nie Mountain, north of Manzanita, on October 1, 1913. The Tillamook County Museum has the ship's bell.

1488   The first vessel recorded to be built in the Northwest was by the English in 1788. It was a small schooner, *Northwest America*, launched September 20, 1788.

1489 The first steam vessel to navigate the Pacific Ocean and Oregon waters was the Hudson's Bay Company's steamer *Beaver*, which departed Gravesend, England August 27, 1835, and arrived in Fort Vancouver April 10, 1836.

1490 The last passenger ships operated with a Portland base were three sisters, *General Sherman, General Pershing,* and *General Lee,* which States Lines operated to Japan, China, and the Philippines from 1932-37.

1491 Port Orford is the farthest west of Oregon's ports.

1492 The only mail boat serving Oregon residents and one of three nationally is the Rogue River Mail Boat which transports mail and people 32 miles to Agness and has operated continuously since 1895. Another mail boat operates along the Snake River and Hell's Canyon area, but it serves only postal customers in Idaho.

Pony Express and Stage Coaches

1493 Some mail transportation during the territorial days was by Pony Express. Newspaper editor and postmaster general William G. T'Vault set up the earliest Pony Express route (1846). It looped around Tuality, Yamhill, and Polk counties, and to the Oregon Institute in Champoeg County, north to French Prairie, and returned to Oregon City.

1494 Hugh Daniel Burns was the Oregon Territory's first Pony Express rider. He rode east over the Rocky Mountains. He carried mail on horseback to Weston, Missouri, in 1846, making the round trip in four months.

1495 The first and only wheeled mail route in the Oregon Territory was between Salem and Oregon City in 1850. It was run by Charles Frederick Ray, who also operated the first mail route out of Portland.

1496 The first stage line began in 1857. In 1860, stagecoach service from Portland to Sacramento was on daily basis.

Trains and Streetcars

1497 The first streetcar system was the horse line established in Portland in 1871.

1498 The first electric trolley car line, the Willamette Bridge Railway, began operations on November 1, 1889, from Albina over the bridge to Third and Glisan. It was established by Swigart and Campbell.

1499 The first locomotive used in the Oregon Territory was the *Oregon Pony*. It was built in 1862 for the Oregon Steam Navigation Company and used at The Cascades (now Cascade Locks) to move freight and passengers past the rapids above Bonneville. The first railroad tracks were laid by Joseph Ruckell and Herman Olmstead in 1859.

1500 The first railroad constructed through the Willamette Valley from Portland was in 1870.

1501 Oregon Railroad and Navigation Company was the first railroad with tracks into Portland from the east (The Dalles, 1882). The first Northern Pacific transcontinental train arrived in Portland on September 11, 1883.

1502 The first railroad sections built connecting Portland all the way to Seattle were laid by 1895.

1503 Prineville is the nation's first city to own a railroad. The City of Prineville completed the 19.4-mile railroad in 1918 to transport pine timber to the Oregon Trunk Line northeast of Redmond.

Wagons

1504 The first wagon brought from Fort Hall to Fort Walla Walla in 1840 by Robert "Doc" Newell, Joseph Meek, Caleb Wilkins, and Francis Ermatinger.

1505 The first wagon to cross the Cascades was led by Samuel K. Barlow in 1846. He opened the road so settlers could bring their wagons into the valley. He started in October, 1846, with 40 people and 20 wagons. They made the journey of 80 miles in two months and 24 days. The wagons were left at Fort Deposit near the top east side of the mountain (1846).

VINEYARDS

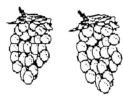

1509   The first wineries were established in the 1890s in Grants Pass and western Washington County. They were gone before or by Prohibition.

1510   The state's oldest fruit and berry wineries, which started before Prohibition, are Honeywood in Salem and Henry Endres in Oregon City.

1511   The first post-Prohibition planting of vinifera grapes for the purpose of producing varietal wines was the Hillcrest Vineyard (1961) in Roseburg, started by wine pioneer Richard Summer.

1512   Montinore Vineyard in Dilley has the largest planting of grapes.

WEATHER

Few states have as wide a range of weather extremes as Oregon. Annual precipitation ranges from 128" in the coastal range to 7" in the Alvord Desert. The average annual precipitation at the Portland International Airport is 37.39 inches.

Oregon's climatic diversity was evident during the first week of April, 1990, when Governor Barbara Roberts declared drought conditions in seven Oregon counties and flood conditions in Tillamook County.
From late 1992 until early 1993 all Oregon counties had drought conditions.

1513   The peak wind gust was 96 miles per hour in Astoria during the infamous Columbus Day storm, October 12, 1962.

1513•   On the other hand, the weather can be calm. The first national record held by an Oregon weather station was the "lowest annual average wind speed, 4.3 miles an hour at Roseburg."

1514   The least precipitation in one calendar year was measured at the Warm Springs Reservoir in 1939 (3.33 inches).

1515   The most snow that has ever fallen on Portland in one 24-hour period (January 31 to February 1, 1950) was 16 inches.

1515•   The most snow that has ever fallen on an Oregon locale in one storm was at Crater Lake, March 16-25, 1975, totalling 119 inches.

1516   The most snow that ever fell at a locale in one month was at Crater Lake in January, 1933, with 256 inches, or over 21 feet.

1517   The greatest snow depth ever recorded in Oregon was 246 inches at Timberline Lodge in Clackamas County on March 19, 1950.

1517•   The greatest snowfall in one season was at Crater Lake, 879 inches or 73 feet (1932-33).

1517•   The greatest measure of snowfall in twenty-four hours was 39 inches at Bonneville Dam, January 8-9, 1980.

1518   In 1898, Oregonians in the eastern and central communities of Pendleton and Prineville experienced the hottest temperature ever recorded in Oregon, 119° F.

1519   In February, 1933, the two communities of Ukiah and Seneca recorded Oregon's lowest temperature: -54° F.

1519•   Cottage Grove resident Earl Stewart has been recording the weather for the National Weather Service since 1917, longer than anyone else (75 years). He's recorded over 27,000 observations.

WEAVING

1521   The first flax wheel was brought out over the Oregon Trail by Nancy Morrison, as were flax seed, bobbins, weaving sleighs, and all the necessities to manufacture clothes. Women did almost all the cooking, dairy management, spinning, weaving, and soapmaking on the Oregon Trail and in early Oregon.

WHISKEY

1522   The first moonshine whiskey was made in Oregon City in 1838.

WILDLIFE REFUGES

1523   Hart Mountain is the largest Federal Wildlife Refuge in Oregon, with 240,374 acres.

1524   Murderer's Creek is the largest State Wildlife Refuge, with 21,037 acres.

1524•   The only wilderness in Oregon where people cannot go is the Oregon Islands National Wilderness. This animal refuge includes 1,400 island rocks and reefs for sea bird colonies from Tillamook Head to Bandon (Goat Island).

Dubious Firsts and Lasts

Not all chronological and ranking firsts are positive. Defining firsts as dubious depends upon your perspective, e.g., first gas tax versus high gas taxes. Some firsts are notorious, others can be disappointments, and still others big embarrassments, but most are learning experiences.

1525 Hugh DeAutremont (age 19) and his twin brothers Ray and Roy (age 23) staged **the last** great train robbery in the nation on October 11, 1923, south of Ashland in Southern Oregon. The brothers were looking for gold, and blew up a U.S. mail car, killing the mail clerk and the engineer. The fireman and brakeman were shot dead. The DeAutremont brothers murdered four men but did not get any money or gold. Millions of WANTED posters were printed in at least six languages. Hugh was arrested in Manila, Phillipine Islands, in 1927 and his twin brothers were later arrested in Ohio. The three DeAutremonts were sentenced to life in the Oregon State Penitentiary. This was the only recorded occurrence of a train being held up in a tunnel during daytime.

1526 The world's **first successful skyjacking** of a commercial airliner started in Portland, Oregon, when "D. B. Cooper" boarded a Northwest Orient Airlines Boeing 727 at Portland International Airport on November 24, 1971. "D. B. Cooper" gave a stewardess a note demanding $200,000 and claiming he had a bomb in his briefcase. The airline provided the $200,000 at a brief stop at the Sea-Tac Airport. Above southwest Washington, perhaps near Ariel, "D. B. Cooper" parachuted with the money at about 10,000 feet into a freezing rainstorm wearing loafers with a business suit.

1527 In 1979, the Wage and Hour Commission promulgated a rule that lowered the minimum wage for minors in an attempt to get more people into the job market. This made Oregon **the first state in the nation to lower the minimum wage, as a training wage.** KIDS AGAINST THE CUT fought it, sued the state, and won when the Court of Appeals invalidated the rule and the 1981 Legislature took away that minimum wage for children.

1528 The 14-state regional telephone company which serves 70% of Oregon, U S WEST Communications, received the **largest fine levied ($10 million) by the U. S. Department of Justice. By manufacturing equipment, U S WEST Communications** violated the 1984 Modified Divestiture Judgement, the anti-trust break-up of the AT&T Bell System monopoly.

1529 During the late 1980s until 1992, Oregon was the only state in which the statewide Poison Control Center was not listed on the inside front cover of telephone directories. In 1981 legislation required that only the **911** emergency response telephone be listed on the inside front cover of directories. Other 24-hour emergency services (e.g., Poison Control, FBI, Coast Guard, etc.) were deleted. 1991 legislation allows Enhanced 911 and listing of Poison Control with other 24-hour emergency numbers (including suicide prevention/mental health) on the inside front cover of directories.

1530 The Washington Public Power Supply System (WPPSS) was involved in the largest municipal bond default in U.S. history in 1982. WPPSS bonds were sold from 1972 to 1981. Of five nuclear power plants which were begun, only one (WNP #2) at Hanford is successfully operating and creating nuclear waste. Over $2.25 billion worth of bonds were issued, and over $5.15 billion interest accrued over 30 years to maturity totals of about $7.4 billion.

Many northwest residents lost a lot of money in this debacle, WHOOPS!

There were 115 total organizations in WPPSS from Oregon, Washington, California, Idaho, Montana, Nevada, and Wyoming. WPPSS, which started in 1957, was comprised of over twenty public agencies in Washington and also included **the following 31 Oregon public and private utilities.**

Public and Peoples' Utility Districts
Central Lincoln Public Utility District
Clatskanie Peoples' Utility District
Northern Wasco County Peoples' Utility District
Tillamook Public Utility District

Municipalities
City of Bandon
City of Canby
City of Cascade Locks
City of Drain
City of Eugene
City of Forest Grove
City of McMinnville
City of Milton-Freewater

City of Monmouth
Springfield Utility Board

Cooperatives
Blanchly-Lane County Cooperative
        Electric Association
Columbia Basin Electric Co-op., Inc.
Central Electric Cooperative, Inc.
Columbia Power Co-op. Association, Inc.
Consumers Power, Inc.
Coos-Curry Electric Co-op., Inc.
Douglas Electric Cooperative, Inc.
Harney Electric Co-op., Inc.
Hood River Electric Co-op., Inc.
Lane County Electric Co-op., Inc.
Midstate Electric Cooperative, Inc.
Salem Electric
Umatilla Electric Co-op. Association
Wasco Electric Cooperative, Inc.
West Oregon Electric Co-op., Inc.

Investor-owned Utilities
Pacific Power & Light Company
Portland General Electric Co.

1530• In 1992, the American Rivers Council declared the Columbia River **"the most endangered river system in the United States."** Native species of fish are endangered by the hydroelectric dams and low-water flows. The Hanford Nuclear Reservation in the State of Washington, one of the largest nuclear waste dumps in the world, was built on ceded tribal lands beside the river. The Columbia River flows through the nuclear reservation. The Hanford site will be one of the costliest sites in the U.S. to clean up. Plutonium is radioactive for thousands of generations. There will be **more dam controversy.**

GREEN
MOUNTAIN
WATERSHED COMMITTEE

1531 **Oregon is the last state** (hopefully) **to try to site a long-term landfill near the top of a mountain.** In 1987, the Oregon Department of Environmental Quality and the Environmental Quality Council selected, among 58 sites, one near the top of Green Mountain in the coastal foothills northwest of Banks for a 50- to 60-year landfill for the Portland metropolitan area. Residents formed the Helvetia-Mountaindale Preservation Coalition and the Green Mountain Watershed Committee to fight the siting. Victories in legal proceedings prevented the siting on Green Mountain.

Instead, a site was chosen near Arlington in Central Oregon which wanted the landfill and where there's little rainfall and leachate evaporates. Over $120,000 in private funds was spent to fight the Green Mountain selection.

1532 From 1988 to 1991, Oregon ranked as the **nation's No. 1 bank robbery state per capita.** Robbers held up an average one bank a day in Oregon in 1988, running up an in-state record of 363 holdups. While Oregon ranks far ahead first per capita, it ranked fourth in 1988 and sixth in 1989 numerically with only the states of California, New York, Florida, Michigan, and Massachusetts having more bank robberies.

1533 **The 1990 property tax limitation** (Ballot Measure 5) was passed with 53% approval and 47% disapproval of the voters. A citizen initiative co-authored by Don McIntire of Gresham and Tom Denehy **is the first state-wide property tax limitation approved by voters that gives so large a portion of the tax benefits to business property owners, especially out-of-state corporations.** Whereas the totals of voters from urban areas supported this form of tax relief, voters in rural counties did not. Renters received no relief. The consequences of the property tax limitation will change the face of Oregon government, affecting the quality of life for years to come, and creating the need for more innovations. *(See also #230)*

1534 Initial effects of the tax limitation include, for example, the longest legislative session (1993) (207 days). In 1991, Governor Barbara Robert's Conversation with Oregon, which used Ed-Net, was an experiment in electronic democracy to understand taxing issues. This Conversation with Oregon was a discussion of government services and how to pay for them following voter approval of the wide-ranging property-tax limitation. Five hundred meetings were arranged with 10,000 randomly-selected voters. Two-way audio was used with one-way video at 60 locations.

1535 In May, 1992, voters in the City of Springfield were the first in the nation to approve an **anti-gay rights initiative** (Ballot #20-08) into law. Chief Petitioner was Loretta Neat of Springfield Oregon Citizens Alliance. The initiative limits civil rights of some Oregonians (gays and lesbians) and restricts government. In June, 1993, four counties (Douglas, Josephine, Linn, Klamath) and two cities (Canby, Junction City) passed similar initiatives, the most in the nation. The 1993 Oregon Legislature passed a pre-emptive statute preventing anti-gay rights laws at the local level.

1537 The official fall 1992 State of Oregon **Voter's Pamphlet** was the first one in the nation to be printed and distributed with **a warning label**. Secretary of State Phil Keisling warned readers, "Some arguments for and against ballot measures that have been submitted for inclusion in the pamphlet contain language that citizens and parents may find objectionable."

1538 Gasoline prices in Portland were higher ($1.26/gallon) than any of 42 major U.S. cities surveyed by *Oil and Gas Journal* on September 13, 1993.

1539 **The nation's first felony conviction for spreading the HIV virus that causes AIDS** was given to Alberto Gonzalez, a 29-year-old Portlander. In November, 1992, a Multnomah County jury found Gonzalez guilty of murder and assault with a deadly weapon. He was sentenced to nine years in jail, but it's uncertain he will live that long.

1540 Five-term U.S. Senator Bob Packwood spent $5.4 million more than his opponent Congressman Walter (Les) AuCoin for Oregon's U.S. Senate position in 1992. This spending difference was the greatest spending gap between any incumbent U.S. senator and a challenger that year.

1541 Despite numerous denials to reporters from major newspapers and to Oregonians during the campaign, after the November, 1992, election the junior U.S. Senator from Oregon, Bob Packwood, was accused by over two dozen women lobbyists and former employees of making uninvited and unwanted sexual advances over a period of twenty years. Though it is not a chronological first, this ranks by far as the **most public accusations of sexual misconduct against any United States Senator**.

These sexual misconduct allegations posed legal **"matters of first impression"** for the United States Senate. In January of 1993, the U. S. Senate Rules Committee held a hearing on this case as a result of **unprecedented action,** receipt of five petitions signed by 250 Oregon voters asking that Bob Packwood not be seated because he won the election by fraudulent means.

Senator Packwood may have set another precedent when his actions represented the first time a United States senator failed to cooperate in an ethics committee proceeding: a request to provide his complete diaries. The full U.S. Senate debated two full days, and voted overwhelmingly (94 to 4) to enforce a subpeona on Senator Robert Packwood for his diaries. The Senate Ethics Committee investigation report had not been released and possible censure or expulsion decisions not made when this book went to press.

The voters' powers to recall elected officials exist at state and local government levels *(see #223)* but not *(yet?)* at the federal level.

Future Firsts

Oregon Benchmarks

Upon the request of Governor Neil Goldschmidt, the Oregon Legislature established the Oregon Progress Board in June, 1989. The Oregon Progress Board is a nine-member group, chaired and appointed by the governor. Its mission is to keep Oregon focused on those actions and opportunities that are fundamental for building a prosperous and rewarding future for Oregon and its citizens.

The Oregon Progress Board adopted the first *Oregon Benchmarks* in 1991. The 157 benchmarks were presented by Governor Neil Goldschmidt to the 1991 Legislature. The Oregon Benchmarks were developed through a citizen involvement process to identify **goals for people, the quality of life, and the economy over the next five, ten, 15, and 20 years. These goals are revised through citizen input.** The benchmarks become tools to achieve goals.

The **Human Investment Strategy** establishes a partnership of citizens, community leaders, higher education, government, and organizational development professionals to achieve a common goal.

Oregon is on the cutting edge of developing and implementing a human investment strategy emphasizing investment in people as a major key to economic and social well-being in the 21st century. The goal of **Oregon's Human Investment Strategy** is to ensure that residents have the preparation and support to be skilled workers, competent parents, and active citizens.

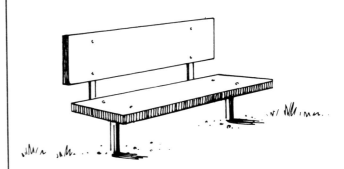

Oregon is the first state with measurable goals approved *(Oregon Benchmarks)*, published, distributed, and being used. Every state in the union requested at least one copy of the 1991 Oregon Benchmarks, as have various countries, e.g., New Zealand, Australia, and sixty different jurisdictions in Canada. The second state to set measurable goals, Minnesota, has printed and distributed its first edition of the **Minnesota Milestones.** Other states which are taking similar planning actions include Arkansas, Indiana, Kansas, North Carolina, Texas, New Mexico, and Montana.

On the following pages is a summary of the **Oregon Benchmarks Report to the 1993 Oregon Legislature.** This summary does not provide all the specific numerical rates and percentages for the five-, ten-, 15-, and 20-year goals.

GOALS FOR PEOPLE

The Oregon Human Investment Strategy is a set of seventy social and health goals or "benchmarks." The following is a summary of problem areas and does not include the annual numeric rates.

HEALTH for Children and Families
DECREASE:
teen pregnancy rate
teen birth rate
child abuse
spousal abuse and violence
homelessness
out-of-wedlock births
HIV-positive child-bearing women
infant mortality by racial and ethnic group

INCREASE:
pregnant women not using illicit drugs, alcohol, tobacco
percentage of citizens above the poverty level
child support paid
adequate prenatal care
healthy birthweight babies
adequately immunized two-year olds

EDUCATION
INCREASE:
student skills (3rd, 5th, 8th, 11th grades)
foreign-language proficiency of high school graduates
baccalaureate graduates
foreign language proficiency of higher education graduates
satisfaction with higher education
high school graduation rate
certified apprenticeship program completion
number of businesses training their workforce
employer payroll dedicated to training and education
percentage of displaced workers employed within 24 months
English literacy skills
information/technology literacy
multilingual skills
geography knowledge
participation in cultural exchanges

DECREASE:
student involvement with alcohol, illicit drugs,and tobacco
sexually transmitted disease rate
number of weapons at school

OTHER MEASURABLE EDUCATION GOALS:
kindergarten teachers
national education
assessmentseconomically disadvantaged urban schools
international reading, math, and science assessments
improve aerobic exercise rate of high school students
high school students with technical education
high school students enrolled in work experience
disabled high school students with successful transition
profile of 25-year-olds
adult formal education attainment

ADULT HEALTH
INCREASE:
number using vehicle safety restraints
number with normal blood pressure
weight-to-height ratio maintenance
number who exercise aerobically.
adults drinking alcohol in moderation
number of adults not smoking tobacco
percent of adults with good health practices

DECREASE:
the occupational illness and injury rate
HIV and AIDS
sexually transmitted disease rate for adults 20 to 44 years old
tuberculosis incidence rate
hepatitis B rate
years of potential life lost
percentage of adults who abuse drugs
substance use death rates
deaths linked to alcohol and drug use

deaths related to tobacco use
deaths due to unintentional injuries
the suicide rate
deaths due to AIDS annually

INCREASE:
successful business ownership
employment in underrepresented
    occupations
percentage of schools with culturally
    diverse curricula
percentage of schools with conflict
    resolution curricula

DECREASE:
hate crimes
workplace civil rights complaints

OTHER MEASURABLE HEALTH
GOALS:
elected and appointed officials

SENIORS
INCREASE:
percentage living independently or with
    adequate support
percentage employed 15 hours/week
percentage living above poverty level
percentage in housing with adequate
    support
percentage living above the poverty level

DECREASE:
elder abuse rate
percentage who aren't employed

DEVELOPMENTALLY DISABLED
INCREASE:
housing with adequate support
percentage employed
percentage above the poverty level

PHYSICAL DISABILITIES
INCREASE:
percentage living with adequate support
percentage who are employed
percentage living above poverty level

OTHER MEASURABLE PEOPLE
GOALS:
Customer Satisfaction Survey
increase skills to compete in a global
    economy
help families and individuals in need
provide primary and secondary education
control drug use

QUALITY-OF-LIFE GOALS
INCREASE/IMPROVE:
air quality standards met
river and stream quality standards met
groundwater quantity
in-stream flow needs met
agricultural land preservation
rangeland condition
forestland preservation
wetlands preserved
wild salmon and steelhead counts.
non-single occupant commuting vehicles
percentage who commute within 30
    minutes to and from work
percentage served by public libraries
eligible citizens registered to vote
eligible citizens who vote
rank of state in percent of voters
number of citizens with 50 hours of
    volunteer time/year
citizens understanding state government
percentage of citizens with a positive view
    of Oregon
percentage of citizens with economic
    access to health care
percentage of citizens with geographic
    access to health care
percentage with access to treatment for
    mental or emotional problems
percentage of seniors seeking nursing
    homes who access them
percentage seeking drug or alcohol treat
    ment who receive it
percentage of offenders needing drug and
    alcohol treatment who receive it
percentage of child care
accredited child care facilities as a percent
    of regulated child care facilities
number of identified child care slots per
    population under age 13
percentage of families for whom child care
    is affordable

QUALITY-OF-LIFE GOALS
(continued)

DECREASE/REDUCE:
carbon dioxide emissions
soil loss, soil erosion rates
miles of limited access highway congested
    at peak hours
transit hours per capita
vehicle miles traveled per capita
homelessness
energy use per dollar of household income
    (BTU per dollar)
property damage due to wild fires
structure fire damage
other crimes punishable by statute
juvenile arrests
reincarceration of paroled offenders
number of arrestees with drugs in system
parole revocations involving substance
    abuse problems
time judicial system takes to resolve cases
felony arrest rate per population
felony conviction rate per population
victimization rates: homicides and hate
    crimes
drinking water not meeting health
    standards
sewage disposal not meeting government
    standards

OTHER MEASURABLE QUALITY OF
LIFE GOALS:
hazardous waste site clean-up
high-level radioactive nuclear
    waste clean-up at the Hanford Nuclear
    Reservation in Washington
solid waste landfilled/incinerated
native wildlife species threatened, endan-
    gered, sensitive, uncertain, and healthy
native plant species threatened, endan-
    gered, sensitive, uncertain and healthy
amount of wilderness public land
multipurpose public land
parks and recreation per population
new developments within walking
    distance of services
existing developments within walking
    distance of services
developments within urban growth bound-
    aries

residences per acre within urban growth
    boundaries
Sub/urban land preserved as natural
metropolitan land preserved as open space
parks and recreation area acreage per capita
affordable housing (% median price)
percentage below median income spend
    ing 30% or less of household income on
    housing
number of families with children in
    affordable housing
public buildings accessible to those
    with physical disabilities
55-mile-per-hour highways
intercity passenger bus, van, or rail service
living within 50 miles of airport with daily
    passenger service
improve local emergency management
    programs capabililty to respond
arts events attended per capita
serious crimes index
community-based plans for law
    enforcement
improve rank of state in per capita arts
    funding
percentage of counties with international
    cultural exchanges
disabled needing in-home support
percentage of injured workers receiving
    adequate support facilities which
    meet established basic standards
customer satisfaction measures

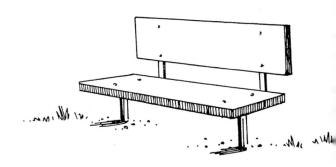

This is a summary of problem areas for
which five-, ten-, 15-, and 20-year goals
were adopted by the Oregon Legislature.
This summary does not include the five-
year numeric rates and percentages to
measure progress in meeting these goals.

GOALS for the ECONOMY

INCREASE/IMPROVE:

per capita income

per capita income among racial and ethnic groups

female-to-male ratio of mean annual incomes

level of real per capita income number of households with net assets over $10,000

average annual pay per worker

percentage of incomes over poverty level

percentage with incomes above 125% of the poverty level

percent employed outside Willamette Valley and Portland

total employment

increase small business startups

companies with high performance practice

percentage of employers with work experience programs

number of employers who engage apprenticeship programs

employer payments dedicated to training and education

percentage of employers who offer child care benefits

improve concentration of

employment in manufacturing

percentage of manufacturing employees outside five largest manufacturing sectors

professional services exported

manufactured goods sold outside the US.

nonstop air flights to cities over 1 million population

direct or non-stop air flights to international cities over one million population

percentage of households with single-party touchtone-capable telephone service

percentage of telephone lines that can reliably transmit data at medium speed

percentage of households with personal computers to transmit data via telecommunications

percentage of households with access to high-speed multichannel telecommunications lines

venture capital invested per capita ranking in federal research and development funding per capita

ranking in private research and development per capita

ranking in patents issued per capita

real per capita capital outlay for public facilities

percentage of public agencies which are high-performance work organizations

percentage of government agencies that employ results-oriented performance measures

improve ranking in national magazine rating of state governments

DECREASE:

worker's compensation costs

rank among states in high health care costs

health care costs relative to 1980 costs (inflation adjusted)

total energy bill as a percentage of personal income

backlog of public bridges in need of repair and preservation

DIVERSE INDUSTRY

producer services

forest products

visitor industry

high technology

agricultural products

environmental services

primary and fabricated metals

software

aerospace

plastics

biotechnology

fisheries

mining

film and video

arts industry

OTHER MEASURABLE ECONOMIC GOALS:

percentage in the middle income range

percentage employed outside the Portland metropolitan area

improve state general obligation bond rating

average electricity rates rank

average industrial electricity rates

natural gas rates

<u>MEASURABLE ECONOMIC GOALS</u>
(continued)
natural gas transmission and distribution
    services to industries
industrial acreage suitable for development
river miles not up to water quality stan-
    dards
developable acres without quality air
percentage of forest land available for
    timber harvest
board feet of timber harvested/year
permits issued within time period
Portland trans-Pacific container
    export rates compared to Seattle and
    Tacoma
taxes per capita as % of U.S.
taxes per capita by type of tax
ranking in per capita state and local taxes,
    by type of tax
business taxes

These goals for people, quality of life, and the economy can and will be revised through citizens' input. If you have questions or suggestions the **Oregon Benchmarks Report to the 1993 Legislature** is available through the

**Oregon Progress Board
775 Summer Street, N.E.
Salem, Oregon   97310
(503) 373-1220**

Projections of Future Firsts

- When plans come to fruition, Portland will have the most bridges lighted for display in North America.

- Planning began in 1992 for a 200th anniversary of the Lewis and Clark Expedition in 2005-2006, which will include displays of more Oregon Firsts.

- Many more firsts locally and worldwide will lead our way into the future.

Prologue

The values applied by Oregonians since pioneer times in developing predominantly positive historical firsts indicate a desire to improve the quality of life for all citizens. The enduring values in many of these firsts signify an active society and a sense of civilization and history being developed in a positive way.

Oregonians have a good sense of nature and they typically understand human values and the importance of "good process" in governing society. The state has a rich history of exemplary citizen participation and popular government. The opportunities and threats of citizen initiatives, referendums, and recall of public officials keep the citizenry thinking about problem-solving. Volunteerism benefits not only the recipient but also the provider.

Societally, we find where we are now from understanding our past, both individually and collectively. Preventing problems is less expensive than having to solve problems after they've been created (but creating problems is a lot easier). People will make progress toward meeting common goals by confronting cutting-edge issues, protecting civil liberties, controlling technology, and making objective evaluations to get positive returns on investments of time and resources.

Someone has to be the first.

Reference Sources/Acknowledgments

Special thanks to the generations of historians, archivists, writers, and librarians whose previous documentary and cataloging efforts made this book possible. Thanks also to librarians for access and maintenance of materials. Many historians have written about early events and some "firsts" have been, or will be, topics of entire books. More details about firsts for Oregon can be found in the following books.

Books

Aikens, Melvin C.; Archaelogy of Oregon, 1986, 2nd Edition

Allyn, Stan; Top Deck Twenty, 1989, Binford & Mort

Attwell, Jim; Columbia River Gorge History, 1975

Avshalomov, Jacob; Music Is Where You Make It, 1979

Barber, Larry; Last Tango Around The Horn, 1990

Belcher, Monika; Gleaning Handbook, 1976

Bingham, Edward; OREGON, 1979, 6/85

Bobinski, George S.; Carnegie Libraries, 1969

Bohrer, Walt, Black Cats and Outside Loops, 1989

Brogan, Phillip F.; East of the Cascades, 1964

Caniff, KiKi; Oregon Free, 1982

Cantwell, Robert; The Hidden Northwest, 1972

Carey, Charles H.; General History of Oregon, 1971

Carpenter, Allan; The New Enchantment of America -- Oregon, 1978

Clatsop Historical; Vol. 1 No. 4

Cogswell, Philip, Jr.; Capitol Names, Oregon Historical Society, 1977

Corning, Howard M., editor; Dictionary of Oregon History, 1956, 1989; Binford and Mort

DeMarco, Gordon; A Short History of Portland, 1990

Dodds, Gordon Barlow; Oregon — A Bicentennial History, 1977

Dodds, Gordon B.; High Technology in Washington County, Manuscript, 1990

Emerson, Charles L.; This Is Oregon, 1936, The Geographers, Inc.

Katz, Vera; Educational Reform Act for the 21st Century, 1991

Encyclopedia of Modern Architecture; Volume III, Harry N. Abrams, Inc., 1964

Freeman, Olga Samuelson; A Guide To Early Oregon Churches, Eugene, Oregon, 1985

First for Clackamas County; Clackamas County Historical Society

Friedman, Ralph; Tracking Down Oregon, 1978

Friedman, Ralph; In Search of Western Oregon, 1990

Goodall, Mary; Oregon's Iron Dream, 1958

Guinness Book of World Records, 1990, 1991

Gullick, William; Roadside History of Oregon, 1991

Harding, Glenn T.; Oregon Historical Calendar and Chronology of Events 1542-1988, Oregon Family Publishing, 1988

Hatton, Raymond R.; Oregon's Big Country, A Portrait of S. E. Oregon, 1988

Hillsboro Historical Notebook, Public Library

Hippely, John Francis; The Mistake Called WPPSS, 1982

Himes, George, First Things Brought to Mind, Early Records of Oregon, VF

Hobson, Howard; Shooting Ducks, A History of University of Oregon Basketball, 1984, OHS

Holmes, Doris; Columbia County History, Col. Co. Historical Society, 1985

Hussey, Champoeg

Jackson, Royal G. and Jennifer Lee; Harney County: An Historical Inventory,

Johnson, Steve; The Portland Book, May, 1979

Kane, J. N.; Famous Firsts Facts, 1980

Klamath County Historical Society; Klamath County History, 1984

Klooster, Karl; Round the Roses, 1987

Latham, Jean Lee; Columbia: Powerhouse of NW, 1967

Lavender, David; Land of Giants, 1956

Lee, Marshall M.; The First 40 Years of Tektronix, 1986

Legacy of the Twenty-six, Multnomah Athletic Club

MacColl, E. Kimbark; The Growth of a City, 1979

MacColl, E. Kimbark; The Shaping of a City, 1976

Maddux, Percy; City on the Willamette, 1952

Marshall, Don; Oregon Shipwrecks, 1984

McArthur, Lewis A. and Lewis L., Oregon Geographic Names, 5th Edition, 1982; 6th Edition

McCarthy, Bridgett; Where To Find the Oregon in Oregon, 1984, 1990

McCormack, Win, and Dick Pintarich; Great Moments in Oregon History, 1987

McCormack, Win; Profiles in Oregon, 1984

McDonald, Lois Halliday, Trade Letters of Francis Ermatinger, (1818-1853)

McGrady, Pat, Sr.; The Persecuted Drug: DMSO, 1973

McPhee, Marnie; Western Oregon, Portrait of Its Land and People, 1987

Meeker, Ezra; Ox Team Days on the Oregon Trail, 1907, Puyallup, WA; New York City

Meier, Gary and Gloria; Whitewater Mailmen, The Story of the Rogue River Mail Boats, 1991

National Geographic, 1990

Neuberger, Richard L.; Memorial in Congress, 1960

Neuberger, Richard L.; Our Promised Land, 1938

Norman, James; Covered Bridges, 1988

O'Donnell, Terrence; That Balance So Rare, 1988

Oregon Biography Index (1976)

Oregon Blue Books, 1918, 1933, 1957, 1985, 1987, 1989, 1991, 1993

Oregon Council for the Humanities; The First Oregonians, 1991

Books (continued)
Oregon, End of The Trail, Binford & Mort, 1956
Oregon Historical Society Vertical Files (1990, 1991, 1992, 1993)
Oregon Provisional and Territorial Records, Archives
Original Journals of Lewis and Clark,
Parrish, Historic Oregon, 1938
Potter, Miles F.; Oregon's Golden Years, 1976
Portland Saturday Market Vendor Handbook, 1990
Potter, Oregon's Golden Years, 1982, Caxton Printers
Price, Richard L.; Newport, Oregon 1866-1936: Portrait of a Coastal Resort, 1975
Purdy, Ruby Fay; Rose City of the World, 1947
Ross, Mary LaRue; Marion County Historical Society
Ruby, Robert H., Brown, J. A., The Chinook Indians: Traders, chapter, *They Drifted.*
Rain Umbrella, Knowing Home, 1981, edited by the staff at *RAIN*
Rees, Helen G., Shaniko, 1982
Reining in the Horseless Carriage, Oregon Dept. of Motor Vehicles,
Saling, Ann; Our Superlative Northwest, Unique Claims to Fame, 1984
Smith, Helen Krebs, editor; With Her Own Wings, Portland Federation of Women's Organizations, 1948
Smith, Kidder, Architecture of the U. S., 1981
Springer, Vera; Power and the Pacific Northwest, 1976, U.S. Dept. of the Interior
Stein, Harry; Kathleen Ryan, Mark Beach; Portland -- A Pictorial History, 1980
The First Oregonians, Oregon Council for the Humanities, 1991
Tollefson, Gene; BPA & the Struggle for Power at Cost, 1985
Tozier, Albert; Wash. Co. Museum, Tozier Collection
Turnbull, George S.; Governors of Oregon, 1959
Vaughan, Thomas; Editor; The Western Shore, Oregon Country Essays, 1976, American Revolution Bicentennial Commission
Victor, Francis Fuller, The River of the West, The Adventures of Joe Meek, 1870, 1983
U. S. Works Progress Administration, Writers Project, 1940, Oregon End of the Trail, revised and edited by Howard McKinley Corning, Binford & Mort
Walling, A. G., 1884, History of Southern Oregon
Webber, Bert and Margie; Single Track To Jacksonville, 1990
Wentz, Walt; Bringing Out The Big Ones, 1983, Oregon Forest Products Transportation Assoc.
White, Robert J.; Sagebrush Heritage, 1987
Wilkins, Lee; Wayne Morse, A Biography and Bibliography, 1985
Wollner, Craig; Electrifying Eden, 1990
Wood, Sharon; Portland Bridge Book, 1989
Woodall, Mary; Oregon's Iron Dream, 1958

Woog, Adam; Sexless Oysters and Self-Tipping Hats, 1991
Works Progress Administration Document, U.S., 1940s
Wright, E.W., Lewis and Dryden's Marine History, 1895

Reference Sources/Acknowledgements
University of Oregon Dissertation
Letter from Johns Hopkins University
Letter from Gov. Robt. Straub to U.S. Administration on Aging, 1976
Letter from Jim Evans, Baker

Magazines, Articles, Reports
City of Portland Homeless Plan, Clatsop County, Historical Quarterly, Golf Digest, Oregon Business, Oregon Coast Magazine, Oregon Historical Quarterly, Oregon Magazine, Oregon Native Son, Oregon Voter, Newsweek, Westways, Cable Age, RAIN Magazine, Northwest Magazine, State Senator John Kitzhaber, National Academy of Sciences, Sporting News; U.S. Independent Telephone Association Bulletin (1991), Portland Winter Hawks, 1982

Newspapers
Daily Capitol Journal, 1909
Hillsboro Argus
New York Times, 1990, 1991
Oregon Daily Journal
Oregon Journal
Real Estate News, 1971
Statesman-Journal (Salem)
The Mountain
The Oregonian
The Scanner
The Times
The Trail Marker
This Week
USA Today
The Washington Post
Willamette Week

Manuscripts
Alvin T. Smith diary
Dodds, Gordon B., High Technology in Wash. Co., 1990
Dorothy O. Johansen of Reed College
Gertie Paisley Meek; Stephen A. D. Meek
Oregon Oddities, Works Progress Administration

Scrapbooks
Oregon Historical Society
Brigetta Nixon

People Credits

In addition to the librarians, historians, archivists, public information officers and writers, **the author gives special thanks** to the many people who answered interview questions, led me to answers, reviewed early drafts of chapters, or made suggestions. Thanks also to my family, friends, the many people who offered encouragement, and all those people who waited patiently for the publication.

C. Melvin Aikens, Terry Aikens, Mark Albanese, Dale Allen, Stan Allyn, Rod Anders, Bob and Betty Ashlock, Jacob Avshalomov, Don Baack, Daria and Gary Barclay, Jim Barlow, George Beard, Gil Bellamy, Pietro Belluschi, James Billington, Mort Bishop, Jr., Katherine Bowman, Bill Bree, Charles Burt, Sam Churchill III, "Bud" Clark, John Clay, Luther Cressman, Sam Dana, Dorothy Danielson, Charles Davis, Bill Day, Doug Decker, Wesley Doak, Dr. Gordon Dodds, Liz Dolan, Ann Donaca, Maynard Drawson, Angus Duncan, David Duniway, Cecil Edwards, Leonard Edwards, Rick Edwards, Gail Elam, Jack Elder, Kris England, Mark and Sue Enloe, Gary Ewing, Mary Eyrie, Amanda K. Failor, Christine Fore, Linda Freidenburg, David Frohnmayer, Elizabeth Furse, Deborah Gangloff, Jose Garcia, Lee Gilson, Judy E. Goldmann, Ted Hallock, Gene and Jeannette Hamby, Bruce Hamilton, Paul Hanneman, Fred Hansen, Dave Hanson, Michele Hascall, Mark Hatfield, Katie Hill, Robin Holdman, Corky Huffsmith, Doug Hutchinson, Lee Lewis Husk, Cheryl Jarvis-Smith, Wayne Jensen, Lee Johnson, Steven Reed Johnson, Trudy Johnson-Lenz, James Jones, Al Jones, Cynthia Kaeser, Louise Kasper, Mike Katz, Debbie Kennedy, Mimi King, Karl Klooster, Jerry Larson, Elizabeth Linder, Stan Link, Runaar Marklund, Richard Matthews, Arthur McArthur, John McKellor, John Meek, Marcia Michel, Fred Miller, Dennis Mulvihill, Bill Naito, Marjorie Napper, Bill Nelson, Maurine Neuberger, James Norman, Sam Oakland, Ralph O'Hara, Rodney Page, Greg Parker, Brian Parrot, Benjamin Peek, Jim & Irene Petersen, Fred Peterson, Stevie Pierce, John Platt, Dan Potter, Richard Read, Stevie Remington, Keith Richard, Betty Roberts, Catherine Ronconi, Carol Satterfield, Jim Scheppke, Jo Shrunk, Charles Sluyter, Joan Smith, Joe Smith, Tricia Smith, Christie Sohn, Vera Springer, Dan Steffey, Quincy Sugarman, Roy Swank, Paddy Tillet, Gene Tollefson, Ron Tonkin, Jon Rogers Tuttle, Sig Unander, George Wasch, Paul Wenner, Jim Westwood, Gordon White, Pat Whiting, Nancy Wilson, John Wolfe, and Carolyn Young.

Special thanks to the following: K. P. Alcott, Virginia Bruce, Nancy Hottenstein, Michael and Leslie Kearsey, Laura P. J. Larsen, Gerald L. Long, Janet W. Long, and Lewis L. McArthur.

<u>Archives</u> State of Oregon Archives, Oregon State University, University of Oregon, City of Portland.
<u>Libraries</u>
Oregon State Library, Multnomah County Library, Wilson Room; Cities of Beaverton, Hillsboro (2), Cornelius, Forest Grove, Salem.
<u>Museums</u>
Oregon Historical Society (vertical file, biography, files, shelves, documents, photographs), Clackamas County Historical Society, Clatsop County Historical Museum, Fort Dalles Museum, Georgia-Pacific Historical Museum, Museum at Warm Springs, Oregon Sports Hall of Fame, Mission Mill Museum, Oregon Maritime Museum, Oregon Military Museum, Tillamook County Historical Museum, Trail's End Heritage Center, Uncle Sam in the Oregon Country (exhibit), Washington County Museum.

<u>Organizations</u>

AAA of Oregon, American Civil Liberties Union Oregon, American Forestry Association, Bicycle Lobby of Oregon, Bonneville Power Administration, Bush House, City of Portland Archives, Dept. of Environmental Quality, Dept. of Education, Executive Department, Forestry Department, Gilbert House, InfoVision, Lang Syne Society of Portland, Long Associates, McLoughlin House, Mission Mill, National Oceanic and Atmospheric Administration, Oregon Advanced Computing Institute, Oregon Dept. of Human Resources, Oregon State Archives (old & new buildings), Oregon State Legislative Historian Office, Oregon Legislative Research, Oregon Barbie Club, Oregon Health Sciences University, Oregon Historical Society, Oregon Public Utility Commission, Oregon Department of Transportation, Oregon Association of Nurserymen, Oregon Trail Coordinating Center, Oregon Wheat Growers League, Portland Fire Bureau, Portland Police Historical Society, RAIN Magazine, State Historic Preservation Office, Southern Oregon Historical Society, St. Vincent Hospital, Tillamook County Cooperative Creamery, U.S. Corps of Engineers, U. S. Forest Service network, U.S. Works Progress Administration Writers Program, Washington County Human Services Coalition, Washington Park Zoo, Portland Water Bureau, and the World Forestry Center.

Visual Credits

COVER PHOTOS
(Cover photos and all photos reprinted with permission, © remains with the source)

Pioneer statue on top of State Capitol, photo by Ron Cooper

Sagebrush Symphony photo courtesy of OHS #14287,#118-A

Joseph L. Meek photo courtesy of Washington County Museum

"Equitable Building" photo courtesy of OHS Neg. #53455

Venezuela and U.S.A. Olympic Basketball Teams before Tournament of the Americas championship game July 5, 1992, Memorial Coliseum, © David L. Minick, 1992, TOTAL ACCESS

PHOTOS from the Oregon Historical Society (OHS) Photograph Library
2 Crater Lake engravement, OHS Neg. OrHi 89395
28 nickel mine photo courtesy of OHS Neg. CN 006313
29 Sagebrush Sandal photo OrHi 88346
126 Courtesy of OHS file
165 Oregon Spectator, OHS
209 Courtesy of OHS file
234 Post Office, Neg. 001875
236 Customs House Neg. 300-a
221 William S. U'Ren, OHS Neg. # 018319
224 Abigail Scott Duniway OHS Neg. Oreg. 4599
page 48 maps, OHS Neg. 87755
297 Wayne Morse photo OHS Neg. #73858
463 Oregon Territorial Capitol, OrHi 533
463 State Capitol, OrHi 18042
466-73 Equitable Building photo OHS Neg. 53455
488 Sagebrush Symphony, OHS Neg. #14287, #118-A
page 105 Forestry Center, OR Hist Neg. 39201
page 105 Blimp Hangar, ORHI 86134, U.S. Navy
page 114 Tideland Spruce, 1905 OrHi 8311

867 Erickson's Saloon courtesy of Fireman Ball souvenir, OHS Neg. #38157
1100 Printing Press Neg. 26237

OTHER PHOTOS
262 Weigh station Oregon Dept. of Transportation
page 60 Governor Tom McCall, courtesy of Audrey McCall
499 Courtesy of RussHeinemann graphics,609 SW Sixth Ave. Portland, OR 97205
501 87 J 1 © Daria Barclay, 1987, ABACI
528 Tabitha M. Brown courtesy of Pacific University
536 Pendleton Library photo, courtesy of Oregon State Library
655 Keep Oregon Green PSA
787 Lang Syne Society of Portland plaque at southwest foot of first bridge
793 Multnomah County Library
873 Courtesy of Gilbert House
881 Phillips screws courtesy of local hardware, copier
1035 Weather Machine from Pioneer Courthouse Square
1055 Courtesy of Keith Townsend
1082 Mary R. Wood from Washington Co. Museum
1126 Trail Blazers Champions
1311 Cecil Edwards photo courtesy Legislative Media
page 216 Wagon train by Bob Cosby of Endersby Graphics

STATE of OREGON
p. 28 Seals of Provisional and Territorial Governments from State Archives
p. 29 With permission from Secretary of State's Office
758 Courtesy of Sen. J. Hamby
1065 Oregon Tribes map from Comm. on Indian Services and Columbia River Inter-Tribal Fish Commission
1311 Courtesy Legislative Media
1414 Courtesy of Treasurer's Office

ILLUSTRATIONS
by Lauren O'Neal of Inklinations Pumpkin
p. 0 Map of Oregon Country
11+1137 Map with mountains
423 Slug
433+1287 Salmon
601 Bottle + can
1541 Bench

by Hugh Hayes
pages 106-7 © KEEP OREGON GREEN Map and #286

by Robert Palladino
494 Calligraphy

by Lynne C. Spinney
121 144 1504 1505
123 Courtesy of OHS files
561 lightbulb drawn by Gary Albertson from BPA photo

LOGOS
136 National Historic Trail
227/268 Citizens' Utility Board
303 Oregon Peace Institute
457+1025 Portland Water Bureau
638-9 Tree by U.S.Forest Service
1532 Beth Weissman for Green Mtn. Watershed Committee

CLIP ART
420 eagle 210 earth
1178 camping 1192 runners

INTERESTING FACTS ABOUT PORTLAND and OREGON FIRSTS GRAPHICS
Black and white reproductions of color computer graphics from graphics database displayed on the northwest's first interactive cable television, CableSystems Pacific Channel 44 (1982-1984) and the InfoVision kiosk in Oregon Pavilion at the 1986 World's Fair, Vancouver, B.C., Canada.
Graphics produced by the author for InfoVision/Community Research Services with help from Deborah White, Scott Gwin, and John Yandell.
#10, 428, 487, 519•, 574, 583, 823-827, 1028, 1084, 1090

Other computer art was created by the author.

COVER DESIGN
Gary Albertson and Jim Long

Firsts INDEX

Chapter Index

First 1993 multi-state Oregon Trail sesqui-centennial wagon train re-enactment crossing the John Day River at 9:45 am on August, 22, 1993

(Photo courtesy © Mark S. Cosby, Endersby Graphics, PO Box 1011, Marcola, Oregon 97454)

Do you want another copy of this book?

Use this order form, copy and complete it, and zip it directly to the publisher or write a letter to the author with comments and/or additions, and to order copies of the most recent up-to-date edition of <u>Oregon Firsts</u>: *Past and Present* for family and friends.

Are you interested in a 1994-1995 Oregon Firsts Calendar?_____ Oregon Firsts Videotape? _____

Oregon Firsts: *Past and Present*   1994 Edition $24.95

I have enclosed a check or money order for $_____ for ___copy(ies) of <u>Oregon Firsts</u>: *Past and Present*.   Copy this form to: **Oregon Firsts Media**
Pumpkin Ridge Productions
P. O. Box 33
North Plains, Oregon 97133-0033

Name:_____

Address:_____

City:_____State: _____ ZIP Code _____

Oregon Firsts: *Past and Present*   1994 Edition $24.95

I have enclosed a check or money order for $_____ for ___copies of <u>Oregon Firsts</u>: *Past and Present*.

Send this form to: **Oregon Firsts Media**
Pumpkin Ridge Productions
P. O. Box 33
North Plains, Oregon 97133-0033

Name:_____   33

Address:_____

City:_____State: _____ ZIP Code _____

Oregon Firsts: *Past and Present*   1994 Edition $24.95

I have enclosed a check or money order for $_____ for _____copy(ies) of <u>Oregon Firsts: *Past and Present*</u>.

Copy this form to: **Oregon Firsts Media**
Pumpkin Ridge Productions
P. O. Box 33
North Plains, Oregon 97133

Name:_____

Address:_____

City:_____State: _____ ZIP Code _____